WILLIAM BRONK

VECTORS AND
SMOOTHABLE CURVES

Collected Essays

NORTH POINT PRESS

San Francisco

1983

North Point Press wishes to thank Mr. James Weil of The Elizabeth
Press for his generous and courteous cooperation in the preparation of this edition. The essays in this collection were originally
published in limited editions by The Elizabeth Press under the
titles *The New World*, *A Partial Glossary*, and *The Brother in Elysium*. The essays in "The New World" first appeared in the *Gros-
steste Review* and *Origin*.

We hold houses in a kind of contempt and give
them nothing, or say we do, as a way to despise
the kinds of things that houses are, all
such kinds of things, the measured entities,
that they should not be what was intended: they fail.
They burn. They fade and sag. They fall away.
We think of a time before we housed the world
or gathered things—spirits were all we saw,
spirit was real, was what there was, was all.
This was man did this, and thought to do well
when he turned away to say, on the contrary, all
the world was what we measured: houses, sums
and angles, vectors and smoothable curves. We turn,
and turn again another way to find
some way to state the world, dissatisfied
none answers.

(From "My House New-Painted")

CONTENTS

We have an imprecise awareness of direction and force which we attempt to locate and quantify: where are the points it translates between and how strong and central are they? Concurrently and in relation we are trying to locate and quantify ourselves because however direct and immediate our awareness may be it is also devoid of external reference and its strength and centrality is uncertain. Vectors, therefore, no matter how exact and quantified, are proposals of location and force whose only referential field is internal—not ultimately oriented. We can be grateful for their stabilities even aware as we are of an arbitrariness with them. There are metaphors which we can recognize as not wholly arbitrary though that's as far as the line goes. We like to assume that there is somewhere a truth, a description of reality in conformance with reality itself however hard to arrive at or accept the arrival. But even in Shakespeare or the Bible, even in the cosmologies of particle physics, it isn't there. Reality is brought to mind by the inadequacy of any statement of it, the tension of that inadequacy, the direction and force of the statement.

THE NEW WORLD

AN ALGEBRA AMONG CATS

To go to Machu Picchu one goes first to Cuzco, the chief Indian city, still, of Peru and once their capital when the Incas ruled. The very ground where Cuzco stands is more than two miles high; and, as though this were high enough, Cuzco lies close and low to the ground and seems pushed and scraped together from it, from mud and stones and from clay baked into tiles. Seen from above, from the hill outside of town, where the enormous fortification and refuge still stands four centuries since the Spanish siege, the tiles of the roofs of Cuzco make one vast roof like a camouflage net pierced only here and there by the squat domes or heavy towers of churches. It is an old city and ruin seems endemic; after each earthquake, it rubbles back again to its essential stones and clay. Not all the city, however. Those massive, unmortared walls which were built before the Spanish conquest and have served since as foundations for later buildings are still there as unmoved as the mountains.

To go to Machu Picchu, we rose early in the morning and went to the railroad station. We had been told it would be cold, but it was only damp and cheerless. On the steps of the station, and on the street in front of the market opposite, which was not as yet open, there were Indian women quietly waiting like people who had come early to watch a performance and they were as free from early morning bustle as though they might have sat there all night. Their wares were beside them ready for buyers, their baskets of bread and of fruit, or on tiny charcoal fires, their kettles of soup, their pans of stew. The railroad yard was deserted. Presently, the station-master came and unlocked his office. Alberto spied our car at the end of the yard and went to get it as one might go to get a horse from the pasture. He came back with the driver and a kind of station wagon mounted on railroad wheels. We got in and immediately started; no one else was going to Machu Picchu that day. Switching backwards and forwards, we climbed for a little, crossed a ridge and descended to a river valley—the valley of the Urubamba, the Sacred River of the Incas, which rises almost in sight of the Pacific, flows down out of the high Andes to join the Amazon, and so crosses the whole wide continent and empties at last into the Atlantic.

3

The valley swells and narrows. There are wide plains where battles were fought, there are steep terraces far up the mountainsides, there are forts and ancient towns and flowers—whole sunlit clouds of yellow broom. Back of the near mountains are higher ranges covered with snow. Toward the end of the trip, almost abruptly, the rocky, arid look of the high altitudes becomes the green thicket of the jungle. When the train comes to a stop near a bridge, the mountains have almost pushed the roadbed into the river and we are nearly a mile lower than when we started at Cuzco. From here to the ruins on the ridge of Machu Picchu it is five miles of winding highway which takes us back up again in that distance a third of the height we have come down.

The river's sound is everywhere, and the sight of it is almost underfoot though a long way under. Full and vigorous from the high mountains and constricted by them, it has a tension like a piece of steel strapping, and entangles the mountains. It presses close to the east base of Machu Picchu ridge, includes the slender upthrust of Huayna Picchu and doubles back abruptly to follow the western base. The site is almost surrounded by the river. The mountains are all around us like a crowd. They are so massive it seems impossible that so many could be so close. We are *in* them. It is like lower Manhattan seen from a position halfway up from the ground, from a setback on one of the buildings. For in these mountains as with those buildings, all other possible attributes have been suppressed in favor of closeness, in favor of rising. Or, if one is reminded of music, it is music as it might sound to someone standing in the very middle of a trumpet voluntary, exultant and assertive and serenely composed. So, in the otherwise complete quiet, we hear the river below us and see the mountains all around us as though hearing them.

Whoever built this city must have been sensitive to its situation and drawn here by it. Before the conquest, the Indians of the high altitudes had a civilization much more highly developed than that of the jungle Indians. The river valley led down to the jungle. It has been reasoned that Machu Picchu was a secure outpost against the jungle Indians. It was undoubtedly secure. The Spanish, for example, who were mad for gold and searched everywhere for it, enduring no matter what hardship, never even found Machu Picchu. Nor is there any indication that it was ever attacked or captured by hostile tribes who were aware of it. The moat of the river and the steep mountainsides leading up to the city give it an almost obsessed security. But the whole aspect of Machu Picchu is of serenity more than obsession. Certainly a security as great as anyone might want could have been attained in any number of nearby places with far less effort. So there must have been some other reason. No doubt it was a holy place; it is easy to feel that it was. Very probably the sun was worshipped here as elsewhere in the Andes, perhaps some lesser gods as well, and the creator god, Viracocha. But these are not enough to account for the quality of Machu Picchu which is not merely beautiful but is beautiful in a special way. There are temples in other places and gods in other places and most of the places are ugly or at least of limited beauty. Holy places are so seldom beautiful that when they are, it is as though some outside god had intervened and taken over. Today, it is this Outside God that seems to have been worshipped at Machu Picchu.

There has been a special reverence here for the site itself. The site is so wonderfully impressive and it has been so successfully developed that reverence seems a proper word. This consideration for site is supposed to be a quality of the best modern architecture and sometimes it is. This ancient city had that quality a long time ago. The terrain and its background have been probed for their best values in much the same way as a piece of stone to be carved is said to be studied by the sculptor who intends to develop his conception from it. And indeed, there is a great reverence at Machu Picchu for stone. Here and there, a rock has been left standing where it must always have stood, but on a spot made conspicuous now with the building of the city around it. A few small planes have been cut away from its natural surfaces to make little shelves on which perhaps offerings were set. In one place, there is a massive ledge or upthrust so situated as to form a cave underneath. The rock on the right of the cave's entrance is beautifully carved into broad facets in a manner we would now call abstract. The top of this same upthrust has been used as a foundation for the wall of a rounded building something like the Temple of the Sun in Cuzco. Inside this temple—or this building, for we don't really know what use was made of it—the natural rock has been left as a rough obstruction, covering most of the enclosed area. It is plain that natural rock itself was valued and respected. The city is built on sloping ground and has many stairways as a consequence. Some of these are laid up, and others are simply cut into the rock slope. The stairways lead finally to the high point at the end of the ridge. There is another rock here, a carved one. Perhaps, cut would be a better word, for it is not ornamented; but the relationships of its planes and surfaces are those of sculpture. The whole area is hardly six feet high.

5

Above the broad base, the rock has been shaped to form a blunt, four-sided post. This is the post to which the priests tied the sun at solstices to force it back again when it had reached its farthest decline. The Spanish found such posts-to-tie-the-sun, or intihuatanas, as they are called in the Indian language, elsewhere in Peru, and destroyed them as objects of pagan veneration. They never found this one. It is very beautiful, at once simple and subtle; and though placed here as the climax to the city, it is so modest that it achieves its effect by being that almost unique thing, an understated monument. To come upon it now, unchanged and unmoved after so many centuries, has the kind of transporting excitement that must go with the opening of an unrifled Egyptian tomb.

The qualities of the Intihuatana, the modesty, the effectiveness, and beauty of stonework are characteristic of the whole city. It is hard to say how it can be that plain grey stone can make such an effect. Hiram Bingham, who discovered this city standing intact but empty in 1911, and cleared away the jungle that had grown over it, refers to one wall at Machu Picchu as the most beautiful wall in America. It may be meaningless to insist on his superlative, but there is no reason to quarrel with it. Even if we know that these builders had no iron or steel tools we feel no need, when we look at this wall, to make an allowance for primitive techniques. No tools or knowledge we know could have made it finer. One might think, a world away, of the Shakers who in their work with wood achieved a similar plain perfection. These stone surfaces have been worked and smoothed to a degree just this side of that line where texture would be lost. Where one stone meets another the surfaces recede slightly forming a small indentation at all the joints. And no doubt it is the joints more than any other one factor which make the perfection. Since no mortar was used it was necessary for each stone to match perfectly all other stones that it touched and these are not like brick or building block that are regular, interchangeable units. Probably no stone was cut quite like another. In many cases they are roughly rectangular, but each one has its variations in size and shape. An inner angle of one is perfectly reflected by an outer angle of the one adjoining, and even after all the intervening time, there is no space at all between. This correspondence, moreover, was not merely of the surface but extended as deep as the stone. What periods of patient effort each one must have required to give us now the great satisfaction of harmonious order, of the pieces for once put together even if the pieces in this instance are only stone.

There is other stonework at Machu Picchu of equal beauty to this. There are also buildings and parts of buildings in which jagged pieces of rock are laid up almost at random in thick clay. One such rough building, surprisingly, faces on the small open space which Bingham calls the Sacred Plaza because the other two sides (the fourth is a precipice) are occupied by fine buildings he believes to be temples. Really huge stones, weighing many tons, in one of these must have been very difficult to quarry, to shape, and to move into place. And there are other instances of technical triumph. In a small building behind this temple there is a stone cut with a pure virtuosity which seems almost playful. Set in the corner, it forms part of two walls and there are thirty-two different angles cut into its sides. And there is that building already mentioned whose curved wall is keyed to an upthrust rock on which it is based. Since this wall slants inward, like most of the Indian walls, the surface of each stone which composed it had to be given whatever small degree of both outward curve and inward slant it needed to contribute to the total shape of the building. It is customary— and of course justified—to speak of the engineering skill of these builders and to admire their techniques, or the results rather, of their techniques since we have not discovered really how they worked. And yet, to modern eyes, the deep impression of the city as a whole is not one of technical skills. Admirable as these may be, we have nevertheless surpassed them long ago in tools and methods. But nothing we have been able to do in this medium surpasses Machu Picchu in beauty. It is something more than an engineer's or stonemason's city. Over and over again one stands in admiration before the imaginative concept of a wall or a building or a prospect to the realization of which the proficient skills were only a tool, however necessary. It is in this sense that Machu Picchu is an important place, and in this sense also that we have not advanced, that time since then has wavered backwards and forwards as we have tried with the encumbrance of our far more numerous and varied skills to achieve a degree of perfection which was reached so simply here so long ago. We are not likely to do better.

When the Spanish adventurers first reached western South America in the sixteenth century, they found the whole Andes area dominated by a group of Indians whose ruler was called the Inca. The term Inca was extended to refer to the Inca's people and their civilization. This dominant group said of themselves that they had come from the Tiahuanaco region near Lake Titicaca, but it seems probable that it was actually from the area near Cuzco that they first began to spread through the mountains, much

7

as the Romans spread through the Mediterranean. And like the Romans also, they absorbed and made use of other high civilizations which had preceded them. They were thus, by their own invention or that of predecessors, in possession of many well-developed skills and products. Corn and potatoes, among other foods, had been hybridized and grew abundantly on thousands of artificial terraces constructed on the steep mountainsides to which water was brought from sometimes many miles away through stone canals. The terraces and canals can still be seen. There were fine textiles of intricate design and beautiful, sophisticated pottery. They could work bronze and precious metals and the Spaniards, who were familiar with some of the finest European stonework at home, were overwhelmed by massive constructions which they saw in Cuzco, and nearby. There was a concept of organization which had conquered and ordered a vast empire and interlaced it with thousands of miles of well-paved roads some parts of which are still in use. This empire and its roads were quite certainly the creation of the Incas and not of some earlier people. Post houses stood along the roads at frequent intervals, and in them were relays of trained runners so that messages could be sent with great speed from one end of the empire to the other. It is claimed that several hundred miles a day were traveled. So well-developed in so many ways was this civilization that it is curious that they had no written language. The messages which the runners carried over the roads were in the form of quipus, or groups of colored cords knotted in various ways at various intervals. Here was a people who, in the development of written language, had skipped completely over any form of picture writing to an abstract system as remote from spoken language or visual images as our own stenotype tapes or punchcard systems.

It is conceivable that this serenely ordered and largely abstract city was built by the Incas. In the absence of written records there is only oral tradition. The conquistadores had direct contact with the oral tradition but they never saw the city, and though they did refer to places they had not actually seen, such references are necessarily uncertain and confusing. After long investigation, Hiram Bingham who found the city, concluded that it was much older than the first ruler to be called Inca, though he concluded also that after the conquest the last ruler to be so called was secreted there from the Spanish. He associated the origins of the city with the Aumatas, whose civilization had declined many centuries before that of the Incas arose. We don't know. Can we doubt that a large part of the tremendous appeal of Machu Picchu is in our failure to account for its origin? It is outside of the tradition and descent of western civilization. This is not our heritage nor were these our ancestors. Moreover this city is inconsistent with our common idea of primitive people. The impact which Machu Picchu makes on us is unsoftened by data and explanations. One thinks of the sea captain in Conrad's story, *The Secret Sharer*, confronted by his unsuspected double, his own naked image come up out of the sea and over the side of the ship. For the image which we see as though behind these walls, or walking these passageways and stairs, is our own, and the impact is more powerful for being unexpected and unaccountable. Not that this city resembles in any outward way a modern capital or even a small modern village, any more than the Inca costumes on mannequins in the museums look like anything we might be likely to wear, even in adaptation. The resemblance—but it is not really a resemblance at all, it is an identification—is on a much more obscure and broader level which ignores the particulars of a location or period to strike toward a community of aspiration and value. It is somewhat as it is when we hear a new language whose words and grammar, or even whose very sounds, are entirely foreign to us. Yet, not only do we recognize human speech, we hear our own intonations and understand emotional attitudes which are expressed or groped for or dissembled. We can be strongly attracted or repelled without an interpreter. And these ruins are almost more eloquent than language. What a small city this was, after all. The grandeur of its temples was not in their size which would have admitted only a few priests and attendants. Its houses are only cold, tiny rooms in spite of the refinements of their stone walls. But it is a city. No one speaks of it in terms of less respect. Much more extensive modern places are unmistakably towns and villages. It is the entire essentials of a city, a complete and perfect abstract of a city. And its houses are real houses and we want to live in them the way we wanted to live in the houses we built to play in when we were children. They speak to us with that kind of immediacy and perfection. We belong here because we are human and because these builders were human in the strongest and best way we can imagine though they used other words and grammar in their language, and their tools and materials were different from ours.

One feels that the buildings at Machu Picchu which must have been old at the time of the Spanish conquest, are nevertheless more of our own time than buildings which must have been erected afterwards—the churches of Cuzco, for example, in the crumbled and rubbled remains of their baroque splendor. These Spanish colonial buildings are now so obviously antique: they are, as we say, 'dated'. The buildings at Machu Picchu, on the other hand, are not shabby and out of fashion, and they are literally not dated; their time of origin is unknown. One curious result of this contrast is that it leads us to reflect on the shallowness of the centuries of our own European tradition, as full of unimportant details as a dull afternoon, and as essentially trivial as the changes in costume fashion from year to year. At Machu Picchu, it is as though time were not a single, orderly progression in which all human events took their place in the same scale. It is at least as though there were several separate scales of time; it is even as though for certain achievements of great importance, this city for example, there were a continuing present which made those things always contemporary. Common sense has huge limitations; and though it may be in some respects what experience has taught us and conforms to experience, it is often our non-sensical experiences which are made to conform, in turn, to common sense.

This is a fantastic city. It is not common sense that a savage and primitive group, in a remote period, would have built, in this inaccessible spot in the middle of the high Andes, a city of such beauty at the cost of so much labor and care. Yet here it is, and we must accept it as reality, not as common sense. It is true of almost all our experience—of reality—that we reject it, that we ask for our senses to be confirmed. We say, 'What was that noise?' or, 'Did you see a flash?' Over and over again, without even being asked, we explain to children what the children see and hear, or are assumed to have seen and heard. This is common sense on its simplest level—whatever we agree in common to have sensed; and as we agree more widely, and experience confirms our agreements, we cease gradually to reject the external world, and the common sense of a society develops in complexity. Perhaps even the idea of the external world as a common sense matter develops in this way. It is interesting, for example, to contemplate what might be the attitudes toward external reality of one human being in complete isolation without anyone else to confirm and corroborate those sensual impressions which it seems to be our instinctive first reaction to reject and refuse as reality. Would there be any world? There is an old philosophical question which asks if sound exists where there is no one to hear it, as when a tree falls in an uninhabited forest. But maybe the question becomes more important, and tells us more about ourselves, if we ask how much one person who had always been alone in that forest as its single occupant, with no one to confirm his sensual impressions, could hear as an outside sound. But of course we don't live alone in a forest. We live with other people who can confirm our impressions as external. The ideas of common sense are enlarged and change. It is almost completely common sense in our world today that if we fly east out of New York and continue in the same direction, we will come back soon across the United States from the west coast. Even more fantastic things than that are beginning to be believed matter-of-factly; and yet, what wild, strange impressions we continue to have. For the most part we deprecate these impressions and adjust them to make them conform to common sense as it exists—to what has already in the past been agreed upon. We continue to reject reality unless it has already been confirmed and accepted elsewhere by other people. Of course we do this in varying degrees. In the arts, and in theoretical science, for example, reality is not always refused and common sense is sometimes enlarged or altered by new replies to such questions as our senses propose.

One thinks again and again how strange this city is. It lies in a kind of saddle between the two peaks, Machu Picchu and Huayna Picchu. The second peak is high, steep-sided and so close-in that it always looks as if it were seen through a telescope. Near its top, in such a position that it seems that the supporting walls must surely slide away, extensive agricultural terraces have been built; and above these in a kind of room formed by a rock overhang, there are some beautifully constructed niches and doorways. This is about a thousand feet above the city proper. The path up and the view down are terrifying to anyone not inured to heights. The traveler easily loses his nerve, and is glad to come down from places in which the old inhabitants moved undoubtedly with ease and composure. And yet it is easy to imagine that what happened to the Indians after the Spanish conquest was roughly similar to this—loss of nerve and composure in a whole society. In hardly more than a year, a well-organized, well-armed, vast and prosperous empire was disarmed and broken by a handful of Spaniards. The Inca, a divine descendant, was robbed and murdered. Thereafter the society broke down rapidly and was never restored.

And yet not everything was destroyed. Machu Picchu is an empty city now and has stood empty probably for several centuries. If it has a compelling interest for us today, the interest is something other than the purely antiquarian—though it may be that, of course, just as it may also be nothing, as it was to the man in the hotel lobby in Cuzco, to whom it was 'an interesting ride, but there's nothing there.' How true it is that we reject the external world, that it becomes too fantastic to believe, and we may come out of an encounter as if no impression at all had been made on us unless the experience of our senses is confirmed in some convincing way. So much of experience, here or elsewhere, disturbs and bewilders us, is plainly beyond common sense. We make what we can of it. What we make is conditioned, and indeed, almost determined by the long tradition of a civilization which has come down to us through our known history from the early civilizations in Europe and the Middle East. That tradition in its various forms is so widespread today that hardly anywhere escapes it. What civilized place or people is outside any longer? Even if, unlike the man in Cuzco, we accept our experience, the external reality constructed within our tradition loses something in reality and interest because there is no one sufficiently 'outside' to confirm it. How satisfying it is that the Indians that Gheerbrant found on his expedition to the jungles of the upper Amazon, were moved and delighted by Mozart's music. It appears that there may be such a reality as man, and that our tradition is not entirely one of accidentals and eccentricities. Machu Picchu is entirely outside our tradition, so remote from us in time and space as to be untouched by it. It confirms and corroborates us. We find here our own image reflected, and it is as though we were to find an algebra among cats, or a Christianity among the people of Mars.

AT TIKAL

That the ideas of time are absurd and arbitrary does not destroy their usefulness nor deny that they are based on experience. We see that light and darkness alternate in a roughly uniform pattern and we make a unit of time from this experience without which we could hardly speak of our lives; but one has only to think of the polar regions to know that days are neither universal nor absolute. In much of the world there are seasons which make a perceptible repeated cycle of temperature or rainfall. Where seasons are not varied, and so less important, the year still shows in a more sophisticated observation as a progress of stars and sun along the horizon or over it. The phases of the moon are a repeated change which are often noticed. We experience the *units* of time as change which is recurrent. If the unit of the week seems artificial to us, so that often we are at a loss to say what day of the week it is without reference to a calendar, it is no doubt because the week is almost pure recurrence without a perceptible change. And in the same way we lose track of the day of the month, but this is artificial also and removed somewhat from experience. Time is most easily remarked when the experiences of change and recurrence are both strong. The recurrent movement from dawn through light and dark to dawn again, or from spring through the seasons of the year to spring again, in the course of which vast changes occur, are among our most powerful experiences of time, circular experience, in which we periodically reach a point from which we had moved away, only to move away again and so return. It is a circular movement and so endless though it may be given a linear appearance by counting the revolutions and numbering them successively. But there is also a linear experience of time which is immediate and forceful, our growth and aging and decline, and the same process as seen in the people around us. The experience is neither circular nor recurrent. It begins at a definite point, follows a linear course, and comes to an end. It is true though that, seen from a little remove, the process of birth, generation and death in succeeding generations appears recurrent and circular. But we are not removed from our own experience. Mortality faces us with an end to time and we are conscious of it. Change is so important a

13

part of experience as to be almost all of it. It is almost so that experience is the impression of change. And change is the essence of time. It is the essence of time that a condition which was is not now, or a condition which is anticipated is not yet, or a condition which is now was not before and will soon not be any longer. It is undoubtedly true that most experience of change is individual and particular, that our time, so to speak, is our own. But there are, as well, changes in the external world, as astronomical movements and their subdivisions, more or less accessible to everyone at will. It is in terms of these, usually, that we speak of time. And it is in these terms also that 'it doesn't seem possible that it is four o'clock already' or 'that the month is all gone' or 'that the summer will ever be over.' Perhaps 'it seems only yesterday' that some long since over happening occurred. For, while bowing to the public time which is regular and impersonal, we continue to live at several speeds at once in private times of our own. The public time is a public metaphor of those incessant changes, arbitrary and mysterious, which we observe and undergo.

At Tikal in Guatemala, as elsewhere in the Mayan area, men accumulated time through centuries as misers accumulate money. One can go there now, where the jungle has overgrown their wide plazas and climbed like a flood up the steep sides of their high temples, and read their accounts, the dated stones erected as monuments to time itself, to the regular passage of accumulated years—not to any great event of those years. They are monuments to simple duration that say, in effect, 'On this date we have endured another twenty years.' Tikal may well be the oldest of the Mayan cities. Somewhere near here time was invented and elaborated and refined quite independently of any similar process elsewhere. Mayan agriculture was based on the burning of the fields toward the end of the dry season, and the planting of corn at the time when the annual rains would fall. It is sometimes thought that this cycle is the impetus and core of their calendar. No doubt these seasonal calculations were important, but it is doubtful that they made an elaborate calendar necessary. To say that the calendar was devised for religious and ceremonial reasons is to avoid the question, for so close was the relation between time and worship as to suggest that time itself was the object of that worship. The nine gods of the underworld succeeded each other endlessly as patrons of successive days. The nineteen months each had its divine patron, and each of the twenty names of days was a god. Time was perceived in these circular patterns of recurrence. To the twenty days were appended thirteen numbers (the numbers were also gods) and a circle of 260 days was made. The names of the days were Ik, Akbal, Kan, Chichan, etc., and one counted 1 Ik, 2 Akbal, 3 Kan, etc., through thirteen days when the number count returned to 1, but the names of the days continued to the twentieth and last which was Imix, and joined to the number 7. Then the number 8 was joined to the first day name, Ik, and so the count continued until each name of a day had been joined to each of the numbers and the whole cycle was repeated again at the conclusion of 260 days, starting as before, 1 Ik, 2 Akbal, 3 Kan, etc.

This formalization of the cycle of repeated change and recurrence seems to have been the oldest reckoning of time by the Mayas, and apparently came before any coupling of time with the apparent movement north and south of the sun. To be sure, the *unit* of the cycle, the day, was a unit at all only by reference to the sun. But the closing and repetition of the cycle after 260 of those units seems arbitrary to us, accustomed as we are to the solar year of (normally) 365 such units. However, if the experience of time is, on its simplest terms, an experience of change and recurrence without external reference, any ordering of that experience is as valid as another. If there is an absolute of time the Mayas had not seen it. The special pertinence for them of 260 may have been in the combination of the thirteen gods of the upper world with the Mayan system of counting, not as we do in tens and powers of tens, but in twenties and its powers.

The Mayas did, however, watch the point on the horizon at which the sun rose in the morning, and saw that the point gradually moved south on successive days, then north again, and returned to its farthest north point after 365 days. They divided this movement into eighteen periods of twenty days and an additional period of five days, and so formed their months. The days of the month were numbered from zero to nineteen (or zero to four in the case of the one short month). After the establishment of the solar year, any particular day was designated not only by its position in the 260 day system, but by its simultaneous position in the system of numbered days of the month with which they intermeshed the first system, somewhat as we do the days of the week with days of the months of the solar year. We count by tens as units, tens, hundreds, thousands, always forming the next higher order by multiplying any order by ten. This seems natural to us if not inevitable. But it is equally possible, and indeed historical, to enumerate in other ways, as twelves, for example: units, dozens, grosses; or by sixties (as the Babylonians did): units, 60's, 360's, etc. The Mayas counted units, 20's, 400's, 8000's, 160,000's, multiplying each time by 20 (rather than, as we do, by 10) to arrive at the next higher order. But when they counted days, they counted single days, units of twenty days, and then units of 360 days (18 × 20 instead of 20 × 20), units of 7200 days (20 × 360), and units of 144,000 days (20 × 7200). The irregularity in the third order was apparently an attempt to make an order which approximated the solar year.

How suggestive it is that the solar year in terms of days can only be approximated, that it runs over the period of even days into a fraction of another. We think naturally of time in terms of days because there is light and dark, and in terms of years because of the succession of the seasons; and the shorter units seem to add up to the longer units and so compose time. But whatever time may be, we have not referred to it directly in terms of days and years. We have referred to two separate aspects of the earth in relation to the sun: to the earth's rotation and to the tilting of its axis. The second movement is not the accumulated result of the first. The year is not an accumulation of days. And one might well wonder what either of these movements of the earth in relation to the sun has to do directly with human time. Neither is the year an accumulation of the changes in the shape of the moon, or the movements of the planet Venus. Both of these movements, however, were observed and marked by the Mayas, and the phase of the moon was incorporated in their statements of time.

The Mayas had really three units which we might call years—the period of 260 days formed by joining the twenty day-names to thirteen numbers, the period of 365 days which, with a correction like our leap year correction for the fractional day, took note of the solar year, and the period of 360 days, a round number in their system of counting, which was an important period in counting long duration. Twenty such 360 day periods were called a katun. The ending of a katun was the occasion for the erection of one of those monuments to duration and the passage of time that one still sees at Tikal. Time monuments were also erected at half katuns and, rarely, even at quarter katuns.

The early Mayan time inscriptions, called the long count, contain detailed information: the number of elapsed days since the beginning of their computation of time, the name of the day in the year of 260 days, the name of the day in the cycle of the nine days, the lunar month and the phase of the moon within that month, and the name of the day according to the months of the solar year. Later inscriptions are reduced to the number of even katuns elapsed since the beginning of the computation of time, and the name of the day which ended the elapsed period stated in terms of the 260 day year and the 365 day year together. Later still, the only information given in a date was the name of the last day of the katun according to the 260 day year. This was a designation not only of that particular day, but of the whole period of twenty cycles of 360 days each which had led up to it. It is true that the designation was reasonably precise and specific, since it would not be used again for more than 250 years—until, that is, thirteen katuns had elapsed. Therefore it was no doubt all that was needed to specify a time which would be understood by those who were using it. And yet, the suggestion is almost unavoidable that the days of the cycle of 260 days, which are thought to have been the oldest part of the Mayan calendar, have come finally to their old importance as the summary and expression of time, as though one could say of time only that it was composed of repeated cycles of recurrent change.

At Tikal, they counted the days. Over and over, through century after century, they counted the days. 1 Ik, 2 Akbal, 3 Kan, the 260 days repeated themselves endlessly, and the count went on. Twenty days were a uinal, eighteen uinals a tun, twenty tuns a katun, twenty katuns a baktun, twenty baktuns a pictun, twenty pictuns a calabtun, twenty calabtuns a kinchiltun, twenty kinchiltuns an alautun—this largest unit was composed of 23,040,000,000 days. The 260 days repeated themselves, but the accumulation of days could go on indefinitely, growing larger day by day. It is the absurdity of time that although it is a finite measurement, it has neither in logic nor experience any beginning or end. It is true that experience would seem to indicate beginnings and endings for individuals. Time then, is like a thread or cord laid up by the twisting together of many individual fibers of varying lengths and definite measure. The individual fibers end, and the cord stretches on indefinitely. There is an idea of time as pure continuance, existing endlessly before now and after now—a finally absurd idea if time is a measure, for a pure, abstract continuance is immeasurable. Any segment is all.

The end of time is often predicted; the beginning of time must be assumed as starting from some event: from the founding of the city; from the birth of Christ; from the flight of Mohammed from Mekka. We say, 'in the thirty-second year of the king's reign,' or 'in the seventieth year of the Independence of the United States.' Time as a measure is a measure of the duration of some new condition, of some change. At Tikal, in the old inscriptions, we do not know from what event they counted duration.

Something happened or was assumed to have happened, some new condition, whose duration was being measured, came into being nearly 3500 years before the earliest recorded dates that have been found. This would place the beginning of the Mayan era at somewhere near 3000 B. C. in our chronology. The nature of the happening or new condition is never stated and we do not know what it might have been. One only supposes that they did not then start counting time, that it was only afterwards that they looked back over their shoulders, as it were, and decided to base their calculations on that chosen point in the past. It implied a beginning of time, as though that were the date, perhaps, of the creation of the world, before which there was nothing or at any rate, no familiar world. Absurd as it may be, it is difficult to know any alternative to this action of the Mayas of setting a distant point from which to calculate time forward, unless it is our present practice of setting a point—the birth of Christ—from which we calculate both forward and backward, a point from which time extends indefinitely in both directions beyond any view. It is evident that one speaks of time as two things—as an indefinite continuance and as a finite duration of a special condition. Thus, one might speak with some validity of the years or the period, the *time*, of the Mayan civilization, during which special conditions came into being, prevailed and expired. But it would be more valid to speak of the time of Tikal or some other Mayan city, of the Mayan Old Empire or New Empire, or the time of the Mayapan Federation, or of some particular katun. For in a long duration, those special conditions whose endurance the accretions of time assert and measure do not, in fact, endure in their fullest strength and without change. The very unit of time is a unit of change, of the alternations of light and dark, and the special and temporary concomitants which, by association, seem to accompany the coming of darkness or a new day. Thus, brief durations have the greatest validity and although a long duration is not impossible, its content is so altered by change as it lengthens as to be lost or to become meaningless. It is as though we were counting oranges and found that for some time now we had actually been counting the seeds of oranges, or orange trees, or perhaps even apples, and were not able to say at what point the change had happened. We have been counting, not a finite duration, but an indefinite continuance which is uncountable, and have been using a unit of change to count the unchanging. We can speak of the weather and say that it was fair for five days but that since then we have had two days of rain, and the statement has meaning; but who can say how many days in all there have been of the varying weathers, or even that days in that sense are countable? Logically, but not in any real sense, the days can be added indefinitely—two cloudy, one warm, four rainy, three cold, or even three dry years and ten that were wet. But, in truth, the weathers do not accumulate over really long periods. There is only *the weather*, which changes but is not increased. As with the weather, so with time, which we note as changes and could not note without changes, the light and the darkness, movement, growth and decline, the various temporary hungers and revulsions. The sum of the changes as it increases over really long periods becomes increasingly meaningless, has a kind of static resistance by which the additions make, not more and more, but only whatever it was that we started with. There is a quirk to counting, which is a linear progression, which reminds us of the great bending force bringing us back again to our starting point in any attempt to lay a straight and level line accumulating inch by inch along the earth. It is only within limits that linear accumulation is possible. Not only do numbers become unreal to us as they increase in size, but we are conscious of the circular as an overriding force.

One thinks again of how at Tikal in counting the accumulated years, some starting point, probably arbitrary, had to be set from which the beginning of the katuns was marked. And one thinks of the late Mayan inscriptions in which a katun is marked by only the name of its last day. They had a strong feeling for time as a circular movement: the circle of the nine days, the circle of the twenty days, the twenty days combined with numbers to make a circle of 260 days, the circle of fifty-two years which started again the correlation of day-names between the sacred and the solar years, the circle of thirteen katuns before the repetition of the name of the last day. Their calendars were round.

In Guatemala today, they no longer count the katuns, but the twenty days are remembered and even venerated. An old man will speak of his age by recalling the time of a president long out of power, or the eruption of a certain volcano. The time of the Mayas is over, their long duration has disintegrated. Our duration is still in progress as though from some beginning, as though to some end. The Mayas were conscious, as we are, of changes, and they saw the same apparent movements of sun and stars as we do, yet their expression of time and, indeed, their very system of counting was different from ours. The expressions of time are arbitrary and variable and even absurd, assuming as they do a beginning and an end for which there is no basis in experience. We experience changes whose duration we note and measure as though they were all—or even anything. But we experience as well a continuing present which neither we nor the Mayas approach or depart from, a present which neither develops nor declines. It is there. The changes do not express it.

THE OCCUPATION OF SPACE—PALENQUE

It is not certain that space is empty and shapeless though it must seem so, just as it must seem that we are nowhere except as we occupy space and shape it. Whether we look at the surface of the earth which is endless though not infinite, or at the spaces beyond, whose limits we cannot see or perhaps think of, the need for a sense of place is so strong that we try to limit the vastness, however arbitrarily, and fill the emptiness if only by naming places such as a mountain, a water, or certain stars.

Space has a featureless aspect which corresponds to a kind of experience: space considered as an indefinite extension, mile after mile, is the equivalent of the common experience of life as a maintained existence, an indefinite succession of days getting and enjoying the available satisfactions and avoiding the avoidable discomforts. In such a world the sense of place is the sense of the familiarity of the usual surroundings. Whether or not that existence is sufficient for most men, it is nevertheless an accepted portion in primitive societies and, though less obviously so, in complex civilizations as well. Space, in such a world, has an emptiness and a shapeless quality. It is possible to live in it without affecting its shape or content much and with hardly any awareness of it. It is possible to live in the presence of space, or at least its potential, without occupying it. No doubt there were men living in Yucatan and its adjacent areas before the Mayan occupation of that space. They took sustenance from the land and their labors and when the Mayan civilization came they contributed their labor and allegiance to it and when the Mayan civilization was broken they continued to live there, as indeed they do now, centuries later. But it was the Mayan civilization that occupied that space, and so effectively that the mark of the occupation has outlasted the civilization. The present inhabitants hardly occupy it, and are largely indifferent to its former occupation. But there are others who come there to locate and study the old sites, to clear away the vegetation and debris from them, and to rename those whose old names have been lost. The old occupation still asserts itself, even though the force of its assertion is now in contrast to the surrounding desolation.

If anyone's world were a single room, perhaps not small but definite and measurable, space would be the shape of that room. But our environment does not present itself in so easy a way. Where it seems to end, it continues beyond and is not measurable. All men live in an environment no doubt, but the experience of space is, for many, so vague and fragmentary as to hardly exist. Only by disregarding the large number of men who live almost without it, can we say that to want space, the shape of things, is a universal human need. But it has been wanted by men in all kinds of times and environments. It is a persistent and widespread and recurrent need. If it is a need for room it is also a need for a room, a place with walls or boundaries or a name. We have often wanted something more than a vague 'here' to answer the question of where we are. At the present time, in our own civilization we have maps and other systems of reference to specify our location. Indeed, the availability of so much spatial information shows for how long we must have believed that by searching our environment we could find out where we are. But it is plain that the ordinary answer to the question of where is in terms of shapes we have imposed on the environment, political shapes or reference lines. The names of places are names we have given them. The more precisely we try to locate ourselves, the more we are sent back to the realization that, except as we have imposed a shape on environment by occupying it, it is still as described in Genesis in the first creation, without form and void and with darkness covering the face of the deep. The shape of things has never been something we already knew, or had only to look up to determine. It has been an uncertainty, whose nature we have tried to suppose only to learn that our suppositions were not correct.

The Mayan civilization existed in an area that includes, in terms of today's world, the Yucatan peninsula together with other adjacent parts of Mexico, Belize and parts of Guatemala and Honduras. It was one of several related pre-columbian civilizations. It is not easy to say when a civilization may have started, though it was certainly in existence in the fourth century. A few traces of its culture—some of its characteristic calendar system, for example—survive today, though most of its great cities were abandoned a thousand years ago, long before the Spanish conquest. Its calendar and its cities are its most conspicuous monuments. Few civilizations have dealt so directly and entirely with time and space. They were not conquerors, nor administrators, nor law-givers, nor makers of a great religion, nor inventors of machines and techniques. Of course their civilization had administrative and military and legal and religious and technical skills, as any civilization must have, but these were not its characteristic qualities. The nature of time and space was their great concern. They ordered and memorialized time by erecting stone shafts to its regular passage. Wasn't their response to space equally gratuitous and abstract, and accomplished in a similar way? Just as time, though we tend to lose track of it, would no doubt have passed even if they had not ordered and marked it, so with space. They had room. There is reason to believe that during their era the Mayan area was more densely populated than it is now; still it is populated. It is not for lack of people that the area today seems empty of any occupation since the one which ended a thousand years ago, whose ruins still assert it once was occupied as space, just as the calendric monuments show that there once was time here. The great Mayan constructions of stucco and stone were not houses; the Mayans lived in rectangular thatched huts with rounded ends, almost identical with the ones they still live in today. Even the buildings which have been traditionally termed 'palaces' or, as at Uxmal, 'the Nunnery', which may possibly have furnished quarters for the rulers, would have furnished them at most sites only at the expense of comfort and convenience as compared with the simple thatched house. It was not need or utility that constructed the Mayan buildings. They were ceremonial, even symbolic, as notably in the Rio Bec region, where indeed there are representations of buildings, high on their steep pyramids, which are dummy buildings, and the stairs leading up to them too steep for even the Mayans to climb. Ceremonial buildings can be utilitarian and often have been, and the shape of their structure is governed in part by the nature of the ceremonies to be performed in them. But it is also and more importantly of their nature that they serve to proclaim and glorify the type and force of the civilization that erected them. The Spaniards in the new world thought it of great importance to build many churches there—more than utility required—and they were especially eager to tear down Indian temples and build churches on those same spots. Mayan buildings were inventions of space, a notice that place existed where they had decided that there should be a place as part of a world they were constructing in accordance with an idea of what the world was.

In order to have a world at all we need places with which we identify ourselves. It is very trivial, but a simple and common way to make this gesture of identification is to build a cairn or add a stone to one. One is reminded of cairns when one comes upon a great conical pile of rubble in the brush of Yucatan or the jungles of Chiapas or the Peten. Once, the sides were furnished with steps or filled in and made smooth with stucco, and the top was surmounted by a temple; but roots have torn apart the steps and rains have washed away the smoothing material. That the idea of a cairn is there now suggests that it may also have been there originally— that part of the idea, at least, which is the idea of adding a noticeable feature to the landscape to mark the presence of the builder there. It is a more positive gesture than cutting a gash on a tree or writing a name on a wall. But its motive would seem to be not in the effect of shaping the landscape but rather in the possible effect on the builder, who enlarges his own local sphere by conferring on himself the mark of his presence in distant places. Another civilization might have built a blockhouse or fort as an outpost on the edge of the wilderness, but the Mayan occupation was apparently a peaceful one. And for the Mayan civilization, everywhere was outpost. So little had gone before, that all they knew of the world was all wilderness. They started fresh, and just as they were inventors of time, so were they also inventors of space. The world which they knew should keep such time and have such shape as they gave it. We live in an inherited scheme of time in the crowding bulks of variously occupied and conflicting organizations of space. But our situations are not so different as they would seem to be. Our civilization, too, is almost obsessed with the ideas of time and space. The old concepts of them have seemed so inadequate to our use that it is the areas of our ignorance which have grown and supplied us with an area for starting as fresh as the Mayas started. Perhaps then it is our common interest, fortified with the sense that no occupation has been final and accurate yet, which still endows the Mayan scene with strength and virtue for us. Surely, we feel more than a respect for a successful alien endeavor, we feel a human identification with a kind of human victory which enabled this civilization, starting from an unknown point and taking an unknown direction, to spread out over the Peten, over Chiapas and Yucatan and down into Honduras, all of which was before a wilderness and is now almost a wilderness again, to occupy it and name it for its own, throwing up its enormous temple-pyramid cairns in order to do so and saying, in effect, let there be a place here (where there was nothing) and let there be another place here (where there was also nothing) and let there be a road between them. The mastery and daring are astonishing.

There is a cairn-like structure at Labná in the Puuc region which typifies this aspect of the Mayan occupation. It is so high and sudden on the stripped plain that one is struck first with the bravura and flamboyance of it. It is like a huge banner, a tremendous shout, exulting in the Mayan possession of this place. The other conspicuous structures at Labná are a portion of a wall pierced by a colossal arch, and a palace group. The arch is graceful in itself but the design elements in the wall are heavy and press clumsily against it. The palace group, unlike other similar structures in the Puuc area, is less a unified plan than a seemingly casual accretion of semi-detached units. Is it after we have noted these things that the pyramid-temple, which had seemed at first bold and jubilant, begins to appear only coarse and blatant? There is a curious orientation of these remaining structures. The pyramid-temple has its back toward the palace group and—maybe only because of the destructive accidents of time—stands at the extreme edge of the site, facing outward. The arch, which by its size and form suggests a grand approach to something, is turned and located not to approach properly either of the other two structures. There is an unrelatedness at Labná, unless it is significant that in facing south, the pyramid-temple faces back toward the heart of the Mayan area.

Back toward Tikal, for example, some two hundred miles south of Labná, where the buildings were better oriented to produce a defined space. Tikal, of course, was a prime center and Labná a minor one. At Tikal, there are several high pyramid-temples. They face inward as if to contain and shelter the city, and two of them help in the defining of the central plaza. We get a quite different spatial feeling from this grouping from the one which we get from an outlying cairn, as at Labná, no matter how elaborate and authentic in style the cairn might be. (It is also very different from the feeling of Chichén Itzá whose buildings, of a late period, seem based on specialized and disparate ideas as if at Chichén Itzá the idea of buildings as direct and simple occupation of space were over and space were there being *used* for various special purposes.) When a group of buildings face inward toward a space which they define and enclose, as at Tikal, they point to that space and accent it. It is only necessary to think of an inward facing group of buildings and then to picture the location as it would be if the buildings were reversed, to sense at once the effect of their orientation. It is the difference between here and there. At Tikal, the buildings say 'here'.

If so at Tikal, the more so at Palenque, whose buildings occupy a smaller area, are better preserved, and can almost be included in one view. Palenque lies in the hollow of some hills. To the north, however, a plain falls away toward the distant Gulf of Mexico. Along this side of the city, the only side not naturally enclosed, there is a line of small buildings raised on a platform and facing inward. Opposite this North Group, and turned toward it, is the Temple of Inscriptions on a massive pyramid. To the east of the Temple of Inscriptions, so as to make a kind of independent plaza, is a group of three smaller temples, those of the Cross, the Foliated Cross and the Sun. More or less in the middle of these various groups and buildings is the large, nearly square, rectangle of the Palace. These are the principal buildings. One has an immediate idea of enclosure, of inwardness. The site itself contributes to this. Where the cities of Yucatan are on open plains, Palenque is naturally enclosed by mountains. The orientation of the buildings toward each other reinforces this feeling. To enter the Palace or one of the Temples is to have the feeling of inwardness reinforced in a different way. *Inside* these buildings there is enclosed space. So often with Mayan buildings elsewhere it is only the outside that matters. The outside may be massive, even magnificent, but the inside is nothing. Cramped and dark, it seems a small hole scraped in the side of a mountain. Though such buildings may, as at Tikal, make an external space by their relation to each other, they fail to create an internal space, to enclose anything. Is it a paradox only of terminology that at Palenque the buildings succeed in enclosing an internal space because they have been able to open out? The outer walls are pierced by wide openings. The corbeled vault of the ceilings opens into transepts. It is an almost playful emphasis of the ability of these designers to enclose internal space that the basic plan of the four principal temples is of a building within a building, an idea that is carried one step farther in some of them so that we have a suggestion at least of a second inner building or enclosure. Sometimes in Christian churches the choir screen and the canopy of the altar make a similar effect. The temples have roofs of two slopes like mansards from the centers of which rise high, heavy screens, or crests, called roof combs, which resemble the pierced and decorated backs of Spanish combs. Between their doorways—this is true of the Palace, also—there are panels in stucco relief showing priestly or kingly figures in ceremonial regalia. The Temples of the Sun, of the Cross and of the Foliated Cross are so named from the central motif in similar, though more elaborate and of course better preserved panels which are placed against the back walls of these buildings and are the focal points of their interiors. The tablets from the Temple of the Cross have been carried away to the Museum in Mexico, leaving an emptiness, it is true, but the organization of the interior space is strong enough to survive the deprivation as a still satisfying building. Under the pyramid base of the Temple of Inscriptions, down in the ground like a root or seed, is a great tomb in which a body lay for a thousand years or more in a sarcophagus covered with a huge carved slab and guarded by sculptured figures at the door and on the walls. Though the sarcophagus nearly fills the floor of the room, the room seems spacious, perhaps because of the high, corbeled vault of the roof. Most Mayan dead, no doubt, were simply laid in the earth, though there is evidence elsewhere of vault burials. For this body at Palenque, however, they shaped in the earth a composed and long-lasting space, the roof of which divided it from the massive disorder of rubble which was the core of the pyramid above it.

It is against a less material, though equally massive, disorder of our experience of our surroundings that the serenely composed spatial order of the Palace at Palenque is so impressive. The landscape of Palenque is very beautiful. The contour of the land and its covering, the thick rich green of tropical rain forest, make a burgeoning, luxuriant Eden, especially at the season when the tremendous emergent trees are in flower. But beautiful as such an environment is, it is also aggressive and destructive, and must have seemed an overwhelmingly disintegrative force to a people equipped only with stone tools and fire to fight against it. Though it was repeatedly visited and investigated by early explorers, Stephens found it so overgrown in 1840 that he was unaware of the Temple of the Foliated Cross even after his party had lived for some time in the Palace and the strenuous efforts of a large group of laborers had been spent in clearing and burning. And sixty years later, Maudslay who was aware of the number of times the site had been cleared, would nevertheless have otherwise taken it for virgin forest. Now that the clearing has been restored, we can see the buildings again as the Mayas could; we can see the shape of the land, which without a cleared space around us we could not have seen; we can even see the luxuriance of the jungle, which even more than other woods can be obscured by its trees. Where there had been a shapelessness which was at once both crowded and empty, the builders of Palenque made a space.

The pleasure and beauty of the Palace is the extension of this space. On the perimeter of the building there is an outer corridor through whose wide and frequent openings one looks out across far greater spaces than the building contains. Within, the spaces of the Palace are extended laterally through a series of courtyards and galleries and rooms, vertically upward in a handsome three story tower and even, one might say, vertically downward by the subterranean passages beneath it. The elegance of the quiet order and movement of space from area to area of this building gives the same kind of pleasure as that given by another building quite different in detail, the Alhambra in Granada. It is true that the square tower is reminiscent of the Alhambra's *torres*, that there are frequent miradors and some arches and apertures of a curiously Moorish shape to give the surprising initial suggestion. But the true similarity is the beautiful combination of the closed and the open, and the feeling of care and devotion so successfully expended on a created space.

Palenque was abandoned centuries before the Spanish conquest. One wonders why; for everything at Palenque speaks of possession as permanent and final as that of the great tomb beneath the Temple of Inscriptions. 'This place; here.' It is almost audible as we walk through the Palace or amongst the buildings. We are induced to acknowledge the expressiveness and self-sufficiency of this space. If one thing more than another, more than their particular beauties, distinguishes the buildings at Palenque from the cairn-like buildings elsewhere, it is a feeling that at Palenque the landscape has been humanized, that in its occupation a kind of form in human terms has been imposed upon the landscape. This is almost opposite to the cairn idea of aggrandizing the builders by stamping on the builders the mark of distant places.

Can what happened once at Palenque fail to move us? Palenque emerged like a huge tree emerging from the indistinguishable undergrowth green of the jungle, towering over it and achieving its form. Space occupied here is in so violent contrast to its surroundings that the occupation of space seems the very formal pattern of all man's constructs, material or not.

In the *Popol Vuh*, the sacred book of another Mayan tribe, we read, 'There are generations in the world, there are country people, whose faces we do not see, who have no homes, they only wander through the small and large woodlands, like crazy people.' It seems that we are always in the presence of the small and large woodlands and that it is possible to wander homeless through them like crazy people. But at Palenque, they cleared a space in the woodlands and occupied it, and so created space and gave shape to an otherwise shapeless environment; and the shape that they gave it had focus and symmetry and proportion, qualities which were furnished by the builders, not copied from the natural surroundings. Something similar happened throughout the Mayan area, though not always with so much taste and skill. 'Innumerable,' says the *Popol Vuh*, 'were the places in which they settled, where they were and which they named.'

Yet Palenque was abandoned. Who knows now what name the Mayans gave it? Where the clearing had stood, the woodlands moved in again and erased it, though the buildings which occupied it have not yet been utterly destroyed. If it is true of space that it is featureless and empty except as we limit its vastness and shape it by our occupation, the form of the cities we impose on it, the direction and location of the boundaries and roads, it is true also that our occupation is never quite successful. It is part of the same truth that the limits we set to space are always in some degree arbitrary, and the names we give it are given names not absolute ones. We are always in some degree still nowhere in an empty vastness. Our passionately occupied Palenques are always abandoned. We tire of the forms we impose upon space and the restricted identities we secure from them. We tire finally even of the act itself of imposition.

COPAN : HISTORICITY GONE

The stelas stand in a large grass plaza, blazed in the full sun. One feels a festivity, a real party, though no one is there. Jim, who flew us in and who comes here in various weathers, says he likes it better in the rainy season, misty, mysterious. It has more than one expression, no doubt; but here in the assertive brightness of the light which is somehow joyful and triumphant, it is hard to think for long of any different expression.

And it is not what we expected either, though how should we say what we expected or how we formed our expectation? People were there before and pictured it and wrote about it. We took the wrong idea or failed to take the right one though it may have been there. What is transmissible? Most of the photographs are clear. Catherwood was skilled and patient with his drawings. He and Stephens discarded the first wood engravings made from the drawings and had them done again on steel in order to have truer pictures for their book. But one can sense in Stephens's account a resigned dissatisfaction with even that result. It wasn't quite as he saw it though he said it was the best to be had. And now if we look for what the pictures have shown us, what we find in addition to recognition each time is a start of surprise at how different things are from what we thought we were shown. And indeed, what is this to the rubbled and tree-grown mounds which were there before such restoration as has been done, or the restorations to the constructions they mean to suggest? What are we looking at or for? At the foot of the great stairways, the structure we look out toward is the ball-court, no doubt, or a part of what stood there once and served as one. But underneath this court is another which this one overlies, and under that one, another. We are looking at what we see, which no description gave us, which never existed. What we see is new and if we mean to see it we must look at it as something new. What we see is not what is there, though surely something is there and we seem to see it.

Across the city, on the river side, a section shows where the river veered and cut away the hill which made the acropolis. Earth had been brought and built on, the structures covered and built again at a higher level, a succession which ended in those buildings whose ruins now still stand at the top. We fly by in the plane and see the levels of stratification, the past exposed, so that it ceases, in a sense, to be the past and becomes again a present, a continuing present, contemporaneous with the structures at the top, within its own various levels, and with us, so that it is our present which enlarges, and we see ourselves as we are: more than we were. Students of the past trace and analyze strata to characterize the sequence of cultures; but, more than history, don't we look to find ourselves there, though history is the guise we give ourselves as if we meant not to speak directly of our subject, and history served as that Mayan mask, complexly devised of plumes and false faces, to cover our nakedness. For it is we who are naked here, exposed in layers by the river's cutting away of those successive domestic and ceremonial disguises in which we sought to hide ourselves. It is our absence, indeed, which is our presence: the disguises are there still and we are not there, we are nowhere; we are as we were. What we call the past is an aspect of our present.

How should we say, consequently, who these figures may be, carved on the stelas, half-covered, chubby, epicene, vaguely-faced, though their faces once may have been more special-featured? Their feet, in elaborate boxings and lacings of sandals, turn outward almost all the way; and their hands, held across the breast, are backside under and half-closed, the fingers turned in, as though to conceal the emptiness they hold. It is said they hold scepters, and perhaps they do, but the convention of the hand position seems an unnatural convention to us. We see something of the forearms, a little of the leg above and below the knee, and the face. The rest of the figure and the space around it are encrusted and overlaid with armband, girdle, kilt and headdress so elaborate that, only because they are carved in the same stone mass, does the figure seem able to carry them. It is by its accoutrements that the figure asserts itself; and that we see it at all is as if, in an illustration, it were indicated as underneath by a dotted line. Take the regalia away, is there anyone there? There seems to have been no concern for such a question and no concern is, in effect, a negative answer. These figures—were they priests or kings, perhaps, or gods?—were anything at all only by the force of their iconography invented to distinguish them, and this is forgotten and not discovered again. In the mass of their stone, their anonymity frightens us, and it would hardly help to know what names they bore, as though the names themselves were again another bangle. It was their nothingness which was not faced, or faced rather, was thought to be concealable under a heavy overlay. There are a few carved

31

heads to be found in the ruins which have little or no adornment. Death's heads are very numerous and these are unadorned. Those notably alive were rich in ornament; death was a stripping away. They were often reminded; they did, of course, their own reminding and felt a need to.

At the top of the acropolis, there is a structure with a richly adorned doorway carved with glyphs and figures and the leaves and tendrils of stylized plants. At the base on either side, as finial to the sill or plinth to the side pilasters, is a kind of death's head which seems less a skull than a skinned decapitation. We don't know what it may be which is depicted here. One figure is almost naturalistic; others are only partly anthropomorphic. Does it say that the idea of death underlay whatever was thought to be in the carving above it, that death was basic? Can we read that human experience is expressible in symbols, that one aspect of it is in relation to other aspects, and that this relationship is one of support and generation? Visually diverse elements are brought together in this carving. Even though we don't know what these elements represent as part by part, their existence as a related structure is an affirmation that our experience is structural and is discernible as structure. We can see this much without knowing what definition they gave the elements, though they must have known. This combination of elements, some natural, some other than natural, has seemed to some observers to represent a cosmology and man in the cosmology occupying his space. We do make cosmologies and we treat them on various levels of belief. It doesn't seem urgent that we understand the one here; its statement, if we could read it, seems unlikely to support us. Perhaps it is only in that sense that we take cosmologies seriously if we do at all. And what prevents us from taking them seriously if we do not is a sense that we are not capable of devising a cosmology which is effective in supporting us, a sense that however much we may desire it or however ingeniously we may pursue it, it is not to be devised. Our interest in knowing how to interpret this inscription as cosmology is an interest in knowing how someone else failed as we do too.

There were two panels in Temple 11 covered with hieroglyphs. We would be gratified to read them. And yet we are completely certain there is no great news they could tell us. They know no more than we and their reference is their own. This is not to disparage them but to recognize our own limitations and to say that they were human like us. And behind Temple 11 is the long stairway which leads to another temple and is known as the Hieroglyphic Stairway because its whole vertical surface is an inscription. Scholars can read some dates here as, of course, elsewhere on the various monuments. Their time was another reckoning from ours and we take satisfaction in finding the correlations of the two so as to state one in terms of the other. One duration in terms of another duration would seem to be the nature of time and to make such a statement was a satisfaction of the Mayas as well. It was apparently at Copan that some of the Mayan time statements were sharpened. A heavy, rectangular slab, called Altar Q, carved with glyphs on its surface and human figures on its edges, seems to have commemorated some more precise astronomical reading by which time was reckoned, with the result that their calendar was made to correspond more closely with the movements of heavenly bodies. We recognize here our own uncanny desire to measure ourselves against the sun and stars, counting revolutions, unrolling the concentric circles which surround us, to make them linear and historical. At Copan, the line of history broke a short generation after the dating of the Hieroglyphic Stairway and Altar Q. No monument discovered has a date later than the year we number 800 A. D. They may have continued the reckoning of time after this without recording it in monuments. Perhaps they deserted the city; perhaps they stayed nearby. Life can continue without a reckoning of time. It has a kind of latitude, and time is one way to speak of that latitude. But when time comes to a stop as it seems to have come to a stop around Copan, the latitude remains. Perhaps the people went away. More probably they stayed and not too far from there. They stopped making monuments and may have no longer reckoned the calendar or thought consciously of the temples and sacred precincts, but remained as much or as little as they were before. The whole set of our minds is splinted so in time and history, our thinking structure fails to stand without them, and we are reluctant and uneasy, thinking of timeless man, of man without history. When we come back now to Copan, we feel at home there because, however remote or alien its terminology, we sense through all our ignorance that time and history have been here once. It seems entirely natural, too, the only human reaction, to feel regret and melancholy and bewildered protest that all these structures are empty and fallen, that something stopped here a thousand years ago. We assume of time and history that they are continuous and progressive and always were. The insistent questions that confront us here and characterize us are, "Where did these people come from?" and "Where did they go to?" We are brought to face the discontinuity of time and history, the continuance nevertheless of man, and the equivalence as answers to these questions of *nowhere* and *here*. We assume that we, too, came from somewhere, go someplace; but of ourselves also we would have to answer *nowhere* and *here*, and know that one answer said the same as the other. And, together, the answers say, insofar as we can be characterized, we are they and they are we, timeless and unhistorical. It is true that we have on either occasion invented times and histories for ourselves and, by an act of will, imposed them as long as strength lasted. We invented these the way we invented speech and buildings and costumes and the changes of modes in these; but, whatever we are, we are without them and apart from the changes in them. These things in themselves can be said to have times and histories; but they have little or nothing to do with us. We lean on inventions, though, to give us standing. We dress ourselves in inventions and house ourselves there. We give ourselves mythic identity, find something we ought to do and project rewards. We are never what our pretensions claim though at times we seem to be when our pretensions succeed for awhile, when will and self-denial and force mold us into some image we impose upon ourselves and on those around us, so that common consent gives us the role we claim for ourselves. To say we make something of ourselves is a form of praise for a person or a culture.

There is a large mask on a stairway in the East Court, a wide-eyed human face with symbols beside it that show it to mean the planet Venus. It is something to say of Venus, and what else should we say? But without the label, we should never have found it out. The Mayan culture and this whole site as exemplar are mask and metaphor. So are we.

One of the strongest impressions that we have is that under the mask and metaphor something is there though it is not perhaps man that is there. There is something which is. Nothing else matters. Copan is a liberation. It is all gone, emptied away. To see it is to see ourselves gone, to see us freed from the weight of our own world and its limitations. One aspect of the roles we assume is taken as something more than whimsical self-indulgence. It is the assumption of the responsibility for our own natures and environment. It is to say that both can be bettered and that we know the direction of betterment and can work that way, and that given time enough and good will and energy, we can evolve a world subject to our reason and wisdom which are sufficient for that, and that this then will be the world, the world that is. One supposes that whoever may have lived at Copan may have thought this way and that the development of this city may have been directed toward that end; one supposes that whoever may have lived here is we. That the idea is historically absurd is only in part our own absurdity: it is the absurdity of our historicity. Whatever we are, we are not historical. The world we make and ourselves, so far as we make ourselves, ourselves in the particularities of time and place, as cultural man—all this can be destroyed and make no matter. We are happy at Copan to witness our own destruction and how we survive it. If something may be said to happen, what happens to us is not what happens. The evident destruction of Copan is witness to this as we, in our own lives, are witness to the same things. We are delivered from our continuous failures and frustrations. Perhaps more importantly, we are delivered from our self-limited successes, the awful banalities of the good life.

Joy and desire surround us without our doing, without our understanding.

The world or what we term the world, that medium in which we find ourselves, and indeed whatever of it we set apart and term selves, is not related to what we make of it and not dependent on what we make of the world or make of ourselves. It is not in the least altered, nor is our basic nature altered, by any cosmology or culture or individual character we may devise, or by the failure or destruction of any of these, as all of them fail. If they seem for a time to succeed, they blind us as though they were real; and it is by our most drastic failures that we may perhaps catch glimpses of something real, of something which is. It merits our whole mind. The good society and the good life are more than we could imagine. To devise them or to assert and defend their devising is not the point.

COPAN : FOR SHIRLEY CLARKE

We are in the real world as ghosts are in this world, of doubtful being, almost impalpable. The matter of the real world passes through us and we pass through the matter of the real world though, so to speak, neither is material, materiality being a concept of this world which we wrongly extend to areas where it has no bearing for support. To speak of us as real or to speak of us as material is not, in effect, to speak of us for it is to speak of something we are not.

One supposes there may be reality though the world where we live by custom is not real and one supposes that if *here* and *now* have any direct meaning, reality must be here and now. Nevertheless, our contact with it is uncertain and remote. It is not conceptual as this world is—what else is this world but the forest of our concepts—and though our receptors are open toward reality, we make no concepts of it and it is received negatively most of the time, not as a positive signal but as a kind of static which roughens and shakes our concepts and, in defending them, we fight against it. But it stands; and it stands by the failure of this world which we defend. How should we speak of a real world if this world were real? There would then be only this world and it real. There is this world, to be sure, but it is not real. Consequently, in addition to this world, there is a real world as well.

And we are in the real world however ghostly our existence there may be. There are times when this world seems in some way related to reality and to resemble it. It is the way, for example, that the coasts of continents reflect each other as though they had once been joined, though now a whole ocean lies between them where the joint was separated. Or the link may be a projection without conforming, like the relation between an airplane and its shadow on the earth, which in following the lateral, or better, circumferential flight of the plane, goes up and down with the contours of the ground, or glides level across the water though the plane climbs or descends. These are infrequent occasions.

More often, the one does not reflect the other and this world so little suggests reality we lose the contrast entirely, take this for the only world and end by supposing it may be real, acting as if it were, even perhaps believing it. Had we remained aware the whole time of a real world around us, what might we have done about it? Surely, we might have believed less in this world. It is just as sure that aware and believing as we might have been of the real world, there is nothing we might have done. The real world is not manipulable, not usable by us. We are not used either. Though we may coincide with reality, it is a coincidence in which we remain, nevertheless, apart. It may sometimes happen, for example, that cut off from any real world, we may push all our energies toward some attainment with the kind of avidity and single-mindedness that absence of reality allows. We push as though our object were both real and attainable as it could not be, and when it shows itself to be one, it shows itself to be not the other. When we experience this, that particular pursuit is over but we have, in that awareness, such a vivid experience of reality, that we are shaken even if not moved by it. What we have been through in our almost total separation from reality is like a long thirst or a long hunger, a long deprivation of any kind and its long-delayed relief. Is it possible that we compensate in this way for our inability to deal directly with reality or to have it deal with us? The objects pursued in this deviant course are often the ordinary objects of this world: power of some sort, political goals selfish or selfless, material possessions, possession of one another, surrender. But even though the goals may be this-worldly, the pursuit, in the intensity of its passion, and perhaps in other ways as well, is rebellious. It turns its back on this world and works across the grain, even as it does with reality also. Had it been in harmony with this world, keeping both goals and methods there and thinking them nothing other than that, the goal could well have been attained and nothing happen.

There are maps of the earth called polar projections such that if the projection is centered on the north pole, the whole outer circumference of the map represents the south pole. The real world seems as remote from us and we from the real world as the far circumference of a circle from its center, as remote and as distorted as the opposite pole appears on a polar projection. Nor is there, on such a projection, any coming the whole way around and back to the starting place again as on a globe. But in this opposition between us and the real world any point can be the pole projected on and as the point shifts as the poles of the earth are said to have shifted in the past, what in one projection is remote circumference becomes, in another, closer center and the opposites interpenetrate each other without effect.

37

The real world is wherever; and so are we. We are not at opposite poles. We discover this. Rather, we might be said to be together at the pole opposite to the one projected on so that our true opposition is to that area at the center of the projection which is our immediate surrounding. This world (the one which we call this world), the one projected on, lies close at hand, is sharply detailed and undistorted. The sharpness of detail and the absence of distortion both diminish as the distance from the center increases. Any projection abandons the wide field to concentrate on the narrow one. The lens of its concentration and focus is particularity, not only in the constantly enlarged and sharpened detail, but in the separation of the object from the observer, from its surroundings, from cause and effect, from any relationship. This world has the hard surface, sharp edges, immediacy and vividness we expect of reality and has it most fully when we have been crowded away from it, as reality has been crowded away, by the multiplication of detail and scale. Particularity excludes us; we can't compel the real world. We are in the real world, negatively at least, in our common exclusion from this world. Where else can we go?

When we are young, our formless insubstantiality frightens us and we look with longing at the immediate materiality of this world as though it were real and as though it could salvage us. It doesn't seem true that its definition was gained by excluding reality. But if we put on one of its costumes, we are nothing wearing that costume, the suit of empty armor. Without a costume, we seem of doubtful being and we want to bring ourselves into this world in hopes of sharing in its quality. We try, by one means or another, to locate and specify and characterize ourselves, to cause the ghost to materialize; and we devise, to this purpose, systems of natural science and politics and metaphysics in order to place ourselves there, to have some sharper image of ourselves, or succession of images, views from various angles. Like the clouds which Hamlet examined with Polonius, we seem different things even at one time. We try numbers for strength and opposition for certainty. The one certainty that appears from all these thrusts in the dark is that they are thrusts in the dark and hit very little. We don't know. Whatever costume we may put on leaves us wholly uncovered or, if we like, wholly hidden—uncovered in a way which reveals nothing except that the costume is not our own.

One thing we feel about ourselves—without knowing—is the uncertainty of our separation. If there is a medium in which we may be said to have our being, are we apart from this or part of it? Can we be said to be in the real world as, for example, in this world we say a bird is in the air or a fish is in the water, implicitly affirming not only the discreteness of their entities but that there are such entities? Of ourselves, we can only say we don't know. There are various ways to speak of man within acceptable terms of reason as a theologian might or a biologist or a political scientist. But any of these rational ways stretches our credulousness even farther than the most fantastic ways, and is finally preposterous because we lie outside of acceptable terms of reason and are not knowable. Not knowing is the condition of our motivation or even the motivation itself. It tries to bring us into this world where rational knowledge is a part.

To see ourselves, should we look at each other? Sometimes we seem to each other to be part of the real world as though here, if anywhere, we came to reality directly. Is it symbolically true? We don't relate to each other, we relate, or try to relate, to some outside symbol the other suggests to us; and if the other relates to us, it is again not to us it relates, but to something we had not supposed ourselves to be. The thing related to may be, as it seems to be, a part of the real world, but it is not we.

We are in the real world as nothing in ourselves, as a skin on that world, as a network of nerves, an awareness not of ourselves but of that world, even as though we might be that world's awareness of itself. In this act of union, the self is shed like an exoskeleton and we lie so close against the real world our identity lies there.

COPAN: UNWILLINGNESS, THE UNWILLED

What do we want? Say everyone were healthy and beautiful, were rich and together and would never die: well, hardly. But that or something like it had seemed to be what we want. Just the same, any increase in personal favor, relief from some particular ailment, or to live if only a little longer,— these partial benefits seem good. But, in either case, it is the imminent certainty of deprivation, whether whole or fractional, we stand on. How should we seem to want these things without that certainty?

So; what *do* we want? Sometimes, to go, in other ways also, counter to the truth, to mark ourselves off from what there is around us, and make that subject to our will: to be masters of some sort, of the political-military sort that leaders and conquerors are, or of the intellectual sort that devises a rationality strong enough that it seems to impose that rationality on what there is. But what there is continues outside and beyond any rationality imposed on it, and political-military mastery is brief and apparent. The notion that man's condition can be stated in such a way that there is, for one thing we, and for another, our environment which we master or fail to master, is in itself a wrong idea. It might be said that we are everything, that the only reality is internal, there is nothing outside of us. Or, it might be said that we are nothing, have no real being, that there is only something else whose existence ignores us, and asks us for nothing. The two statements seem to be opposed but may not be. They are equivalent, at least, in denying the duality. Whatever there is, if there is something, we, if we are, are part of it. There are not two realities: man and his medium, of which one is the subject and one the object. It is only by a willful act in the face of the truth that we become an entity separate from what there is around us; and how much the more willful it is to presume to master what we have marked ourselves off from.

There is something which is and we are not separable from it. Then, if we want something, it is something wanted through us; we are the instrumentality of a desire which it would not be quite accurate to call external because we are part of the wanting, but neither is it right to think it personal. If something is wanted, we feel the want but we are not apart in

wanting it. It is always tempting though to transmute the something wanting into personal terms, to look for, or even to find, our own satisfactions
as though that were what was wanted, as it proves not to be. At any rate,
our personal satisfactions, once had, often seem nothing; whatever it was
that was wanted, it wasn't that, and we are puzzled by trophies that seem
to have been won by someone we don't even remember. Not always
though.

The attempt to put personal desires in place of the general want which
we feel, is a simplification, and makes the problem of desire appear to be
something we could hope to solve. Isn't it, at bottom, a trial to be something of our own, a separate part with its own desire? It is interesting that
our separation is rarely a branching and gradual departure, nor is it a process of development by which inherent and hardly perceptible tendencies
express and realize themselves. It is a removal to an existent position as
though it were transferable, as though we were molten and gave ourselves
into some mold that we saw in order to borrow the form of that mold. We
might make much of the implications of external labels which are neither
natural nor inherent—of name and place and time and function. It is the
somewhat removed mold, often, that seems to attract us, though sometimes the removal is only the distance from actuality to pretension. It may
be that the attraction of hypocrisy is only the unnaturalness of the position
which it offers, a position which is well-defined because of its falsity. We
are uncertain where something real begins or ends, or of its nature; the
false can be sharply defined however hollow it is or however little it means.
The human situation seems less a come-as-you-are party than a party to
which we are bidden to come as our favorite character and, though we are
sometimes cheap or shy, we do fairly well. We put on the costume and
badges, the mental attitudes, the facial and vocal expressions of *something*,
of *someone*. Such an action gives shape and clarity to our desires, gives
them poles and simplicity; it sets us up as some sort of marked-off existent.
It is of course evasive. It is hard to face how insanely evasive until we have
watched the fatal despair with which we fight off the loss of an assumed
identity. An assumed identity is made from appearances and lets us be
nothing and yet appear to be something. We don't so much want to be
something as we want to be allowed to look like something, to be granted
general recognition—even acclaim—as what we pretend to be, to win the
prize for Best Costume. A declared identity is an assertion of independence, often an aggressive and defiant assertion as though our separate

person were a prime value; and it is an avoidance at the same time of any person we might have inside lest it look like the nothing it fears to be. Avoidance, removal, displacement: these seem to be the center of our wanting to be something, our assumption of an identity on our own, as though in order to be something it were necessary to move away, to break some existing connection whatever we sense it to be. But it may be the other way: that we want to be something in order to justify our real desire which is to move aside. There are societies where it is recognized as essential to have an assumed name under which to function and to conduct a mature life, suppressing a real name such as it might be. In certain ways, our own society admits the same need.

We may well be nothing or if not, are tenuous and frail. Resoluteness of being which seems to make us something acts to block our emptiness into which something which is might flow. If we start playing a role and let our energies and devisings embellish and serve that role, we are reflecting, however in error, the flow into our emptiness of energies and intentions from what seems outside, but which finds some sort of reception in us. Something enjoys being. Our imitation in our own right, of being, may pass for pious homage or a satisfaction at least, of those self-generated desires. We envy actors who have a role into which their passions can be directed, or else we envy the dead, that melted flesh no longer faced with the question.

If something wants through us, if we are the instrumentality of a desire whose source is not internal, then to interpose our own will or personal desires is an avoidance of reality, and the wants which our willfulness includes are irrelevant wants and may be dismissed as not important, as not what we want, no more than we want, as we seem to, an endless life, endless wealth and fairness and company. Order and security, to be caressed and honored and to caress and honor in turn—we seem to want these things, but in order to make us a separate enclave, a refuge apart from what may be wanted through us. If we are not to falsify life, but to have it for what it is, we must leave ourselves open to it and undefended, observant of what may happen, since our private will is not relevant and we are not capable of apprehending or assisting any other will, and what we observe and feel is perhaps less will than being and the nature of being. We have made up complicated frameworks of activity and attitude on the foundation that somehow we grasp what may be wanted from us, some challenge or imperative. The challenges and imperatives may not be anything like each other in any respect except in this: that they assume our receiving them. But in experience (and on the contrary) nothing is revealed to us of what our nature may be, or of what we must do. Nor, though we spy on it most diligently, do we learn things of consequence about whatever else there may be besides ourselves. We have no inkling of its wants or purposes or whether it has any. There may be some divine or historical or biological or evolutionary determinism and we may be wholly subject to it—it may want something of us—but it is without our consciousness, and we cannot bring our wills to consonance with it, not knowing what it is. I think we are totally unable to affect it: that any action of ours which is contrary is null by its contrariety, and any consonant action is an action not by us but through us, not by our will or any necessity. We have supposed that there are wants and purposes but it seems likely that none exists.

How empty all those schemes are, and they are very many, which propose our necessity or which propose that we need to do this or that in order to assert or maintain our own existence, or to realize what may have been intended for us. Noting that we do devise as a convenience a kind of machinery of social and political and economic organization, we project that a more searching and more diligent devising would make use of what there is and organize reality into the mechanism. Noting that we do personify ourselves, that we devise a characterization by means of, say, the superego, or historical imperative, or evolutionary vectors, moral precept, or what we will, we project that our courage and intelligence have the means to produce in our own person the fulfilled and realized man who has dared to embody reality in himself, not flee from it, and so has permitted reality to have real being. But what there is—we are part of what there is—is what it is regardless of us. It has real being without our help. We are whatever we are, squirm or resolve what we will to avoid it. We can make as though to run away and leave only a token of ourselves behind, but the token we leave behind is what there is. Anything else is pretense and subterfuge. We need not want anything; nothing needs us to want.

There are things which we feel, certain angers, rejoicings, fears. These feelings astonish us. Set beside our expectation of a real world, they seem not to have the habit of reality. They seem unrelated, and there is a lapse of time before we take them as real in the absence of a more expected reality. We learn at last, and accept the learning at last, that these feelings come to us without our willing or acceding or inventing. They come from beyond our skin like approaches to us, like messages; and we respond, trembling

43

and shaking, or vibrating in tune as though we were instruments a music were played on and we arch and turn to have the contact closer. Our responses are presences that tower around us, seemingly solid as stone.

A PARTIAL GLOSSARY

COSTUME AS METAPHOR

We dress ourselves in certain clothes, change our hair and faces in order to look some way we think to look. Appearance changes us and it need not be dissembling. Indeed, what are we? Are we anything? Sometimes, we become what we look to be which we have thought to be. And, on further thought, this may be nothing also though, for the time, it looked to be something. Other times, our dissembling seems wrong in its particular, as a contradiction of another identity as though we had that identity and an assumed one could contradict it. We want to be something: whatever we really are, whatever we could hope to be. But, 'What we really are' is a mystery, and what we could hope to be has only such value as our hope assigned it. Our aspirations are blind and arbitrary and their success is only their own.

Children dress in scraps of costume and play at being what the scraps suggest. They try it and let it go. Later, our commitments are sometimes fuller and the letting go isn't so easy when our interest wanes as it may. We hedge it with other interests on the side, secret selves or contradictory clothes which protest the real me, so that anyone's person may well be multiple and all the multiples tentative and exploratory as children's are. The space remaining for definition—so wide for children, or so it seems— becomes narrow and limited and definition farther and farther off and we accept what we were as if it were what we are or even what we had meant to be. But it isn't. We know so.

When we ask who someone is we get places and ages for answers, occupations and antecedents, what times and places someone has occupied or what other external has occupied him, as though we were all blanks and had no shape or nature except by possession. Our need to possess and our need to be possessed proclaims this. If we really were something in ourselves, could we need anything? Could anything possess us? Possessions hardly satisfy us. They must have been not our need.

But, whatever our need, they must in some sense have been wrong and we sense the wrong not by contrast with some other possession though it must often seem so: the apparent greenness of other pastures or even this

47

same pasture in the approach of some spring. We have hopes for projected futures, for what may someday be in spite of all. In spite of all. In the light of all. How impressive the all is: the endless possibilities whose indefinite endlessness makes absurd any one. How hopeless it is to pose in any particular costume when all we are is limitless and costume denies that, limits us in a role.

What can we ever be if the limitlessness of the all is truly our quality? We can as little be anything as we could if we were nothing as also it seems we are. It is hard to decide; and the decision whether we are all or nothing, based as it is on the same premise, produces the same result; we cannot ever be anything. Though we dress however forcefully or fancifully we will, it is always pretension though the pretense may have its successes, even for a long time.

What of the world? Though there may seem to be nothing outside ourselves, there is a sense in which we observe and the object, as though it were, of our observation we call the world. This is absurd because the world *is* as little as we *are*.

And yet the language has its declensions and its conjugations. If we speak at all we speak in the structure of the language and what we say, whatever it is, may matter far less than our accession to the way the structure of the language divides experience in terms of person and tense so as to say we are (or were, will be), so as to say what was or could, what is, who is the first or second or third person, what is singular or plural, that there are or could have been, that there still might be, certain actions, certain reactions. We speak in tongues however prosaic our speech may be. The boldness of language supervenes our actual experience. It means to say what we don't know. It creates the world as if the world were. Its whole necessity is metaphor.

And language need not be verbal; that is to say our postures and houses, our laws and landscapes, our science and public buildings, share the character of language. They are metaphor also: creations of desire.

Forgive the world, however terrible it is. We dream of horror, impelled by what we don't know, and the world seems to contain it; but it is not a real world and nothing requires our belief.

That we believe in nothing is a hard requirement because we want to believe in something: some political theorem, say, or religious creed or, sparing these, some unevaluated strength of our own as though in our person we might prevail and that prevalence had the salience of some

proof. For what? For our dying? Because we do. Unable to think of ourselves this way, think instead of someone ten thousand years from us one
way or another who will have or had a name, a place and costume no more
and as much as we have. And who is he? Even so far as we know, it is a
pretense of knowing. Abandon that.

Belief in nothing is a positive belief apart from relieving us of partiali-
ties; and, even in that respect, it is a liberation. The world is not partial.
Nothing is all and the world is nothing as we are. What should we say?
Nothing to say of ourselves and the world tells us nothing. The world is a
silence. But we talk of it and to it.

We know nothing of the world and will never know. All we say is metaphor which asserts at once our unknowing and our need to state in some
language what we don't know. How we love clothes; plain clothing or even
our nakedness, speaking the silence of the world, or fanciful costume in
which we praise some aspect of the world we mean to praise. Clothing as
metaphor, not to dress ourselves nor to say what the world is if we knew
but to praise that world however it might be. Rich fabrics and fine leathers,
ruffles and satin, silver and lace, glorious colors and the fragile purities of
clean whites: none of these is the world nor are they all together the world.
Songs only that sing its praise, the earnest entreaties and importunities of
our desire.

DESIRE AND DENIAL

At length, the mental and physical structures of the world lose strength and articulation so we are nearly free of them and we begin to see, through and around and under the clutter they were, the real world which they encrusted. The real world, though not really a world: no world is real. We see how curious it is that we live at once in a world which is not real and a reality which is not a world and how little the two resemble each other, how impossible it is that the other should ever become the one. What we settle for, if we settle, is not important; but the two are, and no doubt will be, in separate ways.

My friend sends me a picture of Mayan monuments from a site which surprises both of us. These were parts of a world we never knew—might never have known. Though it is quite gone, we can a little way, with their aid, feel into it. Reality is, as always, and needs no monuments. It is for anyone there. But it is also true that anyone there wants, in his time and place, to imagine a world and this imagining imagines a time and place constituting the time and place of that world to which monuments are built. No worlds otherwise exist as worlds. But reality exists always—for them, for us, for anyone. It is shapeless and timeless and, one supposes, always the same, so that in spite of those times and places which we imagine, those particular worlds in which we give ourselves sites and sequences, we say we are nowhere and eternal, that is to say timeless and not in the world. This acuity is direct and immediate which we come to without thinking and often fearfully.

Worlds are refuge and sanctuary but how they penalize us and set us apart, how they subvert our experience as though it happened only in a world and could happen only if there, could only be said to have really happened if it can be related to that world's premises and temporal schemes. As we become increasingly at home in a world and more loyally citizens of it, so our experience does seem to happen there,—within those confines. We dismiss it otherwise as of no consequence.

Dreams, of course: we condescend to these most valid experiences as divagant fantasy, impossible of realization, or as clues to a therapy in a world we failed. And it is true that much of what we dream is impossible in the sense that it can never be incorporated in any more tangible world. And it is also true that that world which we imagine, which we call the actual world, has been imagined as a world of consequence and, within its spaces, works that way. Its parts are related in ways that cause and effort make an effect. We see this happening. What we never see is any consequence outside the confines of that imagined actual world. There are no large consequences. Barring not even the total destruction of that actual world, there are no large consequences.

The real is inconsequential and is still reality. Dreams are part of it as the actual world of consequence is not. We suffer things that occur to us that have no place in the actual world. Waking at night or walking out in the morning, we experience irrational joy, irrational despair. They seem causeless and we think of nothing to do with them. We let them pass if they pass and often they do. Apart from the world, we let them be as if apart from us, from our true experience.

What else, however are we, or what else is reality? We know it is not in that imagined world of mundane invention where we try to act it out, try to contain and prove it in games and stories which shape our lives to their shape. Wars and careers. Engaged in these, we feel an outside form in which we participate, escaping our shapelessness.

Desire is our door into the world. We see shapes there and want them and we go after them into the world. But desire is our door out again also when the shapes we saw leave our desires unsatisfied. What could we ever have wanted? More than a door to enter, the world offers us a prospect to peer into whose shapes suggest a reality which they, themselves, are not. And reality is what we want—our own or any other—and reality is shapeless and disparate. We live in reality without possession or occupation and the love of reality unpossessed transfigures us.

How uneasy our lives are: we are denied those shapes and spaces of desire by our desire which rejects them. Shapeless and impalpable ourselves, we want that reality which has no shape to occupy.

THE BROTHER IN ELYSIUM
Ideas of Friendship and Society in the United States

Viola. What country, friend, is this?
Captain. This is Illyria, lady.
Viola. And what should I do in Illyria?
My brother he is in Elysium.

Twelfth Night
WILLIAM SHAKESPEARE

EPISTLE DEDICATORY TO
SIDNEY COX, among many

It is several years now, Sidney, since this book was started in and around your house,–several years and a war in between. I feel now, at the end, even more surely than at the beginning, that much can be said about the nature of society through the medium of these three American writers, who were so deeply concerned with society in both its immediate form of friendship, and its wider form of our relations within the social structure. Each man's approach to the two forms was single, as indeed it may be for all of us, so that there will be no inconsistencies to be found between our real ideas of our friends and our real political desires. Superficially, this will not seem to be so; but I have intended to go beneath the surface.

Thoreau and Melville and Whitman were artists and their statements were in the language of art. There isn't anyone who is capable of translating that most accurate of languages into any other,—the language of history, or sociology, or criticism, for example, and I have not attempted to do so. Art and action, however, may be considered in the same terms. I have wanted to write a kind of essential drama, in which each of the three characters comments on the matter at hand by his own word and deed, and so reveals himself and his subject. If my book makes any statement, therefore, it must be by the relationships that are revealed, by its composition, by a form brought about to the perceptive reader, by that element which is in every line and in no single one. Of course, I have not declined to agree or disagree, or to make other statements here and there directly and by implication. But these statements, taken singly, are not really the point.

Society is based on something more than economics and physical security. I do not mean to argue the point or to prove it, but without it this book is meaningless, and the reader is thus warned. And without it, too, our political conceptions, even the most grandiose, are slight and shallow and will not last long. As it would be foolish to look at society and ignore material desires, so is it more than equally foolish to assume that men desire society only for its material benefits. Men desire society for its own sake; and of course there are other reasons for the desire, wise and stupid and in between. Whitman, for example, looked to the glorious State to solve his own personal deficiencies, and in varying degrees, this is a widely-shared eva-sive desire. But the underlying motives of men's societies,—even of our own American society—are too complex to be simply listed here. If that could be done, there would have been no need to write this book.

This is partly a book about friendship; and I address you, Sidney, as a friend among many friends. And I address you as one among many because you are one person who is aware of the complexities of the social problem among many people who are not. Most men live in the social body as uncon-sciously as cells live in the physical body. Or they are like the multitude of fish in the sea, which cry out the glory of God, but not in a voice which fish can understand or readily discourse in. This would be well enough if their unconsciousness were not continuously exploited by mistaken or cynical men, or if they were never precipitated into, and forced to act in, those recurrent emotional or political or economic crises which enter a few times even into the lives of socially unconscious men. The ideas of society in this book will seem important to you, but their importance will not be seen by many men to whom, in actual practice, they are equally important.

Viola's brother was not in Elysium, though she almost liked to think so; and where she found him it was Illyria. How often when we are on our best behavior, and moved by generosity or loneliness, we are led to speak of society in terms of brotherhood. We are told that all men are brothers, and the inference has sometimes been that a simple acceptance of that dictum leads to no further problems. Are there then no family quarrels, no bitter-ness in the blood? How complex and ambiguous is the problem of brother-hood is shown in the tragic frustration of Thoreau, Whitman's erotic phan-tasy, and Melville's hard-won wisdom. Read, mark, therefore, learn and inwardly digest; here, as some of our contemporary devils might say, are the scriptures.

W.B.
Hudson Falls, N.Y.
November, 1946

SILENCE AND HENRY THOREAU

Friendship

Henry Thoreau lived in Concord in Massachusetts in the middle years of the nineteenth century. His faith in the common interests of man was so strong that he knew that following the dictates of his own conscience would not make him an enemy of society. This faith gave him great independence of thought and action so that he chose his behavior with little regard for the opinions and shibboleths of his neighbors. The resemblance between his behavior and that of his neighbors then became an indication of that commonness and a fair proof. This same mode of living in accordance with one's own rather than society's opinion, he recommended heartily to all men, but they could not understand this fully and so mistrusted him for the little differences and a certain strangeness that they felt between them and him. Actually, in consideration of his abounding benevolence and true humanity, there should have been no cause for this mistrust, but Thoreau and his ideas placed such high demands on them, that the strangeness even for those who knew and loved him well, remained.

"I love Henry," Emerson, for example, quotes with delight, "but I cannot like him. And as for taking his arm, I would as soon think of taking the arm of an elm tree." The usual picture of Thoreau has been that of a friendless, unfriendly, and thereby cold and emotionless man. Certainly he would seem to have been undemonstrative, but such things are a matter of subtlety; and the greatest emotion was not likely to elicit the most obvious demonstration from Thoreau. That there was emotion and that it was, in some way, demonstrated, one can be sure. Thoreau, who was deeply sensible of his relationships to others and so honest with himself and them in facing the true worth of the relationship, and so exacting moreover, demanding that friendship be based on and maintain a mutual respect and independence, has led people from his own time to ours to say that he lacked feeling for his fellow men and lacked the desire and capability for friendship. He refused to pretend to that which had no existence and indeed could not have cheapened real friendship, for which he had the deepest regard and desire, by accepting something else as though it were indistinguishable from what he really wanted, or had equal value with it.

Thoreau himself might not have found the elm tree comparison so unflat-
tering, however it might be used against him. It is the kind of remark to
amuse and delight him who was a master of such arboreal fancies. He
would gladly have taken the arm of an elm tree and at one time had thought
to marry an oak, he said, when won by the beauty of its leaves in December.

"Well-tanned leather on the one side, sun-tanned, color of colors, color
of the cow and the deer, silver-downy beneath, turned toward the late
bleached and russet fields. What are acanthus leaves and the rest to this?
Emblem of my winter condition. I love and could embrace the shrub oak
with its scanty garment of leaves rising above the snow, lowly whispering
to me, akin to my winter thoughts, and sunsets, and all virtue. Covert
which the hare and the partridge seek, and I too seek. Rigid as iron, clean
as the atmosphere, hardy as virtue, innocent and sweet as a maiden is the
shrub oak."

No, this lover of trees would not be soon to take offense when likened
himself to an elm. He had not been maligned. Emerson, thinking to put
his finger on Thoreau's fault, had touched what to him was virtue. The
remark, as the amusement of many readers will testify, was a just one,—
how deeply just only Thoreau would have sensed; for this, the dignity of
persons in social relations, was of great importance to him. Knowing the
loose and easy and loveless way that his neighbors took arms, he could be
proud to be what he was; and he thought that what was commonly called
social virtue or good fellowship was the virtue of pigs in a litter which lie
close together to keep each other warm.

Yet he longed for society and loved it and he hated to see too much
apartness stand in the way of it, and the nature of his region impressed this
on him. When we think of America of the nineteenth century as a boom-
town, frontier country, we forget New England. New England was growing old, her people moving away. Standing under the hill beyond J. Hosmer's and looking over the plains westward toward Acton, Thoreau saw
the farmhouses nearly half a mile apart, few and solitary in those great
fields between the stretching woods, out of the world, where the children
had to go far to school; the still, stagnant, heart-eating, life-everlasting,
and gone-to-seed country, so far from the post-office where the weekly
paper came, where-in the new-married wife could not live for loneliness
and the young man had to depend on his horse for society. He saw the
house to which young J. Hosmer and his wife had returned from the city
in despair, shut off from the world by the deep snows that blocked the

roads. In this place an old man, he thought, might possibly afford to rust it out not having long to live, but the young man pined to get nearer the post-office and the Lyceum, was restless and resolved to go to California. Thoreau who had lived alone himself for two years, near a railroad line, knew that young men here, listening to the rattling of cars at the depot a mile away, might sometimes think that the world was going by and leaving them. In this place the rabbits and the partridges multiplied and the musk-rats were more numerous than ever, and none of the farmers' sons were willing to be farmers, and the apple trees were decayed, and the cellar-holes were more numerous than the houses, and the rails were covered with lichens, and the old maids wished to sell out and move into the village, and had waited twenty years in vain for this purpose, and never finished but one room in the house, never plastered nor painted, inside or out. These were lands which the Indian was long since dispossessed of, and now the farms were run out, and what had been forests were grain fields, and what had been grain fields, pastures; whither the villager never penetrated but in huckleberry time, perchance; where some men's breath smelt of rum, having smuggled in a jugful to alleviate their misery and solitude. This was Thoreau's country and he found it hard to believe that it was that same hopeful young America which was famous throughout the world for its activity and enterprise, and this the most thickly settled and Yankee part of it. Well might one be lonely and long to be closer to his neighbors here, he knew. But such a longing, for one who knew the towns too, was a thing to take calmly and in its proper place. This was not only Thoreau's country but the real world where the sadness of separation was inescapable and not to be avoided by physical nearness. Some people would seem to exalt the attainment of the physical nearness into a final object, the sub-stance of social virtue. And this Thoreau would not have. "It brings men together in crowds and mobs in bar-rooms and elsewhere, but it does not deserve the name of virtue," he said, in reference to the pigs in the litter.

He therefore found the people who made the least fuss about their socia-bility the most congenial and admirable of his neighbors. He went one evening to a party and found it a bad place to go to, what with so many chattering people crowded into a small room. It was warm and noisy so that one heard no one speaking, only a general babble. He wrote in his Journal that he could imagine better places for a conversation, where there should be a certain degree of silence surrounding you, and less than forty talking at once. That same afternoon, even, he had done better. There had been old Mr. Joseph Hosmer and he, eating their luncheon of crackers and cheese together in the woods, and each one heard all that was said, though it was not much to be sure. And then Hosmer had talked out of such a glorious repose, taking a leisurely bite of the cracker and cheese between his words; and so some of him was communicated to Thoreau, and some of Thoreau to him, they trusted.

Taken as a class, it was the farmers that Thoreau admired above all. He had a general preference for rude men over their more mannered cousins in the town. He saw a ruggedness and independence that he liked in farmers, and sometimes he saw an heroic quality that impressed him even more. They were wise and experienced men, it seemed to him, keeping their castles, or teaming up their summer's wood, or chopping alone in the forest,—he liked best to see them working alone,—men fuller of talk and rare adventure in the sun and wind and rain than a chestnut is of meat. These men he knew, had been out not only in '75 and 1812 but every day of their lives; and they were greater he sometimes thought, than Homer or Chaucer or Shakespeare, only they never got time to say so; they never took to the way of writing. But one could look at their fields and imagine what they might write if they ever put pen to paper. Or what had they not written on the face of the earth already, clearing and burning and scratching and harrowing and ploughing and subsoiling, in and in, out and out, over and over, again and again, erasing what they had already written for want of parchment. Thoreau was likely to see in the silent, simple outdoor characters that he knew, the fishers, the hunters, the awkward country boys coming to the fair, a timeless quality that allowed them to borrow greatness from all their forbears and successors. And thus they grew in Thoreau's eyes to a stature greater than their other neighbors would have granted them. Such a one was the old man Thoreau could barely remember, whom nobody else remembered now, who used to fish in the Concord River, and whose fishing was not a sport nor solely a means of subsistence but a sort of solemn sacrament and withdrawal from the world, just as the aged read their Bibles. Such a one too, was Sudbury Haines, whom Thoreau would often meet on the river wearing an old coat, much patched with many colors. Thoreau considered his fishermen as essential a part of the village as judges and lawyers, and Sudbury Haines with his patched coat and improvident life represented the Indian still. "He is the most patient and believing of men," he said. "Who else will stand so long in wet places? When the haymaker runs to shelter, he takes down his pole and bends his steps to the river, glad to have a leisure day. He is more like an inhabitant of nature. The weather concerns him. He is an observer of her phenomena."

Of all farmers, George Minott was Thoreau's favorite and he stopped often to talk to him. He was the most poetical farmer—the one who most realized to him the poetry of the farmer's life, that he knew. Minott did nothing with haste or drudgery but as if he loved it. He was never in a hurry to get his garden planted and yet it was always planted soon enough and none in town was kept so beautifully clean. He loved to walk in a swamp in windy weather and hear the wind groan through the pines. And being an old man, he could remember many things about past times and past customs,—things which Thoreau liked very much to hear.

Rice was another like him. Though Rice was rich and Minott poor, yet he too lived simply and practiced a rare and neat economy. Thoreau was surprised to find him walking for pleasure one day, for that was a thing which few men so successful could have found time to do. But to get his living or keep it had never been a hasty or disagreeable toil for Rice. He worked slowly but surely, enjoying the sweet of it. "It is interesting for me to talk with Rice," Thoreau wrote, "he lives so thoroughly and satisfactorily to himself. He has learned that rare art of living the very elements of which most professors do not know."

These men, unknown in their own time, forgotten now were it not for Thoreau, and often forgotten by him, were great, as Thoreau knew, for their independence. It was because they lived almost without support or even regard from any institution or any philosophy or each other. Self-sufficient, serene, self-contained, they were their own law. "What a piece of work is man!" said Hamlet, likening him to gods and angels. Thoreau, in his own way, says much the same.

"I see the old pale-faced farmer, out again on his sled now for the five thousandth time,—Cyrus Hubbard, a man of a certain New England probity and worth, immortal and natural, like a natural product, like the sweetness of a nut, like the toughness of hickory. He, too, is a redeemer for me. How superior actually to the faith he professes! He is not an office seeker. What an institution, what a revelation is a man! We are wont foolishly to think that the creed a man professes is more significant than the fact he is. It matters not how hard the conditions seemed, how mean the world, for a man is a prevalent force and a new law himself. He is a system whose law is to be observed. The old farmer condescends still to observe this nature and this order of things. It is a great encouragement that an honest man makes this world his abode. He rides on the sled drawn by oxen, world wise, yet comparatively so young as if they had seen scores of winters. The farmer spoke to me, I can swear, clean, cold, moderate as the snow. He does not melt the snow where he treads. Yet what a faint impression that encounter may make on me after all! Moderate, natural, true, as if he were made of earth, stone, wood, snow. I thus meet in this universe kindred of mine composed of these elements. I see men like frogs; their peeping I partially understand."

Charitable as Thoreau was toward Minott and Rice and Cyrus Hubbard and such others as treated themselves and him with respect, yet some of his neighbors really mistrusted him. They could not know in what high regard Thoreau was waiting to hold them. Those who lacked a serene assurance in their way of life were troubled by what they sensed as Thoreau's opinion of them because at bottom they knew it was their own opinion and they feared to admit it. Others were suspicious of Thoreau's life because it was different from their own, or because they were jealous of his greater freedom. Since he worked for hire only enough to supply his moderate wants, the greater part of his time was free to be used in whatever way he saw fit. Much of it he spent in observing nature, something at which his neighbors seldom looked, and in writing, the results of which they rarely saw or cared to see. He was therefore regarded by most as odd or a loafer. Meeting some men hauling logs in the woods, he muses that they think him a loafer and he thinks them drudges for gain, and yet their employment is more alike than they suspect. He has his work in the woods where he meets them, though his logs do not go to the same mill, and he makes a different use of skids.

Sometimes there seemed to be an advantage in being the humblest, cheapest, least dignified man in the village, and Thoreau thought he enjoyed this advantage to an unusual extent. It was a kind of incognito, though not deliberate to be sure, that enabled him to get the whole good of his neighbors and lose nothing himself. There were several coarsely well-meaning fellows, who knew only the skin of him, who addressed him familiarly by his Christian name. Among them was Sam Staples, the constable, who would almost seem to have been born for the sake of pointing up Thoreau's relationship to his society. It was Staples who, without malice but in the line of duty, arrested and jailed him for non-payment of taxes, an incident which gave rise to the great essay on civil disobedience. He offered to pay the tax himself, not realizing it was 'just a matter of principle.' It was Staples again who went to visit Thoreau in his last illness not long before he died, and reported afterwards to Emerson, so much did he value the company, that he had never spent a more satisfactory hour in his life. Sam exclaimed one evening, "Thoreau, are you going up the street pretty soon? Well, just take a couple of these handbills along and drop one in at Hoar's piazza and one at Holbrook's and I'll do as much for you another time." Thoreau was not, as he wrote, 'above being used, aye, abused sometimes.' But it was often a source of annoyance to him to be looked down upon and mistaken. He disliked especially that his private and serious pursuits should be held in low estimate as though they were not the result of deliberate and thoughtful choice, but of slothfulness. That was why he valued Brigham whose boat he borrowed one day. Brigham was quite ready to lend it, and took pains to shave down the handle of a paddle for him, conversing the while on the subject of spiritual knocking, which he asked if Thoreau had looked into, and that made him the slower. "An obliging man who understands that I am abroad viewing the works of Nature and not loafing, though he makes the pursuit a semi-religious one, as are all more serious ones to most men. All that is not sporting in the field, as hunting and fishing, is of a religious or else love-cracked character." Another hard-featured but talkative character at the bridge inquired, as Thoreau was unlocking the boat, if he knew anything that was good for rheumatism; and he answered that he had heard of so many and had so little faith in any that he had forgotten them all.

But charitableness between neighbors was also impossible sometimes because of pride. If mutual respect was necessary, so was a degree of simplicity. It was for this reason that Thoreau preferred rude and unmannered people to grand ones who forbade him to come within ten feet of them. One of his neighbors especially, who was ridiculously stately, Thoreau decided to leave until he should get his manners off. He could see no reason to make politeness of such consequence when one was ready to assassinate with a word, for he would as soon be knocked down with a bludgeon as run through with a rapier. "Why will men so try to impose on one another?" he says. "Why not be simple and pass for what they are worth only? O such thin skins, such crockery, as I have to deal with! Do they not know that I can laugh? Some who have so much dignity that they cannot be contradicted! Perhaps somebody will introduce me one day and then we may have some intercourse. I meet with several who cannot afford to be simple and true men, but personate, so to speak, their own ideal of themselves, trying to make the manners supply the place of the man. They are puffballs filled with dust and ashes."

The worst of all the people that Thoreau knew,—the direct antithesis indeed of what he admired in a man, were certain aggressively benevolent doers of good who showed no respect for him at all, who arrived in Concord all at the same time once like an epidemic.

"Here have been three ultra-reformers, lecturers on Slavery, Temperance, the Church, etc., in and about our house and Mrs. Brooks's the last three or four days,—A. D. Foss, once a Baptist minister in Hopkinton, N. H.; Loring Moody, a sort of traveling, pattern-working chaplain; and H. C. Wright, who shocks all the old women with his infidel writings. Though Foss was a stranger to the others you would have thought them old and familiar cronies. (They happened here together by accident.) They addressed each other constantly by their Christian names and rubbed you continually with the greasy cheeks of their kindness. They would not keep their distance but cuddle up and lie spoon-fashion with you, no matter how hot the weather nor how narrow the bed—chiefly Wright. I was awfully pestered with his benignity; feared I should get greased all over with it past restoration; tried to keep some starch in my clothes. He wrote a book called *A Kiss for a Blow* and he behaved as if there were no alternative between these, or as if I had given him a blow. I would have preferred the blow, but he was bent on giving me the kiss when there was neither quarrel nor argument between us. I wanted that he should straighten his back, smooth out those ogling wrinkles of benignity about his eyes, and, with a healthy reserve, pronounce something in a downright manner. It was difficult to keep clear of his slimy benignity with which he thought to cover you before he swallowed you and took you fairly into his bowels. It would have been far worse than the fate of Jonah. I do not wish to get any nearer to a man's bowels than usual. They lick you as a cow her calf. They would fain wrap you about with their bowels. Wright addressed me as 'Henry' within one minute from the time I first laid eyes on him and when I spoke, he said with a drawling, sultry sympathy, 'Henry, I know all you would say; I understand you perfectly; you need not explain anything to me;' and to another, 'I am going to dive into Henry's inmost depths.' I said, 'I trust you will not strike your head against the bottom.' He could tell in a dark room with his eyes blinded and in perfect stillness if there was one there whom he loved. One of the most attractive things about the flowers is their beautiful reserve. The truly beautiful and noble puts its lover, as it were, at an infinite distance, while it attracts him more strongly than ever. I do not like the men who come so near me with their bowels. It is the most disagreeable kind of a snare to be caught in. Men's bowels are far more slimy than their brains. They must be ascetics indeed who approach you by this side. What a relief to have heard the ring of one healthy reserved tone! With such a forgiving disposition as if he were all the while forgiving you for existing. Considering our condition or *habit* of soul—maybe corpulent and asthmatic,—maybe dying of atrophy with all our bones sticking out,—is it a kindness to embrace a man? They lay their sweaty hand on your shoulder, or your knee, to magnetize you."

It seems that the finest courtesy, the greatest kindness that we know, is to leave each other alone, to respect one another's integrity, to meet with the grace and dignity of elms and only then to link arms. Thoreau could be thankful that Concord was normally free from those who practiced a degenerate Christian love. Looking around among his neighbors, he could be well satisfied with his relations with them. He wrote in his Journal at 39, "How I love the simple, reserved countrymen, my neighbors, who mind their own business and let me alone, who never waylaid nor shot at me, to my knowledge, when I crossed their fields though each one has a gun in his house! For nearly two-score years I have known, at a distance, these long-suffering men whom I never spoke to, who never spoke to me, and now feel a certain tenderness for them, as if this long probation were but the prelude to an eternal friendship. What a long trial we have withstood and how much more admirable we are to each other, perchance, than if we had been bedfellows! I am not only grateful because Veias, and Homer, and Christ, and Shakespeare have lived, but I am grateful for Minott and Rice and Melvin and Goodwin and Puffer even. I see Melvin all alone filling his sphere, in russet suit, which no other could fill or suggest. He takes up as much room in nature as the most famous."

In spite of the strong rejection in the first of these passages and the whole-hearted acceptance in the second, the dominant attitude in both is a single one. He could begin to love his neighbors because they had left him alone, and because they were separate from him. Love, to Thoreau, was almost a kind of pity of the separateness which, much as it might combat separateness, was nevertheless dependent on it and carried therefore its own sadness within itself. Thoreau's reluctant acceptance of separation and his ultimate insistence on it, expressed a desire for society and provided a time when those who might associate stayed by themselves, innocent and ignorant of one another. What is admired in Melvin is his uniqueness, 'all alone filling his sphere in russet suit, which no other could fill or suggest.' It is the hardness of his outline resisting compression into a smaller and more conventional shape that enables him to take up as much room as the most famous. As much could not have been said of a more indefinite, less independent man. And the hardness of outline had been acquired while he was all alone. Thus our admiration and respect for one another, our neighborliness and that which enables us to live together without the revulsion that Thoreau felt toward the reformers is a strong independence.

We know deeper ties than the somewhat casual ones with our neighbors. Certain of those neighbors achieve for us the special relation of friends. As might be expected, Thoreau's views of friendship, taking account of this greater depth, differ from his demands in relation to his neighbors and yet include the same basic conditions of existence. One great distinction that he makes between friends and neighbors is that he is willing to be used by the latter. As a matter of fact he invites it. "My most serene and irresponsible neighbors," he says, "let us see that we have the whole advantage of each other; we will be useful, at least, if not admirable, to one another. I know that the mountains which separate us are high, and covered with perpetual snow, but despair not. Improve the serene winter weather to scale them. If need be soften the rocks with vinegar. For here lie the verdant plains of Italy ready to receive you. Nor shall I be slow on my side to penetrate to your Provence. Strike then boldly at head or heart or any vital part. Depend upon it, the timber is well seasoned and tough, and will bear rough usage; and if it should crack, there is plenty more where it came from. I am no piece of crockery that cannot be jostled against my neighbor without danger of being broken by the collision, and must needs ring false and jarringly to the end of my days, when once I am cracked; but rather one of the old fashioned wooden trenchers, which one while stands at the head of the table, and at another is a milking stool, and at another a seat for the children, and finally goes down to its grave, not unadorned with honorable scars and does not die till it is worn out. Nothing can shock a brave man but dullness. Think how many rebuffs a brave man has experienced in his day; perhaps has fallen into a horse pond, eaten fresh-water clams, or worn one shirt for a week without washing. Indeed you cannot receive a shock unless you have an electric affinity for that which shocks you. Use me, then, for I am useful in my way, and stand as one of many petitioners, from toadstool and hen-bane up to dahlia and violet, supplicating to be put to my use, if by any means ye may find me serviceable; whether for a medicated drink or bath, as balm and lavender; or for fragrance as verbena and geranium; or for sight, as cactus; or for thoughts, as pansy. These humbler, at least, if not those higher uses."

Anxious as Thoreau was that he be used, at least in humble ways, he was also deeply desirous that someone make greater use of him. In his ordinary dealings with men, he felt that he belittled himself to something less than his fullest value. Friendship, in which we correspond to our ideal estimate of one another, was the best use of a man and Thoreau would have been sorry if no one among those neighbors who used him for lesser things or not at all should find this out. To be put to the purposes of friendship, of course, was not really to be used at all, for Thoreau was quite insistent that friends must never, in the ordinary sense of the words, use each other. Friendship was not a mutual assistance league and Thoreau was angered by those who treated it as such. He felt it was very hard to take money or any other help from a friend. He knew, of course, that when people said that so-and-so was their friend, they meant most often that he was not their enemy."What is commonly honored with the name of Friendship," he said, "is no very profound or powerful instinct. Men do not, after all, *love* their friends greatly. I do not often see the farmers made seers and wise to the verge of insanity by their Friendship with one another. They are not often transfigured and translated by love in each other's presence. I do not observe them purified, refined and elevated by the love of a man. If one abates a little the price of his wood, or gives a neighbor his vote at town meeting, or a barrel of apples, or lends him his wagon frequently, it is esteemed a rare instance of Friendship. Most contemplate only what would be the accidental and trifling advantage of Friendship, as that the Friend can assist in time of need, by his substance, or his influence, or his counsel; but he who forsees such advantages, in this relation proves himself blind to its real advantage or indeed wholly inexperienced in the relation itself. Such services are particular and menial compared with the perpetual and all-embracing service which it is. Even the utmost good will and harmony and practical kindness are not sufficient for Friendship, for Friends do not live in harmony merely, as some say, but in melody. We do not wish for friends to feed and clothe our bodies,—our neighbors are kind enough for that—but to do the like office for our spirits."

To nourish and care for the spirit,—this was what friendship was as

Thoreau saw it. There was no series of acts which one could perform for such a purpose. The most one could do for his friend was simply to be his friend. What this could mean in more explicit terms it is difficult to say, since friendship as Thoreau saw it was not an overt performance but a relationship; but in its simplest, most basic form, as the force which motivated all the rest of the complex, friendship was an exalting and powerful love. It was a kind of love that went forth with no particular object in view and was wholly self-generated. It neither arose from, nor was directed toward, anything else in the world. This love without reference is the basis of friendship in Thoreau. It was one thing in his life that never tarnished for him. Some particular friend might disappoint him after a time, but in friendship itself he had faith always. His friends, to be sure, would accuse him of coldness; and sometimes when he was reproached in this way he almost came to believe in it himself. Then he said that, if it were true, he trusted that he would not soon be too cold for natural influences. He was almost driven to believe that a sympathy with man and a sympathy with nature could not consist with one another,—that those qualities that bring you near to one estrange you from the other. And yet he knew that this was not so, and indeed that nature must be viewed humanly to be viewed at all. He knew that a lover of nature was preeminently, as he was, a lover of man. What was nature to him if he had no friend? She ceased to be morally significant. Almost this same humanistic observation he made in regard to literature when he saw that no subject, tried by ordinary standards, was too humble or too trivial for it. All that could interest the reader was the depth and intensity of the life excited. "We touch our subject but by a point which has no breadth, but the pyramid of our experience, or our interest in it, rests on us by a broader or narrower base. That is, man is all in all, Nature nothing, but as she draws him out and reflects him." Nature indeed, as opposed to mankind and friendship for it, could almost lose its interest for one. It could be experienced in a finite and final way. One could be thankful that the experience of friendship was not finite and final, for in that case it could only be followed by disenchantment. "Ah when a man has traveled and robbed the horizon of his native fields of its mystery and poetry, its indefinite promise, tarnished the blue of distant mountains with his feet! When he has done this he may begin to think of another world. What is this longer to him?" The horizon of friendship, however, even that same horizon that one had seen at first long ago, receded for ever, so that no one could make the complaint that the blue faded or disappeared. The horizon's indefinite promise remained, and the relation was beautiful as a consequence. It was impossible to tarnish its blue because, for all that it might be seen, no feet ever walked quite on it. "Constantly, as it were through a remote skylight, I have glimpses of a serene friendship land, and know the better why brooks murmur and violets grow." On this point, whatever his actual friendships might be, Thoreau could never be disenchanted, never cynical. "The heart," he said, "is forever inexperienced." And so he preserved his innocence, never thinking that his disappointments were final, though indeed they became more frequent with the years and disappointment was almost all that he knew.

Since Thoreau's feeling of friendship was based on a self-generated, non-specific love, he saw it as having an all-pervasive, evanescent quality, and this, while assuring its far presence, came close to prohibiting its near presence. Friendship had established no institutions, it was not taught by any religion, no scripture contained its maxims. It had no temple, not even a single column. To embody friendship without losing its essential quality was extremely difficult. To set about this was almost certain to lead to failure. Sometimes it seemed best not to attempt at all to express one's love but to depend upon it to express itself in some unexpected way. Sooner or later, it would be discovered. Thoreau knew how some distant gesture or unconscious behavior that we remember will suddenly speak to us with more emphasis than the wisest or kindest deeds. It is in being made aware of such a kindness of long ago that we realize that there have been times when we were treated with such high regard and consideration that we could not appreciate it and it passed us quite over. We had been treated as though we were as we aspired to be or as the eyes of friendship saw us; and not as we regarded ourselves at the time, wrapped up and lessened in some pettiness of the moment. Friendship was often, then, a remembered thing; for only in our better moments could we know it at all. It was therefore not to be thought of as defined in time and place by the presence of a friend or even by a particular relationship. It was not only remembered from the past but was also anticipated for the future, and so was as likely to come upon us when alone as when in company. In its greatest form it was like the horizon spoken of before,—seen but never attained. As with most of the goods of the world, one seemed no nearer to it now than in Plato's time. "Friendship," Thoreau said, "is evanescent in every man's experience, and remembered like heat lightning in past summers. Fair and flitting like a summer cloud;—there is always some vapor in the air, no matter how long the drought, there are even April showers. Surely from time to time, for its vestiges never depart, it floats through our atmosphere. It takes place like vegetation in so many materials, because there is such a law, but always without permanent form, though ancient and familiar as the sun and moon and as sure to come again. They silently gather as by magic, these never-failing, never quite deceiving visions, like the bright and fleecy clouds in the calmest and clearest days."

Natural, all-pervasive, its vestiges never departing, and yet how rare a thing was friendship really. "One or two persons come to my house from time to time," he relates, "there being proposed to them the faint possibility of intercourse. They are as full as they are silent, and wait for my plectrum to stir the strings of their lyre. If they could ever come to the length of a sentence, or hear one, on that grounds they are dreaming of! They speak faintly, and do not obtrude themselves. They have heard some news, which none, not even they, themselves, can impart. It is a wealth they can bear about them which can be expended in various ways. What came they out to seek?"

No word was oftener on the lips of men than friendship, and indeed no thought was more familiar to their aspirations. All men were dreaming of it and its drama which was always a tragedy was enacted daily. It was the secret of the universe. You might tread the town, you might wander the country, and none should ever speak of it, yet thought was everywhere busy about it, and the idea of what was possible in this respect affected all men's behavior toward all new men and women, and a great many old ones. Nevertheless, there were only one or two essays on this subject in all literature. No wonder that the mythology and *Arabian Nights*, and Shakespeare, and Scott's novels were entertaining,—men were poets and fablers and dramatists themselves. They were continually acting a part in a more interesting drama than any written. They were dreaming that their friends were their *friends* and that they were their friends' *friends*. Their actual friends were but distant relations of those to whom they were pledged. Men never exchanged more than three words with a friend in their lives on that level to which their thoughts and feelings habitually rose. One went forth prepared to say, 'Sweet friends!' and the salutation was 'Damn your eyes!' "Oh, my friend," said Thoreau, "may it come to pass once, that when you are my friend I may be yours."

But it is equally impossible to forget our friends and to make them answer to our ideal. "When they say farewell, then indeed we begin to keep them company. How often we find ourselves turning our backs on our actual friends that we may go and meet their ideal cousins. I would that I were worthy to be any man's friend."

The rarity of human friendship was closely connected in Thoreau's mind with its exceptional fineness and its difficulty; and of course the difficulty was inseparable from the fineness. And so when one speaks of friendship and Thoreau, one is speaking of a powerful complex of urges and prohibitions in which the splendor, almost extravagance, of his conception of friendship is checked and hindered in its actualization by its own splendor. Misanthropy, a lack of sympathy with men, or of desire for friendship, is totally external to the matter. The fact is inescapable that Thoreau understood friendship and desired it deeply for the use which it alone could make of his higher faculties.

"Only lovers," he sensed, "know the value and magnanimity of truth, while traders prize a cheap honesty and neighbors and acquaintances, a cheap civility. In our daily intercourse with men our nobler faculties are dormant and suffered to rust. None will pay us the compliment to expect nobleness from us. Though we have gold to give, they demand only copper. We ask our neighbor to suffer himself to be dealt with truly, sincerely, nobly; but he answers no by his deafness. He does not even hear this prayer. He says practically, I will be content if you treat me as 'no better than I should be,' as deceitful, mean, dishonest, and selfish. For the most part, we are contented so to deal and to be dealt with, and we do not think that for the mass of men there is any truer and nobler relation possible. A man may have *good* neighbors, so called, and acquaintances, and even companions, wife, parents, brothers, sisters, children, who meet himself and each other on this ground only. The State does not demand justice of its members, but thinks that it succeeds very well with the least degree of it, hardly more than rogues practice; and so do the neighborhood and the family. What is commonly called Friendship even is only a little more honor among rogues.

"But sometimes we are said to *love* another, that is to stand in a true relation to him, so that we give the best to, and receive the best from, him. Between whom there is hearty truth there is love, and in proportion to our truthfulness and confidence in one another, our lives are divine and miraculous, and answer to our ideal. There are passages in our intercourse with mortal men and women, such as no prophecy had taught us to expect, which transcend our earthly life and anticipate heaven for us. What is this

Love that may come right into the middle of a prosaic Goffstown day, equal
to any of the Gods, that discovers a new world, fair and fresh and eternal,
occupying the place of the old one, when to the common eye a dust has
settled on the universe, which world cannot else be reached and does not
exist. What other words, we may almost ask, are memorable and worthy to
be repeated, than those which love has inspired? It is wonderful that they
were ever uttered. They are few and rare, indeed, but, like a strain of
music, they are incessantly repeated and modulated by the memory. We
should not dare to repeat these notes aloud. We are not competent to hear
them at all times."

Obviously it is not only for the opportunity of truth that friendship
provides that it is admired and wanted, but for its entire transcendental
character by which it opens up a whole new world to the heart. And yet the
expression of so rare and transcendental a thing was difficult,—for example the words that should pass between friends. He was forced to feel that
the language of friendship was not words but meanings. It was an intelligence above language. When alone, and he did not feel himself strange or
unique in this experience, he could imagine endless conversations with a
friend in which his tongue should be loosed and his thoughts spoken without hesitancy or end; but the actual meeting was far otherwise. Acquaintances could come and go and have a word ready for every occasion, but
what could the friend utter whose very breath was thought and meaning?
Words were so unsatisfactory, so difficult and so inadequate. The stuff of a
friendship could not be in them but in something else, a sensed thing, so
expressive in itself as to defy expression. If one went to say farewell to a
friend setting out on a journey, the most one could do was to shake his
hand. One had no last words to say. "Alas, it is only the word of words,
which you have so long sought and found not; *you* have not a *first* word
yet. There are few, even, whom I should venture to call earnestly by their
most proper names. A name pronounced is a recognition of the individual
to whom it belongs. He who can pronounce my name aright, he can call
me and is entitled to my love and service."

The difficulties of expression led Thoreau to leave his friendships, as
here in reference to language, almost unexpressed. He came to value a
relationship in and for itself without regard for deliberate expression; and
he held a greater respect for such a relationship than for any service that
friends could perform for one another. Thoreau, who was absorbed in
being rather than in expression, was hesitant of names, of words, of forms

of any sort. He was aware of their ambivalent power which is the power of the metaphor, suggestive of truth, suggestive of being, but such that the truth is not literally in it. Thoreau preferred no expression at all to the valuing of expression for its own sake as though it had its own truth and reality. Of the expressions and forms of friendship, he felt that they must remain consistent with our truth and sincerity and then be taken for granted and little notice be given to either their presence or absence. Otherwise he was determined to abandon what usually passed as friendship for the sake of one more real. Thoreau said that he sometimes heard his friends complain finely that he did not appreciate their fineness; but he was not bound to tell them whether he did or not, as if they expected a vote of thanks for every fine thing which they uttered or did. That he had frequently disappointed them by not giving them words when they expected them, or such as they expected, and so led them to call him hard, he knew. "O ye that would have the cocoanut wrong side outwards," he says, "when next I weep I will let you know. They ask for words and deeds when a true relation is word and deed. If they know not of these things, how can they be informed? We often forbear to confess our feelings, not from pride, but for fear that we could not continue to love the one who required us to give such proof of our affection."

Had Thoreau been able to speak more glibly of his affection for his friends; if the usual almost automatic compliments and benevolences had been able to roll off his tongue, the difficulties with his friends would very likely never have arisen, or would have been of some other nature. But there was always something about his throat and his tongue that knotted up and prevented his speaking,—a caution, a reserve, a plainness, whatever one might call it, it was always there. Such expression as his friends apparently desired seems to have appeared to Thoreau not only as undignified and unsuitable but, recalling how deeply he was shocked by the slimy benignity of the reformers, as actually disintegrating and devastating to personal integrity, breaking it down to a repulsiveness akin to bodily decay or disembowelment, and thereby unfitting it for all social intercourse. This is a paradox, of course, that one's social instincts should prevent one's participation in what is usually regarded as society. Thoreau himself recognized it as such, and even apart from his general inclination toward paradoxical thinking, knew that the truth lay somewhere in it. One might wonder why Thoreau of all of his circle should be the only one to experience this difficulty of expression and in so wondering, question the validity of Thoreau's experience. None of his friends seems even to have understood his motives, much less shared them. It is to be remembered, however, that Thoreau had no difficulty expressing himself to his neighbors, a group of people to whom he stood in a relationship the emotional content of which was relatively low. So it is a question really of the depth and strength of the emotion involved. The difficulty enters there.

And so, once again, it is relations that he demands, not words. "If I am thus seemingly cold compared to my companion's warm," he says, "who knows but mine is a less transient glow, a steadier and more equable heat, like that of the earth in spring, in which the flowers spring and expand. It is not words which I wish to hear or to utter but relations that I seek to stand in; and it oftener happens, methinks, that I go away unmet, unrecognized, ungreeted in my offered relation, than that you are disappointed of words. If I can believe that we are related to one another as truly and gloriously as I have imagined, I ask nothing more and words are not required to convince me of this. I am disappointed of relations, you of words."

That his friends should feel unsatisfied or consider him cold left him bewildered and helpless, and not to them but to himself, after such encounters, he tried to explain his warmth, at least metaphorically as in the beginning of the last passage and again as in this: "—but each thing is warm enough of its kind. Is the stone too cold which absorbs the heat of the summer sun and does not part with it during the night? Crystals, though they be of ice, are not too cold to melt, but it was in melting that they were formed. Cold! I am most sensible of warmth in winter days. It is not the warmth of fire that you would have, but everything is warm and cold according to its nature, it is not that I am too cold but that our warmth and coldness are not of the same nature; hence when I am absolutely warmest, I may be coldest to you. Crystal does not complain of crystal any more than the dove of its mate. You who complain that I am cold find nature cold. To me she is warm. My heat is latent to you. Fire itself is cold to whatever is not of a nature to be warmed by it. A cool wind is warmer to a feverish man than the air of a furnace. That I am cold means that I am of another nature." Four months later, as Thoreau records in his Journal some observations on the character of the bottom in Nut Meadow Brook, this same theme seems to recur in a strange way; for he suddenly interrupts himself to say parenthetically, "(I hear the sound of the piano below as I write this, and feel as if the winter in me were at length beginning to thaw, for my spring has been even more backwards than nature's. For a month past, life has been a thing incredible to me. None but the kind Gods can make me sane. If only they will let their south winds blow on me! I ask to be melted. You can only ask of the metals that they be tender to the fire that *melts* them. To naught else can they be tender.)"

Thoreau's evanescent and non-specific love has gradually evolved into an absolute insistence on the integrity of the individual natures of the two people in a friendship, and into a conviction that these two natures are specific for each other beyond any power of word or deed to change. It seems ridiculous to Thoreau that books for young people should give advice on the selection of friends. They could only mean associates and confidants. Friendship took place between those who had an affinity for one another and was so natural and inevitable a result that no professions or advances would avail. Even speech was unnecessary at first. Friendship would follow after silence as the buds in a graft put forth into leaves long after the graft has taken. The conditions of the relationship remained consistent as it developed so that it was foolish to attempt to repair a friendship by apologies or explanations. Thoreau knew that the only serious differences were constitutional and these were so serious that no apologies could explain them away. We had to accept or refuse one another as we were, apologizing only like dew and frost which are off again with the sun, and known to be beneficent. When Thoreau himself was asked to make excuses and explanations, he was very angry, because it was such an insult to the relationship between him and his friend and such a misunderstanding of it. The truly estranged, he felt, were two friends explaining, for friendship was the joy and blessing which resulted when two sympathized by nature. Natures were liable to no mistakes but would know each other through thick and thin. And he felt an awful necessity to be what he was. "My prickles and smoothness," he said, "are as much a quality of your own hand as of myself. I cannot tell you what I am more than a ray of the summer's sun. What I am I am and say not. Being is the great explainer. In the attempt to explain, shall I plane away all the spines, till it is no thistle but a cornstalk?"

But the awful necessity to be himself and not explain was more than a rationalization of social embarrassment; it was the basic condition of friendship,—and it was almost terribly rigorous, so that Thoreau came, as he said, near to shrinking from the arduousness of meeting men erectly day by day. And yet he knew that there was no alternative available to him or to those whom he could accept. He would have us be resolutely and faithfully what we are, and humbly what we aspire to be. He wanted to give men the best of his wares, though they were poor enough, so that the gods would help him to lay up a better store for the future. "Man's noblest gift to man is his sincerity," he said, "for it embraces his integrity also. Let him not dole out of himself anxiously to suit their weaker or stronger stomachs, but make a clean gift of himself and empty his coffers at once. I would be in society as in the landscape; in the presence of nature there is no effrontery." Thoreau wished to know his friends, and wished them to know him so thoroughly that neither of them could ever do or say anything inconsistent with the other's idea of him; and yet in such a way that their daily and ordinary existence should be continually surprising to one another. There is no contradiction in this. Knowledge cannot destroy original mystery if our sense of the latter has been strong enough and real enough to prevent our ever denying it. Knowledge becomes instead a way to the mystery, and once recognized as being of a different order from it, can never replace it. Two friends, each being resolutely himself, can never be entirely known to one another though they have hidden nothing and indeed, serene as they are in the consciousness of their mystery, have no need to hide. Two friends will be eternally strange to one another, not through subterfuge or by blinking eyes, but by nature. Thoreau was insistent on this. He had a friend, as he relates, who wished him to see as right something he knew to be wrong; but if friendship was to rob him of his eyes, to darken the day, he would have none of it. True friendship could afford true knowledge. "I have never known one," he says, "who could bear criticism, who could not be flattered, who would not bribe his judge, or was content that the truth should be always loved better than himself." The strangeness between friends is something beyond and beneath any knowledge of faults and virtues. The difficulty is that we seldom live on the level where it exists but cover ourselves up in sameness of dress, and conduct, and habits of thought. Our sameness lies in these superficialities not in ourselves. Our strangeness for one another and our essential likeness both lie deep. But for the most part we are unreal. We become not persons at all but creatures of convention, of the moment, of the place, of our economic circumstances, or something else. Thoreau's individual nature lay in his inability and his refusal to meet or consider seriously creatures of convention and sameness; but there was no one,—not the feeble-minded, not negro slaves, not rich men, that he would not meet on the level of likeness and strangeness.

We could become the creatures even of our own relationship with one another unless we were much apart. "Society is commonly too cheap. We meet at very short intervals not having had time to acquire any new value for each other. We meet at meals three times a day, and give each other a taste of that old musty cheese that we are. We have had to agree on a certain set of rules called etiquette and politeness to make this frequent meeting tolerable and that we need not come to open war. We meet at the post office, and at the sociable, and about the fireside every night; we live thick and are in each other's way and stumble over one another, and I think, that we thus lose some respect for one another. The value of a man is not in his skin that we should touch him." Or again he says, "Men lie behind the barrier of a relation as effectually concealed as a landscape by a mist; and when at length some unforseen accident throws me into a new attitude to them, I am astounded as if for the first time I saw the sun on the hillside. They lie out before me like a new order of things." And again,—"[When friends] have mutually appropriated their value for the last hour, they will go and gather a new measure of strangeness for the next. They are like two boughs" ('I would as soon take the arm of an elm tree,' said Emerson) "crossed in the woods which play backwards and forwards upon one another in the wind, and only wear into each other, but never the sap of one flows into the pores of the other, for then the wind would no more draw from them those strains which enchanted the woods. They are not two united, but one divided." Finally, he says, "We have to go into retirement religiously and enhance our meeting by rarity and a degree of unfamiliarity. Would you know why I see thee so seldom, my friend? In solitude I have been making up a packet for thee." The place then, where strangeness is gathered and realized, is solitude.

We are led to an important concept in Thoreau, one which illuminates his obscurities and integrates all of his writing. Sometimes it is called solitude, sometimes silence. In silence he prepares for speech; in solitude for society. And so in like manner, the truest society always approaches nearer to solitude, and the most excellent speech finally falls into silence. One recalls that Thoreau found a party a poor place to go to for conversation because there was so much talking going on; he preferred his luncheon in the woods with Joseph Hosmer where a certain degree of silence surrounded the little they had to say. The same principle underlies his love for the neighbors who have so long respected his privacy, prefacing friendship with probation; it accounts for Thoreau's everywhere-nowhere friendship to which solitude was no obstacle, leading even to the paradox of leaving one's friends in order to keep them company. Silence is the origin of the news his friends have such difficulty in telling him, the news that Thoreau calls 'a wealth they bear about them which can be expended in various ways'; it cannot be separated from those nobler faculties which only friendship could call into use. It is akin to his being most sensible of warmth in winter days. Silence it is that makes speech unnecessary to start a friendship, of little help in its progress, and valueless in preventing its end. Silence leads a man to give another the best of his wares and enables him to do so. It is the seat and source of our strangeness.

Obviously silence is not to be taken as the negation of sound or of speech, any more than the seed is the negation of the plant. Sound and silence is a matter of potentialities and realizations. It would be vain to deny that there is opposition between these, but as long as one always has reference to the other and that reference is preserved, they play into each other's hands. So there is no negation of one by the other. There is negation, however, in frivolous speech, which has no reference to silence and so prevents valid speech or sound. Silence is not only the source of sound but its subject, and since the speaker's acquaintance with it is through himself, it is the speaker also. We describe an intensity of noise by saying that we can't hear ourselves think. "Silence," says Thoreau, "is the communing of the conscious soul with itself. If the soul attend for a moment to its own infinity, then and there is silence. She is audible to all men at all times, in all places, and if we will, we may always hearken to her admonitions." But most of Thoreau's contemporaries, as most of ours, had no desire to listen to the silence and never heard it. There are very few problems answered in such communion that do not have ready-made solutions in habit and convention. These solutions are usually found to be much simpler than an attempt to find real ones, and with a little snipping and cutting here, a little squeezing and lacing, or even an amputation there, we make shift to fit one to the other. And we never know because we never really faced ourselves in the problem, whether the restrictions and pains and deadenings we underwent were due to the problem itself or to the conventional solution we chose. Thoreau felt that there were two voices one could listen to, one's own in silence or someone else's. It mattered very little to whom the second voice belonged. The most usual likelihood would be that it belongs to no one at all, but is merely the generalized voice of convention, or of one's region or circumstances, and therefore since it fits no one's particular nature, no one need follow it. Let each man follow his own nature. Such was Thoreau's recommendation, a recommendation which was moreover a sacred duty because he thought so highly of silence. Our existence in any other circumstances became a neglect and abuse of life,—a sacrilege. Likewise our relations with one another became travesty unless we were first of all ourselves and acted according to our silence. That was why we were to give men the best of our wares, our real persons, and not 'dole out of ourselves to suit their weaker or stronger stomachs.' It involved also a desire to be sure that a relationship was real and worthwhile by knowing the worst and best of each other, just as silence was always a way toward knowing because it cut us off from the safely usual patterns of thought and behavior, accepted perhaps without question, and put us where there was nothing known and no way to know; no way to act but our own; and nothing to insulate us from truth however shocking.

Silence is the world of potentialities and meanings beyond the actual and expressed, which the meanness of our actions and the interpretations put upon them threatens to conceal. Yet all actuality is to be referred to it and valued accordingly as it includes or suggests it. Nothing is worth saying, nothing is worth doing except as a foil for the waves of silence to break against. "Silence is the universal refuge, the sequel of all dry discourses, and all foolish acts, as balm to our every chagrin, as welcome after satiety as after disappointment; that background which the painter may not daub, be he master or bungler, and which, however awkward a figure he may have made in the foreground, remains ever our inviolable asylum." An asylum and inviolable; silence was Thoreau's proof against cynicism. Yet it must not be understood from asylum that he escaped cynicism only by the way of easy gratifications in dreams and phantasies. It was quite different, really. He never refused to face his experience, but he did refuse to acknowledge the finality of it and so deny what reality his heart discovered to him. Silence is an asylum not because it enabled him, in any sense, to stop living, but because it made it possible for him to continue to live and always come back for more in spite of disappointments and failures. He says in *Walden* in a cryptic but meaningful way, "I long ago lost a hound, a bay horse, and a turtle dove, and am still on their trail. Many are the travelers I have spoken concerning them, describing their tracks and what calls they answered to. I have met one or two who have heard the hound, and the tramp of the horse, and even seen the dove disappear behind a cloud, and they seemed as anxious to recover them as if they had lost them themselves." It is of primary importance that Thoreau is still on their trail; and so at one time when he feels that a friendship has come to an end, he accepts the disappointment and loneliness, knowing that sooner or later there will be others to stand in the same relation to him as this friend once did. Friendship is 'evanescent in every man's experience,' one remembers from an earlier writing, 'ancient and familiar as the sun and moon and as sure to come again.'

The asylum of silence was inviolable. This it was, ultimately, that prevented the finality of experience. It was the horizon of friendship which was never tarnished, the heart which was forever inexperienced. "It were vain for me to interpret the silence," he says. "She cannot be done into English. For six thousand years have men translated her, with what fidelity belonged to each; still is she little better than a sealed book. A man may run on confidently for a time, thinking he has her under his thumb, and shall one day exhaust her, but he too must at last be silent, and men remark only, how brave a beginning he made; for when he at length dives into her, so vast is the disproportion of the told to the untold that the former will seem but the bubble where he disappeared."

Fortunate for Thoreau that silence was so vast! Its untranslated passages were the source of his freshness and strength. They were the spring of his peculiar innocence, his perpetual virginity. And yet it was the sum of his action always to render the silence into English; to make it the stuff of his friendship, the substance of life every day in Concord and Massachusetts and America. He wanted to go on like the Chinese cliff swallows, feathering his nest with froth so that it might someday be the bread of life for such as dwelt by the seashore. It was difficult, to be sure, but nothing else seemed much worthwhile. "How hard it is," he says, "to be greatly related to mankind! They are only my uncles and aunts and cousins. I hear of some persons greatly related, but only he is so who has all mankind for his friend. Our intercourse with the best grows soon shallow and trivial. They no longer inspire us. After enthusiasm comes insipidity and blankness. The sap of all noble schemes drieth up, and the schemers return again and again in despair to 'common sense and labor.' If I could help infuse some life and heart into society, should I not do a service? Why will not the gods mix a little of the wine of nobleness with the air we drink? Let virtue have some firm foothold in the earth. Where does she dwell? Who are the salt of the earth? May not love have some resting place on the earth as sure as the sunshine on the rock? The crystals imbedded in the cliff sparkle and gleam from afar, as if they did certainly enrich our planet; but where does any virtue permanently sparkle and gleam? She was sent forth over the waste too soon, before the earth was prepared for her." Thoreau devoted his days to providing that some virtue should sparkle and gleam in the earth whether prepared for it or not. He found it largely unprepared. He became more and more deeply and tragically aware that in spite of his earnest attempt to translate the silence into English, it would remain little better than a sealed book. He had known it would be so. His foreknowledge of failure prevented failure from turning him aside to some other problem. There was no other problem. But searching in the silence for his true identity, he sometimes drew a blank.

Freedom

Thoreau dreamed himself into life. The persistence of the moments in which life appeared noble to him had the recurrence of a dream. And like a recurrent dream, these moments which were his most wakeful, were experienced with such frequency and power as to affect the whole of the fabric of his life. Almost unconsciously, he decided against submitting to pettiness. He believed that it was possible to live nobly and that it was his business to do so,—to make life as a whole less petty purely by the main force of his own living.

He lived for most of his life in Concord with his father's family who made and sold pencils in a small shop in the rear of the house. He assisted in this business at various periods. At other times he had kept school and been a tutor. He was a land surveyor as well, and it was chiefly by this means that he made his living. But he never felt that these employments were his real business. And feeling this, he had the unusual good sense not to allow them to interfere with his life or to constrain him. In 1845, wishing to live by himself in the woods and to transact 'some private business,' he built a small house for himself at Walden Pond, not far from the village of Concord which he frequently visited, and he remained there for two years. At the end of this time, he left the woods and went back to the village, feeling as he said, that since he had many more lives to live, he could spare no more for this one. Whenever Thoreau reflected that there were other men in the world and other methods of living, he experienced a sense of expansion and freedom as though the other ways were tributaries emptying into the current of his being, deepening and enriching the channel. He enjoyed the freedom of many possibilities. "Thank Fortune," he said, "here is not all the world. The buckeye does not grow in New England; the mocking bird is rarely heard here. Why not keep pace with the day, and not allow of a sunset, nor fall behind the summer and the migration of birds? Shall we not compete with the buffalo who keeps pace with the seasons, cropping the pastures of the Colorado till a greener and sweeter grass awaits him by the Yellowstone? The wild goose is more a cosmopolite than we; he breaks his fast in Canada, takes a luncheon in the Susquehanna, and plumes himself for the night in a Louisiana bayou. The pigeon carries an acorn in his crop from the King of Holland's to Mason and Dixon's line. Yet we think if rail fences are pulled down and stone walls set up on our farms, bounds are henceforth set to our lives and our fates decided. If you are chosen town clerk, forsooth, you can't go to Tierra del Fuego this summer." Thoreau could always go to Tierra del Fuego, so few bounds were set to his life. He wondered in this same spring where the next spring would find him and the possibilities ranged from South Africa to Siberia and Peru. Because Thoreau was able to sense restrictions and had so few commitments that he could move away when he sensed them, he was free. He could, there-fore, move away from public opinion, government, religion, education, and even society itself. Their forms and their concepts were arbitrary, not binding. "Shall I raise corn and potatoes in Massachusetts," he asks, "or figs and olives in Asia Minor? I may be a logger on the headwaters of the Penobscot, to be recorded in fable hereafter as an amphibious river god by as sounding a name as Triton and Proteus; and how many more things may I do with which there are none to be compared." Thoreau did go to the headwaters of the Penobscot, though not as a logger, and much less as a river god. He never went to the other places he thought of and for the most part indeed, stayed very much at home. He moved away only as far as Walden, and then moved back again after two years. And yet this expan-sive and hopeful feeling of the world opening up before him, much as the geographical world opened up for the men of the Renaissance, was wholly unaffected and an unmistakably actual and necessary factor in his life. "A man may gather his limbs snugly," he says, "within the shell of a mammoth squash, with his back to the northeastern boundary, and not be unusually straitened after all. Our limbs, indeed, have room enough, but it is our souls that rust in a corner. Let us migrate interiorly without intermission, and pitch our tent each day nearer the western horizon. The really fertile soils and luxuriant prairies lie on this side of the Alleghanies. There has been no Hanno of the affections. Their domain is untraveled ground to the Mogul's dominions."

So it is plain that moving away was more than a physical migration to Thoreau; it was moving away just as he had moved away from his friends— into silence, which was a great world nevertheless, and the one where he knew his true business to lie. Thoreau migrated backwards and then still backwards, to the grandeur that underlay pettiness, the silence that under-lay sound, thinking in this way to attend to the grandeur and embody it, to render the silence, as he said, into English. This, then, was his true employment, not tutoring, nor pencil-making, nor land-surveying, but delving into life trying to find its true heart and live close. Realizing that forms, whether of speech or action, and whether within society or without, were inadequate to contain the truth of man's existence, he spoke almost always in metaphors. As he says in *Walden*, "I will only hint at some of the enterprises I have cherished. To anticipate, not the sunrise and the dawn, merely, but if possible, Nature herself! No doubt, many of my townsmen have met me returning from this enterprise, farmers starting for Boston in the twilight, or woodchoppers going to their work. It is true I never assisted the sun materially in his rising but, doubt not, it was of the last importance only to be present at it.

"So many autumn, ay, and winter days, spent outside the town, trying to hear what was in the wind, to hear and carry it express! I well nigh sunk all my capital in it and lost my own breath in the bargain, running in the face of it. If it had concerned either of the political parties, depend on it, it would have appeared in the Gazette with the earliest intelligence. At other times watching from the observatory of some cliff or tree to telegraph any new arrival; or waiting at evening on the hill tops for the sky to fall, that I might catch something, though I never caught much and that manna-wise, would dissolve again in the sun.

"I have looked after the wild stock of the town, which give a faithful herdsman a good deal of trouble by leaping fences and I have had an eye to the unfrequented nooks and corners of the farm, though I did not always know whether Jonas or Solomon worked in a particular field today—that was none of my business. I have watered the red huckleberry, the sand cherry, and the nettle tree, the red pine and the black ash, the white grape and the yellow violet, which might have withered else in dry seasons.

"In short I went on thus for a long time, I may say it without boasting, faithfully minding my own business, till it became more and more evident that my townsmen would not after all admit me into the list of town officers, nor make my place a sinecure with a moderate allowance. My accounts which I can swear to have kept faithfully, I have, indeed, never got audited, still less accepted, still less paid and settled. However I have not set my heart on that."

Thoreau moved away into a larger view of life and did so for the reason that life looked so large to him that he saw no way to live it profitably on a pettier scale. Moving away like this is moving closer. He came to look at things more directly, getting the full brilliance of them, and so never lost his larger view of the world, keeping it always in mind in his actions,— dreaming himself, as it were, into life. Late in his life on a day when he spent the October afternoon on the river, he has this in his Journal,—

"Though the red maples have not their common brilliancy on account of the very severe frost about the end of September, some are very interesting. You cannot judge a tree by seeing it from one side only. As you go around or away from it, it may overcome you with its mass of glowing scarlet or yellow light. You need to stand where the greatest number of leaves will transmit or reflect to you most favorably. The tree which looked comparatively lifeless, cold and merely parti-colored, seen in a more favorable light as you are floating away from it, may affect you wonderfully as a warm glowing drapery. I now see one small red maple which is all a pure yellow within and a bright red scarlet on its outer surfaces and prominences. It is a remarkably distinct painting of scarlet on a yellow ground. It is an indescribably beautiful contrast of scarlet and yellow. Another is yellow and green where this was scarlet and yellow and in this case the bright and liquid green, now getting to be rare is by contrast as charming a color as the scarlet.

"Wood ducks are about now amid the painted leaves. For two or more nights past we have had remarkable glittering golden sunsets as I came home from the post office, it being cold and cloudy just above the horizon. There was the most intensely bright golden light in the west end of the street extending under the elms, and the very dust a quarter of a mile off was like gold-dust. I wondered how a child could stand quietly in that light, as if it had been a furnace."

When we consider the boundless acres of Thoreau's life and the undeceived enchantment of his earlier enterprises, waiting for the sky to fall; when we see how he marveled at a child not excited by the foliage and sunset, then the light in which Thoreau saw existence is apparent. Surely there is a kind of magic and richness about his life, if only for the reason that he happened to sense that life had these qualities and lived in such a way as never to destroy them. And so he was able to return to them when the triviality of experience made a renewal of faith necessary, and this was his moving away. Following the suggestion of his own words, we can say it was a kind of golden age that Thoreau lived in. As a matter of fact, his particular region during his time has sometimes been called golden. Still I think it would be a mistake to refer this quality in Thoreau to any external factors or to the general character of life in New England of the nineteenth century. Thoreau could have been as he was in, for example, our times too. The multitude of roles that he saw opening up before him on this and the other continents, is not to be taken as an example of thinking peculiar to that America of the past which had a frontier, and therefore of thinking no longer applicable. But rather, the basis for this thought, as might be suggested by the fact that one of these roles was that of a Peruvian mail carrier, is a quite different feeling:—"Think how finite after all the known world is."

"Money coined at Philadelphia," he continues, "is legal tender over how much of it! You may carry ship biscuit, beef, and pork quite round to the place you set out from. England sends her felons to the other side for safe keeping." Having called Thoreau's a golden age, we must find its foundations in his own insights rather than in his times. It is true, however, that merely to see life on an heroic scale is nothing remarkable and we need not praise Thoreau for that. The most cynical people usually have some neverneverland, some sacred Utopia, for which they are quick to claim a hearing. But the painters of the beautiful existence have seldom set foot on their promised lands; and they ask for special conditions and support before they intend to do so. We are familiar with the golden age of the unapproachable distance whether past or future. We think it belongs there. Actually, however, the golden age is not an historical period of which we have records from the past, but a concept in answer to a sense of necessity which comes to us in our own lifetimes. We suppose it must have been in the past and it is more convenient to think of it there. The golden age, shadowy perception of the nature of life that it is, is ours to dispose of, and we should do better perhaps, to preserve it in the present. "Wood, water, earth, air," Thoreau said, "are essentially what they were; only society has degenerated. This lament for a golden age is only a lament for golden men." Knowing that the golden age was always present in thought and was made actual only by golden men, Thoreau had that rare desire to live it into being, without going out of his way, and without asking for special conditions, privileges, or support. He tells a story of an Englishman who went to India to get rich in order that some day he could come back to live like a poet. "He should have gone up-garret at once," he said.

There is the riddle that Thoreau makes in *Walden* about the lost hound and bay horse and turtle dove for which he spends his nights and his days searching, which is as exact and suggestive as any other few sentences he ever wrote of himself. Thoreau pursued his life like game wherever he might find it or it might come to him, and no other business was allowed to obstruct the meeting. It was a pursuit that led him in strange and unfrequented ways,—over the back road to Walden Pond, down to Nine Acre Corner, and all across the southern part of the town on the disused traces of the Canoe Birch, and Sudbury, and Old Marlboro Roads, which led away from towns and temptation, and conducted to the outside of earth, over its uppermost crust; where you could forget in what country you were traveling; where no farmer could complain that you were treading on his grass; no gentleman who had recently constructed a seat in the country, that you were trespassing; on which you could go off at half-cock and wave adieu to the village; along which you might travel like a pilgrim, going nowhither; where travelers were not too often to be met; where your spirit was free; where the walls and fences were not cared for; where your head was more in heaven than your feet were on earth; not so luxuriant a soil as to attract men; where earth was cheap enough by being public; where you could walk and think with the least obstruction, there being nothing to measure progress by; where you could pace when your breast was full and cherish your moodiness; where you were not in false relations with men, not dining nor conversing with them; by which you might go to the uttermost parts of the earth. "Sometimes," Thoreau says, "it is some particular half-dozen rods which I wish to find myself pacing over, as where certain airs blow; then my life will come to me, methinks. Like a hunter I walk in wait for it. When I am against this bare promontory of a huckleberry hill, then forsooth my thoughts will expand. Is it some influence, as a vapor which exhales from the ground or something in the gales which blow there, or in all things there brought together agreeably to my spirit? The walls must not be too numerous, nor the hills too near, bounding the view, nor the soil too rich, attracting the attention to the earth. It must simply be the way and the life,—a way that was never known to be repaired nor to need repair, within the memory of the oldest inhabitant. I cannot walk habitually in those ways that are liable to be mended for sure it was the devil only that wore them. The road to the corner! the ninety and nine acres that you go through to get there! I would rather see it again though I saw it this morning than Gray's Churchyard! There I can walk and stalk and pace and plod. Which nobody but Jonas Potter travels beside me; where no cow but his is tempted to linger for the herbage by its side; where the guideboard is fallen and now the hand points to heaven significantly,—to a Sud-

bury and Marlboro in the skies. That's a road I can travel, that the particular Sudbury I am bound for, six miles an hour, or two, as you please; and
few there be that enter thereon. There I can walk and recover the lost child
that I am without any ringing of a bell; on the promenade deck of the
world, an outside passenger. I must be fancy-free. I must feel that wet or
dry, high or low, it is the genuine surface of the planet, and not a little chip
dirt or a compost-heap or made land or redeemed."

Thoreau derived his idea of how life should be spent from the happiness
of man. The streets of the village were much more interesting to him,—as
actually they probably were to his neighbors,—of a summer evening for
example, than by day. Neighbors, and farmers come a-shopping after the
day's haying, chatted in the streets, and he heard frequently the sound of
musical instruments and of singing from various houses. For a short hour
or two, he felt, the inhabitants were sensibly employed. The evening was
devoted to poetry such as the villagers could appreciate. He approved of
these activities and therefore it was not difficult for him to believe that he
could well afford to spend his life as he did. To go to his old roads in pursuit
of his life instead of spending his day as his neighbors did in earning more
means of material subsistence, seemed only sensible to him. We must return again to the expansive feeling of the spring when he sensed the freedom which came when he saw that even the most distant and romantically
attractive of roles was as limited and finite as his place in Massachusetts.
He was free then from them all. There was nothing to do; nothing to do in
the whole world. The art of life, he felt, was not having anything to do, to
do something. He felt that a man's employment should be of his own
choosing. This was directly opposed to the practice and belief, or at least
profession, of his neighbors, most of whom would have claimed that their
inclination was to walk too, if they had the time. They neither shared nor
understood his freedom, his feeling of nothing to do in the world. His
neighbors were like the visitor at Walden who told Thoreau, one of the
poorest men in Concord, that that was the way he would live 'if he could
afford to.' They said that there were certain things like earning a living that
had to be done even though a man might be attracted to pleasanter pursuits
and need to discipline himself and exert his will in order to confine his
business to what was necessary rather than pleasant. It was not an easy life
that they lived. They were aware without being told so that much of their
lives was trivial and apparently meaningless, but they saw no freedom
from it and they liked better to be told of some remote or some future

meaning it might somewhere or some day have. They were willing to live dimly in the present, if need be, and hope for reward in old age or in heaven. Thoreau saw that there was no glory so bright, not the sunset, nor the autumn foliage, nor the sky falling, but the veil of business or other expediency put in the way could hide it effectually. And his hope, though it was not that of his neighbors, was to preserve this glory. "With most men," he said, "life is postponed to some trivial business, and so therefore is heaven. Men think foolishly they may abuse and misspend life as they please and when they get to heaven turn over a new leaf." But Thoreau knew that there was but one leaf in our lives, that if we were ever to get to heaven, we must start now and if there were any heaven in our hearts, live by it,—keeping our golden age in the present. We must live by our hearts, at any rate, whatever was in them. From the heartless existence that most men led, Thoreau withdrew to walk his own way over the fields and woods of Concord. It was impossible for him, he said, to be interested in what interested men generally. The pursuits of most men, of the 'men of society' as he called them, were frivolous; they lived on the surface, they were interested in the transient and fleeting, asking always and only after the news. These men, for whom the enterprises of society so unimportant to Thoreau were sufficing and final, regarded wealth and the approbation of men as the only success. Thoreau said that the grounds of his existence lay beyond, behind them and their improvements, and that society or man had no prize that could tempt him, for that which interested a town or a city or any large body of men was always something trivial, as politics.

Rather than for society therefore, he wished to speak a word instead for nature: for absolute freedom and wildness as contrasted with a freedom and culture merely civil. Man, he claimed, was first of all an inhabitant of nature, a part of the natural world himself, and was only secondarily and unimportantly a member of society. Thoreau saw that the criteria of society, cynical with a false maturity, obscured the real purposes of men, so that only outside of society could one reach maturity. "Whatever a great many grown-up boys are seriously engaged in," he said, "is considered great and good and, as such, is sure of the recognition of the churchman and statesman." A man's purposes might become after a time so completely obscured by such immature enterprises, that he could never discover them again when the time came that his material pursuits which society honored had lost whatever little meaning they had ever possessed, and he wished to find some new thing or return to an old. Thoreau was disappointed in Hosmer, for example, whom he considered the most intelligent farmer in Concord and perchance in Middlesex, because Hosmer, who had admitted that he had property enough for his use without accumulating more, and talked of leaving off hard work, letting his farm, and spending the rest of his days easier and better, could not think of any method of employing himself better than in work with his hands. Much as he was inclined to speculation in conversation,—giving up any work to it for the time,—and long-headed as he was, he talked of working for a neighbor for a day now and then and taking his dollar. The freedom from anything to do in the world was not a liberation to him but a threat. He 'would not like to spend his time sitting on the milldam.' The goods of the farmer's life had been exhausted, but Hosmer was only a farmer still and unable to turn to anything new or better; in becoming a farmer, that is, a member of society, he had ceased to be an inhabitant of nature, and had lost that freedom without which life to Thoreau had no value.

Thoreau wished that Hosmer and that all of us might have a richer, a truer perspective, that we might see how little space was occupied after all, by church and state and school, trade and commerce, and manufactures and agriculture, and politics even, the most alarming of them all.

He wished us to see that most of us were half dead with custom, passively obeying the laws, and despairingly doing things that we had no desire to do because we thought it impossible, and had never tried very hard, to stay here in this world on our own conditions. He sometimes wondered, in spite of all he did for the emancipation of the slaves, that anyone in Massachusetts could be so frivolous as to attend to so gross and foreign a form of servitude as negro slavery when so many subtler masters enslaved the north. The man who was held and set in his ways by economic considerations, for example, had no freedom; and those of his neighbors who were fearful of outraging convention, or those who mistook the purposes for which they had been intended and therefore were underlings of their own ignorance and disdain of themselves, were in bondage more fearful than any negro's. It was deep irony to Thoreau to whom political freedom was meaningless in itself, and only valuable as a means to moral freedom, that on such occasions as the nineteenth of April, those who though free from King George IV, had new masters enough, should celebrate freedom. "We are a nation of politicians," he said, "concerned about the outsides of freedom, the means and outmost defenses of freedom." Thoreau's neighbors were enslaved and deadened by a worship of native customs. For his own part, Thoreau could see no important difference between our customs and the customs of those to whom we sent missionaries. One set was as heathen and barbarous as the other; as for example, the assumed gravity and bought funeral sermon of the parish clergyman, were of a piece with the howling and breast-beating of the hired mourning women of the East. It was when his own countrymen became, as it were, foreigners to him, that he was able to avoid any false notions of reverence either for his native customs or for things actually foreign or ancient. "We have heard enough nonsense about the pyramids," he said. "I believe they were built essentially in the same spirit in which the public works of Egypt, of England, and America are built today,—the Mahmoudi Canal, the Tubular Bridge, Thames Tunnel and the Washington Monument. The inspiring motive in the actual builders of these works is garlic or beef or potatoes. For meat and drink and the necessaries of life men can be hired to do many things. Men are wont to speak as if it were a noble work to build a pyramid,—to set, forsooth, a hundred thousand Irishmen at work at fifty cents a day piling stone. I should not think it worth the while nor be interested in the enterprise." This, as Thoreau saw it, was what it meant to be free, to live as an inhabitant of nature with an absolute freedom and wildness, rather than a freedom and culture merely civil. "I pass from it," he says, speaking of the political world, "as from a bean-field into the forest, and it is forgotten. In one half-hour I can walk off to some portion of the earth's surface where a man does not stand from one year's end to another, and there, consequently, politics are not, for they are but as the cigar smoke of a man."

Thoreau felt that to one who habitually endeavored to contemplate the true state of things, the political state could hardly be said to have any existence whatever. It must be unreal, incredible and insignificant to him, and to endeavor to extract the truth from such lean materials was like making sugar from linen rags when sugar cane was available. He thought that the political news might be written ten years in advance with sufficient accuracy. "Most revolutions in society have not power to interest, still less alarm us," he said, "but tell me that our rivers are drying up or the genus pine dying out in the country and I might attend. Most events recorded in history are more remarkable than important, like eclipses of the sun and moon, by which all are attracted, but whose effects no one takes the trouble to calculate."

He wished for a government so well administered that private men need never hear about it. It appeared to him that those things which most engaged the attention of men, as politics, for instance, were vital functions of society, to be sure, but that their daily routine should go on like the vital functions of digestion and circulation of the blood, which in health we know nothing about. A wise man was as unconscious of movements in the body politic as he was of the process of digestion and circulation of blood in the natural body. These processes were infra-human. A consciousness of them was the equivalent of a dyspepsia.

Thoreau knew with surety, that his business in life was not with such petty and trivial concerns as politics and trade and the conventions of society. He had known in like manner that such an aspect of his life as his relations to friends could not confine itself or even be troubled by the littleness of politeness and favors,—those things which would commonly pass for friendship and were not. And therefore his purposes were so large that at times he felt that the only road that pursued them, his back road, must lead so far west to the sunset brilliance and beyond, that it went out of this world entirely and left all of it behind. He was afraid sometimes that his dream which was to lead him into life might remain a dream, never to be lived, as when at thirty-four he saw that his life was as yet almost wholly unexpanded, and unfolded so slowly indeed that within another thirty-four years that miracle could hardly take place. He was so little of what he anticipated for his maturing, there was such an interval in many instances, between his ideal and his actual, that he might almost say, he thought, that he was unborn. But he was determined, nevertheless, neither to hurry nor to trade his birthright for pottage. Here again is the perpetual inexperience of the heart,—the refusal to accept as final his own disappointments, when acceptance would mean a denial of reality which he sensed as finer and quite possible though as yet unrealized,—the same position he maintained so strongly in his concept of friendship and in his relationship with his friends. The interval between the ideal and the actual could be closed quickly in the usual manner, if he were only to cease to hold the ideal possible and so accept the finality of his disappointments. But Thoreau preferred not to do this but rather to leave the possibilities of growth still open even at the risk,—and it was a terrible risk and he knew it,—of leaving the world behind. "Methinks my seasons revolve more slowly," he said, "than those of nature. I am differently timed. This rapid revolution in nature, even of nature in me, why should it hurry me? Let a man step to the music which he hears, however measured. May not my life in nature in proportion as it is supernatural, be only the spring and infantile portion of

94

my spirit's life. Shall I turn my spring to summer? My spirit's unfolding observes not the pace of nature. The society which I was made for is not here. Shall I, then, substitute for the anticipation of that this poor reality? If life is a waiting, so be it. I will not be shipwrecked on a vain reality. What were any reality which I can substitute?" Or again, besides the slowness of growing which made our full maturity seem impossible in this world, so that we hoped for another world in hoping for the fullness, and in the continuance of that hope rejected an artificial maturity here, and so rejected all of this world's immediacies,—there was, in addition to this, the shortness of the period granted for our growth and our action so that we accomplished but little on any great project, or even wasted our time. The death of his uncle Charles was one occasion at least, on which Thoreau was affected by the consideration that a man might spend the whole of his life after boyhood in accomplishing a particular design; as if he were put to a special and petty use without taking time to look around him and appreciate the phenomenon of his existence. And if so many purposes, he thought, were necessarily left unaccomplished, perhaps unthought of, then we were inevitably reminded of how transient an interest we had in this life. Our interest in our country, in the spread of liberty and truth, strong and, so to speak, innate as it was, could not be as transient as our present existence here. It could not be that all those patriots who died in the midst of their careers had no further connection with the career of their country.

Torn between the presence, yet insufficiency, of this world and the grandeur of what might be thought of as the next, Thoreau did not, as has been charged against him, reject this world and escape it. "However mean your life is," he says in *Walden*, "meet it and live it; do not shun it and call it hard names. Love your life, poor as it is. Do not trouble yourself much to get new things, whether clothes or friends. Turn the old; return to them. Things do not change; we change." Thoreau turned the old and returned to them. His little time and slow pace appeared in keeping with the thing in hand, not to be done with quickly, nor effected at once and by one man only, but always recurrent, slowly emerging, and in this world always, where what was left undone by one would be done, or done again by another, and where though we might do little, it was enough and all we could ask for. It was enough, for example, merely to be connected with the eternal things, and to perform them with hope and faith as a ritual or a celebration. "Hosmer," he says, finding the darkest of his own thoughts almost echoed, "is overhauling a vast heap of manure in the rear of his barn, turning the ice within it up to the light yet he asks despairingly what life is for, and says he does not expect to stay here long. But I have just come from reading Columella, who describes the same kind of spring work, in that to him new spring of the world, with hope, and I suggest to be brave and hopeful with nature. Human life may be transitory and full of trouble, but the perennial mind, whose survey extends from that spring to this, from Columella to Hosmer is superior to change. I will identify myself with that which did not die with Columella and will not die with Hosmer."

Thoreau was a realist who faced in the present whatever reality he found, and then since this was little enough, he set about to cut through and cut away deadwood and convention, to reveal and make actual more. He identified himself with whatever in the present most embodied the things of eternity,—for it was in these that he was most interested, and these which he felt to be the only considerable reality. It is wrong to call this attitude escapism. Just as an individual's purposes are obscured and finally lost in a tangle of business and politics, so Thoreau felt that the nature and purposes of eternal things were obscured and finally defeated by the institutions designed for their fostering. "In my short experience of human life," he says in the *Week*, "the *outward* obstacles, if there were any such, have not been living men but the institutions of the dead." It is a question here again, as with politics, not of the outright badness of institutions but of the lack of perspective with which men viewed them. As a matter of fact, it was Thoreau's feeling that there was an original goodness in institutions which they gradually lost, while still retaining some traces of their origin, just as our worst passions had their roots in the best,—as anger, for example, might be thought of as only a perverted sense of wrong. Like the gradual departure of goodness from institutions was the gradual accumulation of Thoreau's finally strong distaste and hatred for them. When he was only twenty, he spoke mildly of institutions, saying that we must consider war and slavery with many other institutions and even the best existing governments, 'notwithstanding their apparent advantages,' as only abortive rudiments of nobler ones which distinguish man in his savage and half civilized state. A little later he says, "The soldier is the degenerate hero as the priest is the degenerate saint; and the soldier and the priest are related as the hero and saint. The one's virtue is bravery, the other's bravery is virtue. Mankind still pay to the soldier the honors due only to the hero. They delight to do him honor." As he grew older, the discrepancy between the origin of institutions and their present state appeared greater and greater to him as he saw how completely they failed to embody those eternal realities in which he had placed his faith and his hope. He became one of those few who saw that the universe was larger than enough for man's abode, if man was to be a creature of his trivial pursuit and occupations;—one of those who, having been out of doors and out all night, had gone beyond the world of humanity and seen its institutions like toadstools by the wayside.

The fault, of course, was that despite the goodness of their origins, the life departed out of institutions and out of those who paid allegiance to them so that Thoreau was reminded of those monkeys, who being shot, contracted their tails around a limb out of reach of the hunter and so hung there, a dead monkey on a dead limb, until sensible corruption took place.

"Some institutions—most institutions, indeed—have had a divine origin," he said. "But of the most that we see prevailing in society nothing but the form, the shell, is left; the life is extinct and there is nothing divine in them. Then the reformer arises to reinstitute life and whatever he does or causes to be done is a reestablishment of that same or a similar divineness. But some, who never knew the significance of these instincts, are by a sort of false instinct, found clinging to the shells. Those who have no knowledge of the divine appoint themselves defenders of the divine, as champions of the church, etc. I have been astonished to observe how long some audiences can endure to hear a man speak on a subject which he knows nothing about, as religion for instance, when one who had no ear for music might with the same propriety take up the time of a musical assembly with putting through his opinions on music. The young man who is the main pillar of some divine institution—does he know what he has undertaken? If the saints were to come again on earth, would they be likely to stay at his house? Would they meet with his approbation even? *Ne sutor ultra crepidam.* They who merely have a talent for affairs are forward to express their opinions. A Roman soldier sits there to decide upon the righteousness of Christ. The world does not long endure such blunders, though they are made every day. The weak-brained and pusillanimous farmers would fain abide by the institutions of their fathers. Their argument is they have not long to live and for that little space of time let them not be disturbed in their slumbers."

Thoreau became more and more shocked at the enormity of our blind stupidity in mistaking the church for religion, the decisions of the law court for justice, the puny institutionalized reality that we revere, for reality itself. One is reminded of the angry scorn of Keats when, in *Sleep and Poetry*, he turns on the hacks of classicism who had dared to call themselves poets. "The preachers and lecturers deal with men of straw," Thoreau said, "as they are men of straw themselves. If there were any magnanimity in us, any grandeur of soul, anything but sects and parties undertaking to patronize God and keep the mind within bounds, how often we might encourage and provoke one another by a free expression. The church, the state, the school, the magazine, think they are liberal and free. It is the freedom of the prison yard. What is it you tolerate, you church today? Not truth but a lifelong hypocrisy. Let us have institutions framed not out of our rottenness, but out of our soundness. This factitious piety is like stale gingerbread. I would like to suggest what a pack of fools and cowards we mankind are. They want me to agree not to breathe too hard in the neighborhood of their paper castles. If I should draw a long breath in the neighborhood of these institutions their weak and flabby sides would fall out, for my inspiration would exhaust the air about them. The Church! It is eminently the timid institution, and the heads and pillars of it are constitutionally and by principle the greatest cowards in the community. The best 'preachers' so called, are an effeminate class; their bravest thoughts wear petticoats. If they have any manhood they are sure to forsake the ministry though they were to turn their attention to baseball.

"One of our New England towns is sealed up hermetically like a molasses-hogshead,—such is its sweet Christianity,—only a little of the sweet trickling out of the cracks to daub you. It is Christianity bunged up."

And the further one went up country, he found, the worse it was, and the more benighted were the inhabitants. There was always the barroom on the one side, holding the "scoffers," and the vestry on the other, with little to cheer you in either company. It might often be the truth and righteousness of the barroom indeed, that saved the town. There was nothing to redeem the bigotry and moral cowardice of New England in his eyes, he said, for what was called faith was an immense prejudice, and like Hindoos or Russians or Sandwich Islanders, they were the creatures of an institution.

Fearful of real freedom or actual religion, his neighbors erected the prison of an institution around them and so had the safe and make-believe freedom of the prison yard or, as Thoreau said, had Christianity bunged up. But since there was a yard within the prison, the defenders of the institution could constitute themselves defenders of freedom, when they really defended not the space within at all, but the enclosure itself, carrying on in this way a continuously hypocritical and reactionary program, keeping the mind within bounds. Thus, though born free, we undertake as quickly as possible to unburden us of our freedom; we confine ourselves tightly and like liquids, take the shape of the thing that holds us. It was in this sense that Thoreau called his neighbors creatures of an institution; for in another sense they were not even that. The walled structure of an institution is a means of escape from freedom, an avoidance of that full area of existence into which Thoreau moved away and which constituted the boundless acres of his life. But these structures are of two kinds. The walls of the parlor which institutionalized refinement shut men out just as the walls of the prison yard shut them in. Thoreau's neighbors protected the drabness of their everyday lives from the inroads of anything better they could discover by placing the better things aside like curios on the what-not, and then pulled the parlor curtains and shut the door. But they could always point to the parlor as proof of their civilization to Thoreau who lived a life which was so simple in its outward aspects as to be rude. "Would you have us return to the savage state?" they would ask in horror, when Thoreau would advocate his drastic simplicity. His reply, in essence, was that they had never left it.

"Again and again, I am surprised what an interval there is, in what is called civilized life," he said, "between the shell and the inhabitant of the shell,—what a disproportion there is between the life of a man and his conveniences and luxuries. The house is neatly painted and has many apartments. You are shown into the sitting room where is a carpet and couch and mirror and splendidly bound Bible, daguerreotypes, ambrotypes, photographs of the whole family even, on the mantlepiece. One could live here more deliciously and improve his divine gifts better than in a cave surely. In the bright and costly saloon, man will not be starving or freezing or contending with vermin surely, but he will be meditating a divine song or a heroic deed, or perfuming the atmosphere by the very breath of his natural and healthful existence. As the parlor is preferable to the cave, so will the life of its occupant be more godlike than that of the dweller in the cave. I called at such a house this afternoon, the house of one who in Europe would be called an operative. The woman was not in the third heavens but in the third kitchen, as near to the woodshed or to outdoors and to the cave as she could instinctively get, for there she belonged,—a coarse scullion or wench, not one whit superior, but in fact inferior, to the squaw in a wigwam,—and the master of the house, where was he? He was drunk somewhere on some mow or behind some stack and I could not see him. He had been having a spree. If he had been as sober as he may be tomorrow, it would have been essentially the same; for refinement is not in him, it is only in his house,—in the appliances which he did not invent. So it is in the Fifth Avenue and all over the civilized world. There is nothing but confusion in our New England life. The hogs are in the parlor. This man and his wife—and how many like them!—should have sucked their claws in some hole in the rock or lurked like gypsies in the outbuildings of some diviner race. They've got into the wrong boxes; they rained down into these houses by mistake, as it is said to rain toads sometimes. They wear these advantages helter-skelter and without appreciating them or to satisfy a vulgar taste, just as savages wear the dress of civilized men, just as that Indian chief walked the streets of New Orleans clad in nothing but a gaudy military coat which his Great Father had given him. Some philanthropists trust that the houses will civilize the inhabitants at last. The mass of men, just like savages, strive always after the outside, the clothes and finery of civilized life, the blue beads and tinsel and centre-tables. It is a wonder that any load ever gets moved, men are so prone to put the cart before the horse."

Thoreau did not believe that the houses would civilize the inhabitants, and he was not interested in sham civilization. Almost his entire difficulty with society either as groups or as individuals lay in his aversion to its incessant tendency to strive after the outside while he was laboring so diligently from within that he sometimes never achieved a very handsome or at all elaborate exterior. With his devotion to nature and his belief in the productiveness of leisure, he was quite naturally criticized by those who could not see how such a way of life could be productive and so thought him lacking in enterprise. But this failed to shake his faith in his misunderstood ventures and failed to tempt him to engage in more conventional enterprises. "I hate the present modes of living and getting a living," he says. "Farming and shopkeeping and working at a trade or profession are all odious to me. I should relish getting my living in a simple primitive fashion. The life which society proposes to me to live is so artificial and complex—bolstered up on so many weak supports, and sure to topple down at last—that no man surely can ever be inspired to live it, and only 'old fogies' ever praise it. At best some think it their duty to live it."

Thoreau wanted, not to return to the savage state, though he should have preferred it to most that were called civilized, but to achieve a true civilization in nature by growth from within outward. "Here is this vast savage, and howling Mother of ours," he says, "Nature, lying all around with such beauty and such affection for her children as the leopard; and yet we are so early weaned from her breast to society, to that culture which is exclusively an interaction of man on man, a sort of breeding in and in, which produces at most a merely English nobility, a civilization destined to have a speedy limit.

"In society in the best institutions of men it is easy to detect a certain precocity. When we should still be growing children, we are already little men. Give me a culture which imports much muck from the meadows—and deepens the soil, not that which trusts to heating manures and improved implements, and modes of culture only!

"Many a poor sore-eyed student that I have heard of would grow faster, both intellectually, and physically, if instead of sitting up so very late, he honestly slumbered a fool's allowance."

Just as from the standpoint of our life in nature, Thoreau was opposed to any other meaningless form or activity, he was opposed to meaningless enterprise. There was what Thoreau called a coarse, boisterous, money-making fellow in the north part of town. He was going to build a bank wall under the hill along the edge of his meadow and asked Thoreau to spend three weeks there digging with him. Thoreau examined the probable results. He knew that the employer would no doubt thereby get a little more money to hoard or for his heirs to spend foolishly. He knew also that if he took the job the community would commend him as an industrious and hard working man, and that if he chose to devote himself to labor which yielded more real profit though but little money, he was a loafer in the eyes of the community. Thoreau said that he had no need of a police of meaningless labor to regulate him and saw nothing absolutely praiseworthy in the building of the wall, however amusing it might be to the man who suggested it, and therefore preferred to finish his education at a different school.

He was unable to respect enterprises which his neighbors respected, for various reasons. Sometimes it was the end to which labor was put that made it seem waste in his eyes. He sees Hayden, for example, one morning just after sunrise, hauling a heavy hewn stone slung under the axle as he walked beside his team. He seemed surrounded in an atmosphere of honest, peaceful, world-conserving industry, such as all men respected and society had consecrated. "And I thought," Thoreau said, "such is the labor which the American Congress exists to protect,—honest, manly toil. Toil that makes his bread taste sweet and keeps society sweet. The day went by and at evening I passed a rich man's yard, who keeps many servants and foolishly spends much money while he adds nothing to the common stock and there I saw Hayden's stone lying beside a whimsical structure intended to adorn this Lord Timothy Dexter's mansion, and the dignity forthwith departed from Hayden's labor in my eyes."

As a matter of fact the chief objection that Thoreau felt toward this hustling, determinedly materialistic form of activity praised as enterprise, was only that he knew that his business in life, and as he thought, the business of any other sensible man lay elsewhere. It is interesting in the light of Thoreau's withdrawal that his objection to enterprise should be in terms of production. It has sometimes been assumed that because Thoreau would not do as society expected him to do, he was refusing to do anything for the benefit of society. Thoreau's individualism was not selfish but practical. That he regarded himself as a producer and regarded his production as valuable to society can easily be seen, as when he says, "What an army of non-producers society produces—ladies generally (old and young) and gentlemen of leisure so called. Many think themselves well employed as charitable dispensers of wealth which somebody else earned and those who produce nothing being of the most luxurious habits, are precisely they who want the most and complain loudest when they do not get what they want. They who are literally paupers maintained at the public expense are the most importunate and insatiable beggars. They cling like the glutton to a living man and suck his vitals up. To every locomotive man there are three or four deadheads clinging to him as if they conferred a great favor on society by living upon it. Meanwhile they fill the churches and die and revive from time to time. They have nothing to do but sin and repent of their sins. How can you expect such bloodsuckers to be happy?"

It was the gold rush, finally, that hindered the golden age,—that drew the veil most darkly over nature's sunset and autumn foliage. "The recent rush to California," Thoreau said, "and the attitude of the world, even of its philosophers and prophets in relation to it appears to me to reflect the greatest disgrace on mankind. That so many are ready to get their living by the lottery of gold-digging without contributing any value to society and that the great majority who stay at home justify them in this both by precept and example! It matches the infatuation of the Hindoos who have cast themselves under the car of Juggernaut. I know of no more startling development of the morality of trade and all the modes of getting a living than the rush to California affords. Of what significance the philosophy, or poetry or religion of a world that will rush to the lottery of California gold-digging on the receipt of the first news to live by luck to get the means of commanding the labors of others less lucky i.e. of slaveholding without contributing any value to society? And that is called enterprise and the devil is only a little more enterprising! The philosophy and poetry and religion of such a mankind are not worth the dust of a puffball. The hog that roots his own living and so makes manure would be ashamed of such company. If I could command the wealth of all the world by lifting my finger I would not pay such a price for it. It makes God to be a moneyed gentleman who scatters a handful of pennies in order to see mankind scramble after them. What a comment, what a satire on our institutions! The gold of California is a touchstone which has betrayed the rottenness, the baseness of mankind."

Or again he says, facing the subject in a quieter way, "Yesterday, toward night, gave Sophia and mother a sail as far as the Battle-Ground. One-eyed John Goodwin the fisherman was loading into a handcart and conveying home the piles of driftwood which of late he had collected with his boat. It was a beautiful evening and a clear amber sunset lit up all the eastern shores; and that man's employment so simple and direct—though he is regarded by most as a vicious character in whose whole motive was so easy to fathom—thus to obtain his winter's wood—charmed me unspeakably. So much do we love actions that are simple. They are all poetic. We, too, would fain be so employed. So unlike the pursuits of most men, so artificial or complicated. Consider how the broker collects his winter wood, what sport he makes of it, what is his boat and handcart?" Thoreau felt that it was such a joy to satisfy any of our wants simply and truly that he never liked to buy anything of what was necessary to his life if he could make or grow it himself. To him, time spent in earning the money for something he wanted was a postponement of life, for he wanted not merely to eat his food or burn his wood, but to get the good of it twice by producing or securing himself what he wanted. It would be to give no account of his employment to say that he cut wood to keep himself from freezing or cultivated beans to keep from starving. The greatest value of those labors was received before the wood was teamed home or the beans harvested. Such was the simple

life in the manner of Goodwin and Thoreau. No trade, however, was simple, but artificial and complex. It went against the grain, and if the first
generation did not die of it, Thoreau said, the third or fourth did. In the
face of all statistics even, he would never believe that it was the descendants
of tradesmen who kept the state alive, but rather the descendants always of
simple yeomen and laborers. "Postponing instant life," Thoreau says of
the broker, "he makes haste to Boston on the cars and there deals in stock,
not quite relishing his employment,—and so earns the money with which
to buy his fuel. And when, by chance, I meet him about this indirect and
complicated business, I am not struck with the beauty of his employment.
It does not harmonize with the sunset." Moreover, Thoreau saw very little
to be accomplished by such employment. He says of the railroad that to
make it available to all mankind would be equivalent to grading the whole
surface of the planet. "Men have an indistinct notion that if they keep up
this activity of joint stocks and spades long enough, all will at length ride
somewhere, in next to no time, and for nothing; but though a crowd rushes
to the depot and the conductor shouts 'All aboard!' when the smoke is
blown away and the vapour condensed, it will be perceived that a few are
riding but the rest are run over—and it will be called and will be 'a melancholy accident!' No doubt they can ride at last who shall have earned their
fare, that is, if they survive so long but they will probably have lost their
elasticity and desire to travel by that time."

Getting his living, engaging in an enterprise, was a question that deeply
concerned Thoreau. He wanted to do it properly. And it must be by now
apparent that such a question was a difficult one for him to answer. Immediately to be reckoned with was his aversion to the trivial and forgetful. His
occupation must, by all means, have some of the wonder and respect for
life and for nature of the autumn and winter days spent outside the town
trying to hear what was in the wind and carry it express. "I wish to suggest," he said, "that a man may be very industrious and yet not spend his
time well. There is no more fatal blunderer than he who consumes the
greater part of his life getting his living. All great enterprises are self-
supporting. The poet, for instance, must sustain his body by his poetry, as
a steam planing mill feeds its boilers with the shavings it makes. You must
get your living by loving. But as it is said of merchants that ninety-seven in
a hundred fail, so the life of men generally, tried by this standard, is a
failure, and bankruptcy may be surely prophesied." Though he felt devoted to higher pursuits and so did not wish to spend his life getting a

living, yet in another sense, he did wish to spend it this way, and complained as we have seen of the brokers who having postponed life, spent their time in getting the means of getting a living rather than the living itself. He spent days, like Goodwin, gathering wood. Though this may seem contradictory at first, it is only that he did want to spend his life getting his living if it meant, as it so seldom did, getting his life at the same time.

Thoreau, we may say, continued in his earlier enterprises, though he might seem to have paused. It will be recalled that he concludes the recital of his first employments with a passage that seems to end them. "In short, I went on thus for a long time," he said; "I may say it without boasting faithfully minding my own business, till it became more and more evident that my townsmen would not after all admit me into the list of town officers, nor make my place a sinecure with a moderate allowance. My accounts which I can swear to have kept faithfully, I have, indeed, never got audited, still less accepted, still less paid and settled. However I have not set my heart on that."

He follows this passage with a story about an Indian who brought baskets to sell at the house of a well-known lawyer. "Do you wish to buy any baskets?" he asked. "No we don't want any," was the reply. "What!" exclaimed the Indian as he went out the gate, "do you mean to starve us?" The Indian, having done his part in weaving the baskets, was surprised to learn that society might not buy them and so cooperate. Thoreau himself, having woven as he said, a kind of basket for which there was little market, continued nevertheless to weave them though in so doing he lived in the woods for a while and was thankful that his wants were very few. Society will not always reward us for what we consider the most congenial as well as valuable action, nor will it make as high a use of us always as it might. It was so in regard to Thoreau's lectures.

"I am reminded of Hayden, the painter's, experience when he went about painting the nobility," he says in speaking of his surveying. "I go about to the houses of the farmers and squires in like manner. This is my portrait painting,—when I would fain be employed on higher subjects. I have offered myself much more earnestly as a lecturer than as a surveyor. Yet I do not get any employment as a lecturer; was not invited to lecture, once, last winter, and only once (without pay) this winter. But I can get surveying enough, which a hundred others in this county can do as well as I, though it is not boasting much to say that a hundred others in New

England cannot lecture as well as I on my themes. But they that do not make the highest demands on you shall rue it. It is because they make a low demand on themselves. All the while that they use only your humbler faculties, your higher unemployed faculties like an invisible scimitar are cutting them in twain. Woe be to the generation which lets any higher faculty in its midst go unemployed! That is to deny God and know him not and he, accordingly, will know not of them."

Thoreau knew that society did mean, as the Indian said, to starve us. Accepted on its own terms, it made only such low use of a man as to starve his spirit, and by refusing to feed his body otherwise, attempted to force acceptance of spiritual starvation. But he also knew that unemployment of higher faculties was death anyway, both to one's self and one's society, and therefore that only by refusing to accept society on its own terms could one hope to survive. It did mean, indeed, to starve us though sometimes it failed and by persistence such failure could be forced. One needed however to expect and to be content with very little, and to be able to dismiss the likelihood of being rewarded by society for what it had not wanted.

In 1860, Thoreau found a Canada lynx in Concord, an animal whose appearance in those parts was so rare as to be almost unheard of. But one man to whom Thoreau related the happening, immediately asked, "Have you got the reward for him?"

"What reward?"

"Why the ten dollars which the state offers," he replied, and continued to speak only of the reward, not caring at all for the lynx itself. "Yes," he said, "this state offers ten dollars reward."

"You would say that some men," Thoreau wrote with this in mind, "had been tempted to live in this world at all, only by an offer of a bounty by the general government—a bounty on living—to anyone who will consent to be out at this era of the world, the object of the governors being to create a nursery for their navy. A thing is not valuable—e.g. a fine situation for a house, until it is convertible into so much money, that is, can cease to be what it is and become something else which you prefer. So you will see that all prosaic people, who possess only the commonest sense, who believe strictly in this kind of wealth, are speculators in fancy stocks, and continually cheat themselves, but poets and all discerning people who have an object in life and know what they want, speculate in real values. The mean and low values of anything depend on its convertibility into something else—i.e. have nothing to do with its intrinsic value."

Thoreau had an object in life and knew what he wanted. "The aim of a laborer," he said, "should be, not to get his living, to get 'a good job', but to perform well a certain work."

Thoreau's business in life, which was to make life less petty, achieved its objects simply by living, not by trading. Since all of his values were intrinsic, he could bear that society would not pay him for what he liked best to do, that it was not immediately willing to make any but a low use of him. He went on with his work as before, knowing that the community had no bribe with which to tempt a wise man, for though you might raise money enough to tunnel a mountain, it would still be impossible to raise enough to hire a man who was minding his own business. An efficient and valuable man does whatever he can, whether the community pay him for it or not. Thoreau knew that his life was in nature, not in society, just as whatever community life as has value and is truly existent is in nature too. That, however, is not society. He was content that a society which he had rejected anyway should not reward him. They would have been hardly anxious to. However high the sometimes hypocritical or heavily qualified regard in which we hold Thoreau today, to most of his neighbors Thoreau must have often seemed a most unimportant and dubious member of the community. It is one of the prices of a freedom as complete as Thoreau's. What really mattered were the returns from what he called in financial terms, his speculation in real values. The knowledge which he ultimately fronted included the diminishment even of these. It was a knowledge beyond his accounting and he never offered to make one.

Social Action

"I came into this world," said Thoreau, "not chiefly to make this a good place to live in but to live in it, be it good or bad." He lived as we know, by silence, and therefore, unlike the goodness of those who were waiting and planning until the time should be more opportune,—until they should have converts enough, or until through some change in external conditions goodness could exist unhindered,—his goodness was little affected by the goodness or badness of his neighbors or society. It sprang and grew through obedience to his own nature, and without fear of the consequences, for it was after this fashion that silence had counseled him to live. And if such obedience should sometimes bring him into conflict with society or the state, he felt no obligation either to yield to the state's demands, or to change the state or repair it. He was not responsible for the successful working of the machinery of society. He perceived that when an acorn and a chestnut fell side by side, the one did not remain inert to make way for the other, but both obeyed their own laws and sprang and grew and flourished as best they could, till one, perchance, overshadowed and destroyed the other. "If a plant cannot live according to its nature," he said, "it dies; and so a man."

All over New England, and thence spreading west, the social revolutions of the mid-nineteenth century had begun to blossom like some unexpected kind of flower. The country was full of reformers, ranging in scale from vegetarians to abolitionists, all of them men who were discontented with the world for various reasons, all of them teaching their doctrines and their panaceas in lecture halls or wherever a number of people would hear them and become their disciples, as many did. The reformers found some indeed who were willing, if others were persuaded to join them, to abandon whatever previous positions they had held, to pull up stakes, and become a member of one of the numerous colonies for social experiment which were then projected. No matter what kind of life a man might lead, he seemed to believe that it was only necessary to reconstitute society and change the external conditions of existence in order that he should lead a better.

Thoreau knew that there was evil and injustice in society, and he was not indifferent to it. He knew that only a few of his contemporaries had led what could be called a good life, and he was interested that all men should lead a better. But the whole kernel of his social thought is contained in the statement of why he came into this world. In 1843, reviewing a book which contained a proposal for remodeling society according to the theories of Fourier, he confesses the book is to be praised for its objects at least, which were far beyond the usual complacent trivialities. "We confess," he says, "that we have risen from reading this book with enlarged ideas, and grander conceptions of our duties in this world. It did expand us a little. It is worth attending to if only that it entertains large questions."

And it had, indeed, entertained large questions. "Fellow men!" the author had said, "I promise to show the means of creating a paradise within ten years, where everything desirable for human life may be had in superabundance, without labor, and without pay; where the whole face of nature shall be changed into the most beautiful forms, and man may live in the most magnificent palaces, in all imaginable refinements of luxury, and in the most delightful gardens; where he may accomplish, without labor, in one year, more than hitherto could be done in thousands of years; may level mountains, sink valleys, create lakes, drain lakes and swamps, and intersect the land everywhere with beautiful canals, and roads for transporting heavy loads of many thousand tons, and for traveling one thousand miles in twenty-four hours; may cover the ocean with floating islands movable in any desired direction with immense power and celerity, in perfect security, and with all comforts and luxuries, bearing gardens and palaces with thousands of families, and provided with rivulets of sweet water; may explore the interior of the globe, and travel from pole to pole in a fortnight; provide himself with means, unheard of yet, for increasing his knowledge of the world, and so his intelligence; lead a life of continual happiness, of enjoyments yet unknown; free himself from almost all the evils that afflict mankind, except death, and even put death far beyond the common period of human life, and finally render it less afflicting. Mankind may thus live in and enjoy a new world, far superior to the present, and raise themselves far higher in the scale of being."

The author of this astonishing book believed that powers existed in nature to effect the changes which he proposed, and he wished to demonstrate this thesis. His plan called first for the formation of a phalanx or community, after the model of Fourier, the members of which should live together in harmony, and begin to employ to their full extent the powers of the wind, the tide, the waves, and the sunshine. It was in the *Mechanical System*, a sequel to this book, that the specific application of the powers was to be found. In the present work, the author was content to indicate what ends might be accomplished.

Thoreau, too, would have the powers of nature employed to a fuller extent. "Already nature is serving all those uses which science slowly derives," he said "on a much higher and grander scale to him that will be served by her. When the sunshine falls on the path of the poet, he enjoys all those pure benefits and pleasures which the arts slowly and partially realize from age to age. The winds which fan his cheek waft him the sum of that profit and happiness which their lagging inventions supply."

Moreover, there were the moral powers which no one would presume to calculate. "Suppose we could compare the moral with the physical and say how many horse-power the force of love, for instance, blowing on every square foot of a man's soul would equal. . . . But though the wisest men in all ages have labored to publish this force, and every human heart is, sooner or later, more or less, made to feel it, yet how little is actually applied to social ends! True it is the motive power of all successful social machinery; but as in physics we have made the elements do only a little drudgery for us,—steam to take the place of a few horses, wind of a few oars, water of a few cranks and hand mills,—as the mechanical forces have not yet been generously and largely applied to make the physical world answer to the ideal, so the power of love has been but meanly and sparingly applied, as yet."

The Paradise within the Reach of all Men, without Labor, by Powers of Nature and Machinery, as the book was called, is in essentials, the familiar work of reformers and social planners, in spite of the fact that certain changes in the fashion of reform, like changes in fashions of dress, may make it appear so plainly fantastic today. In our own time, the hope of many reformers and their followers is placed in plans which, in all important respects, are the equivalents of this,—plans which while projecting or securing changes, even good and desirable changes from the standpoint of comfort and convenience in the external world, fail to bring the good life by any appreciable distance closer, or to make it the living pattern for a greater number of men. It is not that a reformer's plans are too lofty to be realized, as they are sometimes said to be, for one can note in this instance how many of the marvels which the author projects have been accomplished or overshadowed. It is only that, once their realization has been brought about, their marvelous and effective quality pales. One who came into this world not chiefly to make this a better place to live in but to live in it, be it good or bad, has been in no way benefited. For him to have busied himself with reform of this character, would have been to waste the time which he sorely needed for other business. For the reformer, who thought he had imagined a paradise, will be found to have imagined a world which is little different from the one already existent. He spends all his strength in changing externals only. As Thoreau said of this author, "His castles in the air fall to the ground, because they are not built lofty enough; they should be secured to heaven's roof."

To be sure, Thoreau did feel that if we were to reform our outward life truly and thoroughly, we should find no duty of the inner omitted. It would be employment for our whole nature; and what we should do thereafter would be as vain a question as to ask the bird what it will do when its nest is built and its brood reared. "But," he said, "a moral reform must take place first, and then the necessity of the other will be superseded, and we shall sail and plow by its force alone. There is a speedier way than the 'Mechanical System' can show to fill up marshes, to drown the roar of waves, to tame hyenas, secure agreeable environs, diversify the land, and refresh it with 'rivulets of sweet water', and that is by the power of rectitude and true behavior. It is only for a little while, only occasionally, methinks, that we want a garden. Surely a good man need not be at the labor to level a hill for the sake of a prospect, or raise fruits and flowers, and construct floating islands for the sake of a paradise. He enjoys better prospect than lie beyond any hill."

Thoreau would therefore have no part in reform; and his rejection of it reveals one of his most characteristic traits. He met suggestions from the outside which concerned his behavior with a strong resistance, rejecting and refusing the action recommended, from a sense that to recommend the action to him was impertinent, because he had already been suffi-ciently aware of the problem involved to have settled it in one way or an-other,—either by including the action in the general pattern of his behav-ior, or by deciding it was something apart from his particular business. Having thus some inner criterion for judging the pertinence and necessity of an action, he could reject actions which were apparently perfectly fair and reasonable and socially valuable, merely because he felt no need to do them. It seemed to him foolish to choose actions like diversions, turning one to another, in response to some desirable qualities they might have, as though one had nothing better to do,—no truly compelling business to occupy one's mind.

Thoreau's attitudes, far from being arbitrary or irresponsible, were basically consistent with one another, the facets of one large point of view. If Thoreau was in error, it was a basic and irredeemable error. His views of philanthropy, for example, were the same as his views of reform,—a restatement, so to speak, of a theme. "There are those," he said, "who have used all their arts to persuade me to undertake the support of some poor family in the town; and if I had nothing to do, for the devil finds employment for the idle,—I might try my hand at some such pastime as that. However, when I have thought to indulge myself in this respect, and lay their Heaven under an obligation by maintaining certain poor persons, in all respects as comfortably as I maintain myself, and have even ventured so far as to make them the offer, they have one and all, unhesitatingly preferred to remain poor. While my townsmen and women are devoted in so many ways to the good of their fellows, I trust that one, at least, may be spared to other, and less humane pursuits. Probably I should not consciously and deliberately forsake my particular calling to do the good which society demands of me, to save the universe from annihilation; and I believe that a like, but infinitely greater steadfastness elsewhere is all that now preserves it."

This steadfastness in one's own nature was the pattern that Thoreau held for conduct. Thoreau believed that a man who was truly good in his being, was free from any need for doing good which was deliberate, so great was the power of his being, self-sufficient and all sufficing. "Men say practically," he said, "begin where you are and such as you are, without aiming mainly to become of more worth, and with kindness aforethought, go about doing good. If I were to preach at all in this strain, I should say rather, set about being good. As if the sun should stop when he had kindled his fires up to the splendor of a moon or a star of the sixth magnitude, and go about like a Robin Goodfellow, peeping in at every cottage window, inspiring lunatics and tainting meats, and making darkness visible, instead of steadily increasing his genial heat and beneficence until he is of such brightness that no mortal can look him in the face, and then, in the meanwhile too, going about the world in his own orbit, doing it good, or rather, as a truer philosophy has discovered, the world going about him, getting good."

Thoreau said that if he knew for a certainty that someone was coming to his house with the conscious design of doing him good, he should run for his life as from a simoon, for fear of getting some of that man's good done him.

He saw that the chief failing of reform and philanthropy was their false approach to goodness. When he said that he intended to live in this world, be it good or bad, he spoke with the full knowledge that for him, living included as near an achievement as possible of true goodness within himself; but he saw that philanthropy was only concerned with doing good, and reform aimed at a coating of goodness on the outside, or a goodness concentrated on mechanical aspects. Neither of these, of course, was in Thoreau's opinion a plan for effective social action; and in any event, they were unsuited to his nature because he placed a greater value on being than on doing. Thoreau's concept of being was not a rejection of action, but a step toward acting consistently from one's whole nature, as though from a surplus of being. He asked from his personal associates, 'not words and deeds, but relationships,' and so again in our relations with society, he recognized that the effective factor was not what we might assume to do, but our true worth and nature. Nothing we might do to conceal or alleviate this truth seemed desirable or of importance to him. If we are truly mean, let us know it.

Neither in terms of what it claimed to be, nor most certainly, in terms of the nature of man, was philanthropy worth-while. Thoreau saw both these truths in the light of one of his neighbors near Walden Pond, Johnny Riordan, to whom he one day carried a coat, and whose strength, in spite of his miserable condition,—walking a mile to school every day, over the bleakest of causeways, with only one thickness of ragged cloth over his shirt for all the wildness of the weather, and with only worn out shoes into which the snow got, on his feet,—was greater, Thoreau thought, than that of all the charitable people in Concord, was greater even than that of the Persian army or a thousand Indras. "The thought of its greater independence and its closeness to nature diminishes the pain I feel when I see a more interesting child than usual destined to be brought up in a shanty," he said. "While the charitable waddle about cased in furs and finery, this boy, lively as a cricket, passes them on his way to school. Our charitable institutions are an insult to humanity,—a charity that dispenses the crumbs that fall from its overloaded tables! whose waste and whose example helped to produce that poverty! I see that, for the present, the child is happy, is not puny, and has all the wonders of nature for his toys. Have I not faith that his tenderness will in some way be cherished and protected as the buds of spring in the remotest wintry dell no less than in the garden and summer-house?"

Thoreau placed his faith in a kind of essential Fortune, a benevolence of existence, a providence of God, and prevalence of man, rather than in philanthropy. Philanthropy seemed to him, not love for one's fellow man in the broadest sense. It was again, a misunderstanding of our being, something less than life itself. "A man is not a good *man* to me," he said, "because he will feed me if I should be starving, or warm me if I should be freezing, or pull me out of a ditch if I should ever fall into one. I can find you a Newfoundland dog that will do as much." We thus find Thoreau seeking as a quality of social behavior what, in almost the same words ('We do not wish for friends to feed and clothe our bodies,—our neighbors are kind enough for that.') he had heretofore sought in a friend, stating that friendship was the highest use to be made of a man, beside which lesser uses paled to insignificance. In using the same criterion for the wider as for the narrower relationship, Thoreau was more consistent than confused, more wise than quixotic. "I want," he said, "the flower and fruit of a man; that some fragrance be wafted over from him to me, and some ripeness flavor our intercourse." It seemed, however, that the philanthropist too often gave one instead the hulls and blemishes; he surrounded mankind with the remembrance of his own cast-off griefs as an atmosphere, and called it sympathy. Likewise with the reformer. He believed that what saddened the reformer was not his sympathy with his fellows in distress but, though he were the holiest son of God, his private ail. "Let this be righted," Thoreau said, "let the spring come to him, the morning rise over his couch, and he will forsake his generous companions without apology." Philanthropy and reform, it was obvious to Thoreau, could not be supported by our best energies, were not consistent with our highest purpose, and in the light of our full development faded to nothing. As social action, they were therefore effective in a different direction from the one in which Thoreau wished to travel.

Thoreau, who traveled toward the west and the sunset brilliance, wanted to proceed to the highest expression of the individual. The only method that he knew for this was to keep him separate from the mass. A man, as Thoreau felt, must remain free from the mass of men, partly for his own sake, but partly also that he might have some value for all of mankind. Such value, unless he kept himself apart, was impossible. "The mass," he said, "never come up to the standard of its best member but on the contrary degrades itself to a level with the lowest." Thoreau was continually disappointed when he approached men and women to find himself confronting not real persons but false exteriors with no particularity. "One goes to a cattle-show," he said, "expecting to find many men and women assembled, and finds only working oxen and neat cattle. He goes to a commencement, thinking that there at least he may find the men of the country; but such, if there were any, are completely merged in the day, and have become so many walking commencements, so that he is fain to take himself out of sight and hearing of the orator lest he lose his own identity in the nonentities around him."

It was this trait of men that was responsible for Thoreau's amusement when someone spoke of the freedom of the press. Thoreau was not concerned so much about government interference or any other external censorship as he was about a more pernicious limitation,—the restrictions imposed by society as a whole. We sometimes speak,—and not without justice,—of the misrepresentation and distortion of the news by particular sections of the press as though a few members of a group were, in each case, the only ones involved in the decision as to what should appear in the papers. But the divergences of the press are within society and each group appeals to us in society's terms; and all of us as members of society are as responsible for the distortions as anyone, and we welcome the distortions and foster them. We exult in a society which is held in balance or allowed to run wild by a conflict which we know to be false or largely false. Should we begin to think for ourselves from a point outside of society, calling into question the assumptions our era takes most matter-of-factly for granted, then the inadequacies not only of the reactionary press but of the liberal journals as well would become immediately apparent in some measure. We are exhorted by one group within society to unite against the lies of the other, and exhorted by the other group to cast out the propaganda of the first, as though the division of the truth were on class or economic or even political lines, and as though narrowness and stupidity were to be routed by shouting. A little perspective, a few things known and more suspected that society never told us, are a defense against false and inadequate statements from either side or from both, for the two are agreed essentially in the rules of deception. Thoreau knew that the latest liberal journal, which thought itself liberal even to boldness, would not publish a child's thought on important subjects; and if it had been published at the time of the famous dispute between Christ and the doctors, it would have published only the opinion of the doctors, and suppressed Christ's. "There is no need of a law," he said, "to check the license of the press. It is law enough and more than enough to itself. Virtually, the community have come together and agreed what things shall be uttered, have agreed on a platform and to excommunicate him who departs from it, and not one in a thousand dares utter any thing else." This gregariousness of men was, to Thoreau, their most discouraging and contemptible aspect. It prevented the only kind of social reform in which he was interested because it offered no basis from which to work. The lively germ, the growing point of the individual man was not to be reached, hidden away as it was by the masses of men, and abandoned there where it had been sacrificed for the safety, the relief from thought and responsibility, which is to be found so readily in numbers. "Apparently in ancient times," Thoreau said, "several parties were nearly equally matched. They appointed a committee and made a compromise, agreeing to vote or believe so and so, and they still helplessly abide by that. Men are the inveterate foes of all improvement. Generally speaking, they think more of their hen-houses than of any desirable heaven." Always one had to contend with this stupidity of men which kept them and kept one's relations to them on the surface. It was like a hard-pan, and if one went deeper than usual, one was sure to meet with a pan made harder even, by superficial cultivation. Men were obedient not to ideas, but to words, and minded names more than things; so that one could read them a lecture on education, calling it that, and they would think it something important. But if one called the lecture 'Transcendentalism' they would immediately pronounce it moonshine. Or again, one could halve the lecture, and put a psalm at the beginning and a prayer at the end, and men would pronounce it good without thinking. Although we commonly regard a change in names or a change in other outward aspects a momentous one, because we accept men on their own terms, as though no other level besides the surface existed, or were possible, such change is merely political and Thoreau was not interested. Effective social action which would carry the individual, and with him, society, towards a fuller meaning, must inevitably begin with separation. "If you aspire to anything better than politics," Thoreau said, "expect no cooperation from men. They will not further anything good. You must prevail of your own force, as a plant springs and grows by its own vitality."

It was more than a mechanical separation for which Thoreau asked; it was a true prevalence by one's own force, an assertion of the power of the individual, a coming into one's sovereignty, for as he said, each man is the lord of a realm by which the earthly empire of the Czar is but a petty state, a hummock left by the ice. He was shocked and puzzled to find that we reject the privilege of our individuality, making ourselves commoners rather than kings, selecting granite for the underpinning of our houses and barns, building fences of stone, and not ourselves resting on an underpinning of granitic truth, the lowest primitive rock, the foundation of democracy, the unyielding granite of the individual. "The excitement about Kossuth," he said, when the Hungarian patriot came to America, "is not interesting to me, it is so superficial. It is only another kind of dancing or of politics. Men are making speeches to him all over the country but each expresses only the thought, or the want of thought of the multitude. No man stands on truth. They are merely banded together as usual, one leaning on another, and all together on nothing; as the Hindoos made the world rest on an elephant, and the elephant on a tortoise, and had nothing to put under the tortoise. You can pass your hand under the largest mob, a nation in revolution even, and, however solid a bulk they may make, like a hail cloud in the atmosphere, you may not meet so much as a cobweb of support. They may not rest even by a point on eternal foundations. But an individual standing on truth you cannot pass your hand under, for his foundations reach to the center of the universe. So superficial these men and their doings, it is life on a leaf or a chip which has nothing but air or water beneath. It is unimportant what these men do. Let them try forever, they can effect nothing."

Thoreau saw them continually trying. He saw men banded together to effect some object, and it was often suggested to him that certainly more could be accomplished by several working together than by one man alone. But Thoreau had little faith in the effectiveness of group action. He was skeptical of what the church, for example, might do. Here was one, he said, of a minister, unable to butter his own bread, who had just combined with a thousand like him to make a dipped toast for all eternity. And unlike others in New England, he hoped for little from the experiment at Brook Farm or from Fourierism in general. "Talking," he said, "with Bellew this evening about Fourierism and communities, I said that I suspected any enterprise in which two were engaged together. 'But,' said he, 'it is difficult to make a stick stand unless you slant two or more against it.' 'Oh, no,' answered I, 'you may split the lower end into three, or drive it single into the ground which is the best way; but most men, when they start on a new enterprise, not only figuratively but really, *pull up stakes*. When the sticks prop one another, none, or only one, stands erect.' "

One of the great objects of Thoreau's life was to make everything personal that could be made so, and to discount the rest as irrelevant. The separation of the single man from the mass was an important action in Thoreau's eyes, since the mass represented for him the impersonal and the irresponsible. By such separation the inertia of the mass was destroyed, as bit by bit the mass became personalized through the assertion of the individual. "When I ask for a garment of a particular form," Thoreau said, "my tailoress tells me gravely, 'They do not make them so now,' not emphasizing the 'They' at all, as if she quoted an authority as impersonal as the Fates, and I find it difficult to get made what I want, simply because she cannot believe that I mean what I say, that I am so rash. When I hear this oracular sentence, I am for a moment absorbed in thought, emphasizing to myself each word separately that I may come at the meaning of it, that I may find out by what degree of consanguinity, *They* are related to *me* and what authority they may have in an affair which affects me so nearly; and, finally, I am inclined to answer her with equal mystery, and without any more emphasis on the 'they',—'It is true they did not make them so recently, but they do now.' "

Such an assertion of one's own person and assumption of responsibility, simple as it sounds in respect to one's clothing, was Thoreau's principle for greater matters as well. He realized that the most common obstacles to the good life were not the doers of evil, but those who consented to the evil,—not the creators of fashion but those who irresponsibly and impersonally followed. One could not truly and successfully avoid responsibility by following the leader. For example, Massachusetts, as one of the Union, was involved in such matters as slavery and the Mexican War. Claim as she might that she was helpless to end troubles some other state had started and was carrying on, the real promoters of war and slavery were not a hundred thousand politicians at the South, but a hundred thousand merchants and farmers at home who were more interested in commerce and agriculture than they were in humanity. Thoreau's quarrel was not with far-off foes but with those near to home who cooperated with and did the bidding of those far away, and without whom the others would be harmless. Thoreau saw it was not a primary need that the forces of wrong or of evil be destroyed. So long as there was absolute goodness somewhere to leaven the lump; so long as individual resistance could prevent the mass from lending the weight of the whole people to whatever wrong was most prevalent at the time, there was little to be feared.

But against this remedial action the state was a leading obstacle. Thoreau, from time to time finding himself in opposition to the state, maintained himself there. One afternoon during the sojourn at Walden, when he went to the village to get a shoe from the cobbler's, he was arrested by an embarrassed and puzzled constable, Sam Staples, because he refused to pay a tax to, or recognize the authority of a state which, as he said, sold men, women and children like cattle at the door of its senate house. As he stood then in the jail, considering the thickness of the walls and of the doors, and watching the light streaming through the grating, he was struck with the foolishness of the institution which treated him as if he were mere flesh and blood and bones, to be locked up; and he wondered that it should have concluded at length that this was the best use it could put him to and had never thought to avail itself of his services in some other way. "I could not but smile," he said, "to see how industriously they locked the door on my meditations, which followed them out again without let or hindrance, and they were really all that was dangerous. As they could not reach me, they had resolved to punish my body; just as boys, if they cannot come at some person against whom they have a spite, will abuse his dog. I saw that the State was half-witted, that it was timid as a lone woman with her silver spoons, and that it did not know its friends from its foes, and I lost all my remaining respect for it and pitied it."

He would have preferred not to be in conflict with the state could it have been avoided. For one thing, the physical strength of the state was greater than his or any individual's. And therefore the state always confronted one's body, not one's sense, either intellectual or moral, and in the physical realm, was easily victorious. Secondly, it was apparent from one point of view that this particular state, this American government, was in many respects a very admirable and rare thing to be thankful for, such as a great many had described it; but seen from a point of view a little higher than this, it was most certainly what he had described it to be; and seen from a higher still and highest, Thoreau wondered who might say what it was, and whether it was worth looking at or thinking of at all.

The comparative worth of the American government was most vividly represented to him by a visit to Canada. He saw that a private man was not worth so much there as in the United States, and that anyone whose property consisted largely of being private and peculiar had best stay here. It was evident that the Englishman, not to speak of the other nations, habitually regarded himself merely as a constituent part of the English nation, holding a recognized place as such; and was proud of his nation. Whereas the American, it appeared to Thoreau, cared little for these things, and therefore greater freedom and independence were possible to him. He was nearer to the primitive condition of man. He let government alone, and government let him alone. Quite obviously, not all Americans measure up to this; and Thoreau criticized America for that reason, wishing to accentuate the peculiarity of his country in order to bring its native and highly valuable elements to greater and greater strength.

These were negative elements so far as they pertained to the state. They were notions, not toward the aggrandizement or strengthening of the government, but toward its gradual atrophy and final disappearance. Even when given its fullest powers, Thoreau felt that the state's ability to effect anything worthwhile was very slight, because the only cooperation which was possible between men was exceedingly partial and superficial. True cooperation was always only as if it were not, and was therefore beyond the state and not to be striven for. But the power given to government, though unable to effect much good, could be in many cases harmful. Thoreau objected to a standing government, as one would object to a standing army. Government, which he saw as only the mode which the people had chosen to execute their will, was liable to great abuse and perversion before the people could act through its agency. He felt that this was the case with the Mexican War,—the work of comparatively a few individuals, using the standing government as their tool; for in the outset, the people would not have consented to such a measure. And thus the state worked directly counter to its own purposes:—while the law held fast the thief and the murderer, it let itself go loose. When Thoreau refused to buy from the state an unwanted protection by paying the tax which the state demanded of him, then the state robbed him; when he asserted the liberty it had itself presumed to declare, then it imprisoned him. The state was incapable of providing the protection whose provision was the excuse for denying the liberty that it denied. For the sake of a liberty so absolute that it became a security from each other, Thoreau was willing to abandon any other security ever offered. The state denied that security. "If, for instance, a man asserts the value of individual liberty over the merely political commonweal," he said, "his neighbor still tolerates him, sometimes even sustains

him, but never the State. Its officer, as a living man may have human virtues and a thought in his brain, but as the tool of an institution, as a jailer
or constable it may be, he is not a whit superior to his prison key or his staff.
Herein is the tragedy; that men doing outrage to their proper natures, even
those called wise and good, lend themselves to perform the office of inferior and brutal ones. Hence come war and slavery in; and what else may
not come in by this opening?"

The crux of the matter is that Thoreau believed that all evil did come in
through the opening formed when any man might so betray his own nature
as to lend himself to perform an inhuman office. While it might be con-
tended that good and evil are something to be done at will and according to
will, without reference to our own constitutions,—that we are of indifferent or irrelevant moral quality ourselves, and are able to choose between
a good act and an evil one and so determine by the excess of one kind of
action over the other our own moral quality and the moral quality of the
world, yet it was Thoreau's contention that the process by which good and
evil came into being was more exacting and natural, less arbitrary than
this. He believed that it was always necessary to make the choice between
good and evil whenever such a choice was presented, but he also believed
that in most cases, the choice was not presented, and that evil resulted in
some mysterious way without anyone's willing it, or being aware of it, and
even to everyone's surprise and chagrin. Thoreau accounted for this phenomenon by saying that being is more important and more effective than
doing. Anything therefore might happen to us which was consistent with
the nature we took for ourselves, even though the process by which the
happening came about was so subtle or so complicated that we missed the
apprehension of it, even after its end. If, as Thoreau said, we do outrage to
our proper nature,—if we take our identity from the state, then we become
liable to the evils of the state, and have no defense against war and slavery,
since it has none. It is only by refusing to do the office of inferior and brutal
natures that we can hope to escape, on our own part, treatment which in its
brutality is suited to inferior natures. We must be treated according to the
nature which we determine shall be ours. We can win or lose, or act in any
other way, only in accordance with terms we set for ourselves.

The identity which Thoreau wished us to find, which left no opening
for the evil we claimed to deplore, was most certainly not to be found in the
state; and neither was it to be found in any other external form, for its
essence was personal. It was to be found only through that steady com-

munion with one's deepest desires and insights, which was called silence. He found no evil and little that was ambiguous in silence. It is easier to see now, of course, why Thoreau rejected philanthropy and reform, since to find one's identity, to become personal, was truly to ennoble one's being; it was to enjoy those moments of serene and self-confident life which were better than whole campaigns of daring; it was to combat evil directly by leaving no opening by which it could enter. Philanthropy's method was less direct. It offered the goodness of actions as an excuse and substitute for being. Reform was an attempt to avoid a change in true form by changing the surface only.

Thoreau, walking through Concord, found in the elms the virtues of men in the good state. "I have seen many a collection of stately elms," he said, "which better deserved to be represented at the General Court than the manikins beneath,—than the barroom and victualling cellar and groceries they overshadowed. When I see their magnificent domes, miles away in the horizon, over intervening valleys and forests, they suggest a village, a community, there. But, after all, it is a secondary consideration whether there are human dwellings beneath them; these may have long since passed away. I find that into my idea of the village there has entered more of the elm than of the human being. They are worth many a political borough. The poor human representative of his party sent out from beneath their shade will not suggest a tithe of the dignity, the true nobleness and comprehensiveness of view, the sturdiness and independence, and the serene beneficence that they do. They look from township to township. A fragment of their barks is worth the backs of all the politicians in the union. They are free-soilers in their own broad sense. They send their roots north and south and east and west into many a conservative's Kansas and Carolina, who does not suspect such an underground railroad,—they improve the subsoil he has never disturbed,—and many times their length if the support of their principles require it. They battle with the tempests of a century. See what scars they bear, what limbs they lost before we were born! Yet they never adjourn; they steadily vote for their principles, and send their roots further and wider from the *same centre*. They die at their posts, and they leave a tough butt for the choppers to exercise themselves about, and a stump which serves for their monument. They attend no caucus, they make no compromise, they use no policy. Their one principle is growth. They combine a true radicalism with a true conservatism. Their radicalism is not cutting away of roots, but an infinite multiplication and extension of them under all surrounding institutions. They take a firmer hold on the earth that they may rise higher into the heavens. Their conservative heartwood, in which no sap longer flows, does not impoverish their growth but is a firm column to support it; and when their expanding trunks no longer require it, it utterly decays. Half a century after they are dead at the core, they are preserved by radical reform. They do not, like men, from radicals turn conservative. Their conservative part dies out first; their radical and growing part survives. They acquire new States and Territories, while the old dominions decay, and become the habitations of bears and owls and coons."

Thoreau had occasionally known a man with the virtues he found in the elms, but for the most part, men avoided the real problems of moral worth and social behavior by dodges such as philanthropy or superficial reform, or such as the law, which never made a man a whit more just, though by their respect for it, even well-disposed men were daily made the agents of injustice. "A common and natural result," Thoreau said, "of an undue respect for law is, that you may see a file of soldiers, colonel, captain, corporal, privates, powder-monkeys, and all, marching in admirable order over hill and dale to the wars, against their wills, ay, against their common sense and consciences, which makes it very steep marching indeed, and produces a palpitation of the heart. They have no doubt that it is a damnable business in which they are concerned; they are all peaceably inclined. Now, what are they? Men at all? or small movable forts and magazines, at the service of some unscrupulous man in power? Visit the Navy Yard and behold a marine, such a man as the American government can make, or such as it can make a man with its black arts, a mere shadow and reminiscence of humanity, a man laid out alive and standing, and already, as one may say, buried under arms with funeral accompaniments."

Thoreau knew that the mass of men served the state thus, not as men mainly, but as machines, with their bodies. These men constituted the standing army, and the militia, jailers, constables, *posse comitatus*, and the rest. In most cases, there was no free exercise whatever of the judgment or of the moral sense; but they put themselves on a level with wood and earth and stones; and wooden men could perhaps be manufactured that would serve as well. Such men, in Thoreau's eyes, commanded no more respect than men of straw or a lump of dirt. They had the same sort of worth only as horses and dogs. "Yet such as these even," he said, "are commonly esteemed good citizens. Others,—as most legislators, politicians, lawyers, ministers, and office holders—serve the state chiefly with their heads; and as they rarely make any moral distinctions, they are as likely to serve the devil, without *intending* it, as God. A very few, as heroes, patriots, martyrs, reformers in the great sense, and *men*—serve the state with their consciences also, and so necessarily resist it for the most part; and they are commonly treated as enemies by it."

Thoreau knew that he who gave himself entirely to his fellow-men appeared to them useless and selfish, while he who gave himself partially to them was pronounced a benefactor and philanthropist. But he felt that a wise man would not give himself in less than his entirety, that he would not consent to be used as less than a man. He wished to keep his serenity and confidence in himself as a man, not lose it and be hastened to set about some outrageous actions to attract attention to himself, to assure and justify his existence. He wanted to remain confident enough of the goodness of life to be able to maintain without impertinence, his own good living. He felt that it was only because of a widespread loss of confidence and serenity that the evils of war were a serious threat in 1856. "The papers are talking about the prospects of a war between England and America," he said. "Neither side sees how it can avoid a long and fratricidal war without sacrificing its honor. Both nations are ready to take a desperate step, to forget the interests of civilization and Christianity and their own commercial prosperity and fly at each other's throats. When I see an individual thus beside himself, thus desperate, ready to shoot or be shot, like a blackleg who has little to lose, no serene aims to accomplish, I think he is a candidate for bedlam. What asylum is there for nations to go to? Nations are thus ready to talk of wars and challenge one another, because they are made up to such an extent of poor, low-spirited, despairing men, in whose eyes the chance of shooting somebody else without being shot themselves exceeds their actual good fortune. Who, in fact, will be the first to enlist but the most desperate class, they who have lost all hope? And they may at last infect the rest."

In at least one instance, Thoreau lost his own serenity and despaired. Because of his human sympathies, there was a deep intersection of his orbit with that of the state's, even though their identities were separate. Some years after he had refused the state his taxes and had gone so briefly to jail, and had thought himself quit of the matter, the state of Massachusetts sent a negro, Anthony Burns, back south into the slavery from which he had escaped. Thereafter, Thoreau found himself living with a sense of having suffered a vast and indefinite loss. He thought that every man in Massachusetts capable of the sentiment of patriotism must have had a similar experience. He was surprised that men were going about their business as if nothing had happened, that the man whom he had just met on horseback was so earnest to overtake his runaway cows, since all property was insecure, and if they did not run away again, they might be taken away from him when he got them. "Fool!" Thoreau said, "Does he not know that his seed corn is worth less this year,—that all beneficent harvests fail as you approach the empire of hell? No prudent man will build a stone house under these circumstances or engage in any peaceful enterprise which it requires a long time to accomplish. Art is as long as ever but life is more interrupted and less available for a man's proper pursuits. It is not an era of repose. We have used up all our inherited freedom. If we would save our lives, we must fight for them.

"I walk toward one of our ponds; but what signifies the beauty of nature when men are base? We walk to the lakes to see our serenity reflected in them; when we are not serene we go not to them. Who can be serene in a country where both the rulers and the ruled are without principle? The remembrance of my country spoils my walk. My thoughts are murder to the State, and involuntarily go plotting against her."

But in spite of this darkness and disappointment, Thoreau resumed his walking, and he chanced finally one day on some fragrant flowers just come into blossom. They burst up so pure and fair to the eye, and so sweet to the scent, as if to show what purity and sweetness reside in and can be extracted from the slime and muck of earth. He thought he should not so soon despair of the world, notwithstanding slavery and the cowardice and want of principle of northern men. The fragrance of the flowers suggested,—not rationally but nevertheless truly,—what kind of laws had prevailed longest and widest and still prevailed, and that the time might come when man's deeds would smell as sweet. If nature could compound that fragrance still annually, he would believe her still young and full of vigor, her integrity and genius unimpaired, and that there was virtue even in man, too, who was fitted to perceive and love it.

But in the case of John Brown at Harper's Ferry, it was Thoreau who defended the use of force and militarism, the rest of the country and the government itself that condemned the use and hanged the offenders. Here, for once, Thoreau thought, the Sharp's rifles and the revolvers were employed in a righteous cause, the tools were in the hands of those who could use them. But even the most prominent anti-slavery paper, *The Liberator*, called John Brown's a 'misguided, wild and apparently insane effort,' and the rest of the papers were, naturally, less restrained in their condemnations, expressing no admiration or true sorrow even, but dismissing the men as 'deluded fanatics,' 'mistaken men,' 'insane,' or 'crazed.' Thoreau was the one man in all America, or one at least of the very few, who could see John Brown, his men, and their actions as they really were. "When we heard at first that he was dead," Thoreau said, "one of my townsmen observed that 'he died as the fool dieth'; which, pardon me, for an instant suggested a likeness in him dying to my neighbor living. Others, craven-hearted, said disparagingly, that 'he threw his life away,' because he resisted the government. Which way have they thrown their lives, pray?—such as would praise a man for attacking singly an ordinary band of thieves or murderers. I hear another ask, Yankee-like, 'What will he gain by it?' as if he expected to fill his pockets by this enterprise. Such a one has no idea of gain but in this worldly sense. If it does not lead to a 'surprise party,' if he does not get a new pair of boots or a vote of thanks, it must be a failure. 'But he won't gain anything by it.' Well, no, I don't suppose he could get four-and-sixpence a day for being hung, take the year round. . . ."

"I do not wish to kill nor to be killed," Thoreau said further, "but I can forsee circumstances in which both these things would be by me unavoidable." And though he was unable to concur completely in John Brown's principles and methods,—being himself of a somewhat different composition,—he knew that for John Brown, that action had been from personal principle and was by him unavoidable. As Thoreau advised in *Walden*,— "I would not have anyone adopt my mode of living on any account; for, besides that before he has fairly learned it I may have found out another for myself, I desire that there may be as many different persons in the world as possible; but I would be very careful to have each one find out and pursue his own way, and not his father's or his mother's or his neighbor's instead." And again he says in relation to John Brown and abolition,—"At any rate, I do not think it is quite sane for one to spend his whole life in talking or writing about this matter, unless he is continuously inspired, and I have not done so. A man may have other affairs to attend to." Thoreau had other affairs to attend to, but not, he knew, John Brown, who was integral to this affair. It was the spectacle of the man that moved him, the deep convictions turned slowly and deliberately to action, the service to the state which was not with his body only, or the force of arms, but with his whole conscience. "When I think of him, and his six sons, and his son-in-law, not to enumerate the others, enlisted for this fight, proceeding coolly, reverently, humanely to work, for months if not years sleeping and waking upon it, summering and wintering the thought, without expecting any reward but a good conscience, while almost all America stood ranked on the other side, —I say again that it affects me as a sublime spectacle."

The great thing was that he came and went, as he informed the citizens of Concord when he visited that town, 'under the auspices of John Brown and nobody else.' Thoreau heard many condemn Brown's men because they were so few, a mere handful to throw their lives away against the full force of the state militia and army. "When were the good and the brave ever in a majority?" Thoreau asked. "Would you have had him wait till that time came?—till you and I came over to him? The very fact that he had no rabble or troop of hirelings about him would alone distinguish him from ordinary heroes. His company was small indeed because few could be found worthy to pass muster. If he had had any journal advocating '*his cause*,' any organ, as the phrase is, monotonously and wearisomely playing the same old tune, and then passing round the hat, it would have been fatal to his efficiency. If he had acted in any way so as to be let alone by the government, he might have been suspected. It was the fact that the tyrant must give place to him, or he to the tyrant, that distinguished him from all the reformers of the day that I know."

Thoreau was not concerned with an uprising of the masses, thrilling as such a thing might seem, but with an upstanding of righteous men, of individuals in any number.

It seemed to him that only those whose whole beings were thwarted by the conditions against which they revolted, only those with a deep and personal conviction, testified to by the loneliness of their positions, only those who in themselves were already in opposition to the state, who had dispensed with its support, in whom, that is, the revolution had been accomplished:—only such as these, for whom the issues at stake were clear, could have it within their power to bring about a revolution within society which should be worthy of the name.

"When the subject has refused allegiance and the officer has resigned his office, then the revolution is accomplished," Thoreau said. Some of Thoreau's neighbors, even the most liberal ones, were embarrassed when he went so far as to refuse to pay his taxes and was therefore placed in prison.

But believing as he did that action from principle, the perception and the performance of right, changed things and relations, and was essentially revolutionary, he acted in that manner. It was always his deep wish to clarify the issues at stake, and to force the clarification of the issue when the rest of the country was at pains to avoid it. The real issue, he felt, which was always at stake, was our humanity; and he, for one, would not submit to be treated as less than his true worth, for he knew to what evils the door was left open by such submission. The government must be forced to consider him not as a voter nor as a taxpayer, but as a man. He had heard some of his townsmen say, "I should like to have them order me to put down an insurrection of the slaves, or to march to Mexico;—see if I would go." "And yet these very men," he said, "have each, directly by their allegiance, and so indirectly, at least, by their money, furnished a substitute. The soldier is applauded who refuses to serve in an unjust war by those who do not refuse to sustain the unjust government which makes the war, is applauded by those whose own act and authority he sets at naught; as if the state were penitent to that degree that it hired one to scourge it while it sinned, but not to that degree that it left off sinning for a moment.

"I meet this American government, or its representative, the State government, directly, and face to face, once a year—no more—in the person of its tax-gatherer; this is the only mode in which a man situated as I am necessarily meets it; and it then says distinctly, Recognize me; and the simplest, the most effectual, and, in the present posture of affairs, the indispensablest mode of treating with it on this head, of expressing your little satisfaction with and love for it, is to deny it then. My civil neighbor, the tax-gatherer, is the very man I have to deal with—for it is after all, with men and not with parchment that I quarrel,—and he has voluntarily chosen to be an agent of the government. How shall he ever know well what he is and does as an officer of the government, or as a man, until he is obliged to consider whether he shall treat me, his neighbor, for whom he has respect, as a neighbor and well-disposed man, or as a maniac and disturber of the peace, and see if he can get over this obstruction to his neighborliness without a ruder and more impetuous thought or speech corresponding with his action."

Thoreau sometimes reflected that even the tax-gatherer meant well, and that he should not therefore give his neighbors pain to treat him as they were not inclined to. When many millions of men, without heat, without ill-will, without personal feeling of any kind, demanded of him a few shillings only, without the possibility, such was their constitution, of retracting or altering their demand, and without the possibility on his side of appeal to any other millions, why should he expose himself to this overwhelming brute force? He did not resist cold and hunger, the wind and the waves thus obstinately. He did not put his head into the fire. But it was just in proportion as he regarded this as not wholly a brute force, but partly a human force, and considered that he had relations to those millions, as to so many millions of men, and not of mere brute or inanimate things, that he saw that appeal was possible, first and instantaneously from them to the Maker of them, and, secondly from them to themselves. It was silence again, the proof against cynicism, the refuge from the finality of experience, that was as effective a truth in social thought as in friendship. "If I could convince myself," he said, "that I have any right to be satisfied with men as they are, and to treat them accordingly, and not according, in some respects to my requisitions and expectations of what they and I ought to be, then, like a good Mussulman and fatalist, I should endeavor to be satisfied with things as they are, and say it is the will of God."

Thoreau believed that a man was his own law unto himself. Most men preferred the laws of the state, economics, expediency or custom. But Thoreau had seen the sovereignty of man through the elms, and long ago recognized its necessity for friendship. Just as the independence of men was necessary there, so was it necessary to a decent state. "There will never be a free and enlightened State," he said, "until the State comes to recognize the individual as a higher and independent power, from which all its own power and authority are derived, and treats him accordingly. I please myself with imagining a State at last which can afford to be just to all men, and to treat the individual with respect as a neighbor; which even would not think it inconsistent with its own repose if a few were to live aloof from it, not meddling with it, nor embraced by it, who fulfilled all the duties of neighbors and fellow-men. A State which bore this kind of fruit and suffered it to drop off as fast as it ripened, would prepare the way for a still more perfect and glorious State, which also I have imagined but not yet anywhere seen."

WALT WHITMAN'S MARINE DEMOCRACY

Fusion

Walt Whitman felt a kindred with the sea. Writing at sixty, he said that even as a boy he had had the fancy to write a piece or perhaps a poem about the sea-shore,—"that suggesting, dividing line, contact, junction, the solid marrying the liquid,—that curious lurking something (as doubtless every objective form finally becomes to the subjective spirit), which means far more than its mere first sight, grand as that is—blending the real and the ideal, and each made a portion of the other." During his Long Island youth and early manhood, for long stretches of time, he haunted the shores of Rockaway or Coney Island, going as far east as the Hamptons or Montauk. Once at Montauk, when there was nothing but sea tossings in sight in every direction as far as his eyes could reach, he felt that someday he must write a book expressing this liquid mystic theme; and later, it came to him that rather than any special literary attempt, the sea-shore should be an invisible influence or gauge and tally for him in all his writing.

As early in his principal book, *Leaves of Grass*, as one of the opening inscriptions, it begins to appear how this could be so. Expressing there a hope he will be read by sailors, he says,

Here are our thoughts, voyager's thoughts
Here not the land, firm land, alone appears, may then by them be said,
The sky o'erarches here, we feel the undulating deck beneath our feet,
We feel the long pulsation, ebb and flow of endless motion.
The tones of unseen mystery, the vague and vast suggestions of the briny
    world, the liquid-flowing syllables,
the perfume, the faint creaking of the cordage, the melancholy rhythm,
The boundless vista and the horizon far and dim are all here,
And this is ocean's poem.

But *Leaves of Grass* is ocean's poem not only because of the distance and dimness of its horizon, the vagueness and vastness of its suggestion, for there is also associated with the sea a constant and clear intensity. "There is a dream," says the conclusion of Whitman's account of the sea's effect on his writing, "a picture, that for years at intervals, (sometimes quite long ones, but surely again, in time,) has come noiselessly up before me, and I really believe, fiction as it is, has entered largely into my practical life—certainly into my writings, and shaped and color'd them. It is nothing more or less than a stretch of interminable white-brown sand, hard and smooth and broad, with the ocean perpetually, grandly, rolling in upon it, with slow measured sweep, with rustle and hiss and foam, and many a thump as of low bass drums. This scene, this picture, I say, has risen before me at times for years. Sometimes I wake at night and can hear and see it plainly."

Whitman's feeling for the sea was no simple concept, and in its metaphorical fullness, no casual one. He went to the sea to bathe, or to lie on the beach; he went after clams or for fish, but these were superficial things. Desire which mingled vagueness with intensity was Whitman's kindred with the sea.

"Oh sea!" he says,
"Where day and night I wend thy surf-beat shore,
Imagining to my sense thy varied strange suggestions
Thy lonely state—something thou ever seek'st and seek'st but never gain'st
Surely some right withheld, some voice, in huge monotonous rage, of
    freedom-lover pent,
Some vast heart, like a planet's, chain'd and chafing in those breakers
By lenghten'd swell, and spasm, and panting breath,
And rhythmic rasping of thy sands and waves,
And serpent hiss, and savage peals of laughter,
And undertones of distant lion roar,
(Sounding, appealing to the sky's deaf ear—but now rapport for once
A phantom in the night thy confidant for once,)
The first and last confession of the globe,
Outsurging muttering from thy soul's abysms,
The tale of cosmic elemental passion,
Thou tellest to a kindred soul."

Whitman speaks to the sea as a phantom in the night, as one who though knowing himself to be part of the universe and activated by desire, yet feels himself a still unspecified part, and feels a still unspecified desire. It was no personal and eccentric longing that made Whitman feel his kinship for the sea, but rather a feeling that both of them shared in some cosmic and elemental passion. On the beach at night alone, he had become aware of a vast similitude which interlocked all. All spheres, grown, ungrown, small, large, suns, moons, planets, all distances of place however wide, all distances of time, all inanimate forms, all souls, all living bodies though they be ever so different, or in different worlds, all gaseous, watery, vegetable, mineral processes, the fishes, the brutes, all nations, colors, barbarisms, civilizations, languages, all identities that have existed or may exist on this globe, or any globe, all lives and deaths, all of the past, present, future, this vast similitude spanned them, and always had spanned them, and should forever span them and compactly hold and enclose them.

This vast similitude was the basis of Whitman's universe, in which, despite diversity there was only one substance, one reality, a single material and a single spirit. Because by contrast with the land, the shapes of the sea were so transitory and blended quickly with one another, and because of a certain immensity and limitless horizon which made it susceptible of vast suggestion, Whitman took the sea as a symbol of this similitude which leveled and interlocked diversity. Even the specified parts of the universe became by virtue of similitude, as seen through Whitman's eyes, much less specific.

Within this universe of all embracing and eternal unity, there was one great cosmic and elemental passion which was the moving force. There was an insufficiency, a loneliness, an ever seeking and seeking, a feeling of repressed expression. Even though the universe excluded nothing, there was a consciouness of lack. But it was a lack of no particular thing. Its only object was a state in which the consciousness of lack no longer existed. Whitman preferred such a consciousness to the contentment which it ended. It illuminated the universe for him, and awakened him to a new life. As such, it was even when unsatisfied, pleasurable to him. He first experienced it one night as a child, when while the early lilacs were in blossom, he heard on the sea shore a bird who was singing and calling, as it seemed to Whitman, for his lost mate. There by the shore, with the stars shining and the winds blowing, the notes of the bird echoing, with angry moans the fierce old mother the sea incessantly moaning and rustling on the sands, the yellow half-moon enlarged, sagging down, drooping, almost touching the face of the sea, the boy ecstatic, with his bare feet the waves, with his hair the atmosphere, dallying,—there, as he said, the love in his heart long pent was finally loosed, and burst forth, at last, in tumult.

"Now in a moment, I know what I am for, I awake," he said,
"And already a thousand singers, a thousand songs, clearer, louder, and
    more sorrowful than yours,
A thousand warbling echoes have started to life within me never to die.

"O you singer solitary, singing by yourself, projecting me
O solitary me listening, never more shall I cease perpetuating you,
Never more shall I escape, never more the reverberations,
Never more the cries of unsatisfied love be absent from me,
Never again leave me to be the peaceful child I was before what there in the
    night,
By the sea under the yellow and sagging moon,
The messenger there aroused, the fire, the sweet hell within,
The unknown want, the destiny of me."

Whitman, convinced that he now shared in the cosmic and elemental
passion, began in the company of such cosmic elements as the night, the
earth, and the sea, to surrender himself to a kind of lonely erotic abandonment.

"I am he that walks with the tender and growing night," he said,
"I call to the earth and sea half-held by the night.

"Press close bare-bosom'd night—press close magnetic nourishing night!
Night of south winds—night of the large few stars!
Still nodding night—mad naked summer night.

"Smile O voluptuous cool-breathed earth!
Earth of the slumbering and liquid trees!
Earth of departed sunset—earth of the mountains misty-topt!
Earth of the vitreous pour of the full moon just tinged with blue!
Earth of shine and dark mottling the tide of the river!
Earth of the limpid gray of clouds brighter and clearer for my sake!
Far-swooping elbow'd earth—rich apple-blossom'd earth!
Smile, for your lover comes.

"Prodigal, you have given me love—therefore I to you give love!
O unspeakable passionate love.

"You sea! I resign myself to you also—I guess what you mean
I behold from the beach your crooked inviting fingers,
I believe you refuse to go back without feeling of me,
We must have a turn together, I undress, hurry me out of sight of the land,
Cushion me soft, rock me in billowy drowse,
Dash me with amorous wet, I can repay you.
Sea of stretched ground-swells,
Sea breathing broad and convulsive breaths,
Sea of the brine of life and of unshovell'd yet always-ready graves,
Howler and scooper of storms, capricious and dainty sea,
I am integral with you, I too am of one phase and of all phases."

It was as integral with the sea, as of one phase and of all phases that Whitman wrote most of his poems and began to illustrate the sea's desire. The simple fact of his common nature was rich and fertile for him. He took great satisfaction in it. Having pried, as he said, through the strata, analyzed to a hair, counsel'd with doctors and calculated close, he found no sweeter fat than stuck to his own bones, and in all people he saw himself. Indeed, in the whole universe he saw himself. He was of that same substance as the sea, which united all substances and all diversity within its similitude. He was large, he claimed, he contained multitudes, and included even contradictory things within himself.

"There was a child went forth . . ." he says,
"And the first object he look'd upon, that object he became,
And that object became part of him for the day or a certain part of the day,
Or for many years or stretching cycles of years."

The desire which had quickened him, and which was still so unspecified, had made the whole world desirable and so beautiful that hearing the beautiful tales of things and the reasons of things, he nudged himself to listen. He knew of nothing but miracles. To him, every cubic inch of space was a miracle, every hour of the light and dark was a miracle, every square yard of the surface of the earth was spread with miracles, and every foot of the interior swarmed with miracles. He rejoiced to himself that there was no imperfection in the present and could be none in the future. "The known universe has one complete lover and that is the greatest poet," he said, anticipating the satisfaction of his cosmic and elemental passion, enjoying its fervor. "He consumes an eternal passion, and is indifferent which chance happens, and which possible contingency of fortune or misfortune, and persuades daily and hourly his delicious pay. What balks or breaks others is fuel for his burning progress to contact and amorous joy. Other proportions of the reception of pleasure dwindle to nothing to his proportions. All expected from heaven or from the highest, he is rapport with the sight of the daybreak, or the scenes of the winter woods, or the presence of children playing, or with his arm round the neck of a man or woman. His love above all love has leisure and expanse—he leaves room ahead of himself. He is no irresolute or suspicious lover—he is sure—he scorns intervals. His experience and the showers and thrills are not for nothing. Nothing can jar him—suffering and darkness cannot—death and fear cannot. To him complaint and jealousy and envy are corpses buried and rotten in the earth—he saw them buried. The sea is not surer of the shore, or the shore of the sea, than he is the fruition of his love, and of all perfection and beauty."

Whitman felt he was of the old as much as the young, of the foolish as much as the wise, maternal as well as paternal, a child as well as a man. Whatever was commonest, nearest, cheapest, easiest, was he, adorning himself to bestow himself on the first that would take him.

"Stop this day and night with me," he could say, "and you shall possess the
    origin of all poems,
You shall possess the good of the earth and sun, (there are millions of suns
    left,)
You shall no longer take things at second or third hand, nor look through
    the eyes of the dead, nor feed on the spectres in books,
You shall not look through my eyes either, nor take things from me,
You shall listen to all sides and filter them from your self."

This primordial indefiniteness of being enabled Whitman to place himself in any situation, resisting as he said, anything better than his own diversity. When the big doors of the country barn stood open and ready and the dried grass of the harvest-time loaded the slow-drawn wagon, when the clear light played on the brown gray and green intertinged and the armfuls were pack'd to the sagging mow, he was there, he helped, he came stretch'd atop of the load. He felt its soft jolts, one leg reclined on the other; he jumped from the cross-beams and seized the clover and timothy, and rolled head over heels and tangled his hair full of wisps. Alone, far in the wilds and mountains, he hunted, wandering amazed at his own lightness and glee. In the late afternoon, choosing a safe spot to pass the night, he kindled a fire and broiled the fresh-killed game, and fell asleep on the gathered leaves with his dog and gun by his side. When the Yankee clipper was under sky sails, cutting the sparkle and scud, his eyes settled the land, he bent at her prow or shouted joyously from the deck. The boatmen and clam-diggers arose early and stopped for him. He tuck'd his trowser-ends in his boots and went and had a good time. Whitman, considering himself as the sea, thinking only of those aspects of himself which placed him in the common stream of humanity, and not at all of those aspects which would make his place in the stream distinct, was able to think of himself as of all times and places, accepting whatever was human. Addressing himself to the priests of all time, the world over, he claimed to hold them in no despite, for his was the greatest of faiths and the least of faiths, enclosing as it did, worship ancient and modern and all between ancient and modern, believing he would come again on earth after five thousand years, waiting responses from oracles, honoring the gods, saluting the sun, making a fetich of the first rock or stump, powwowing with sticks in the circle of obis, helping the lama or brahmin as he trims the lamps of the idols, dancing yet through the streets in a phallic procession, rapt and austere in the woods a gymnosophist, drinking mead from the skull-cup, to Shastas and Vedas admirant, minding the Koran, walking the teokalis, spotted with gore from the stone and knife, beating the serpent-skin drum, accepting the Gospels, accepting him that was crucified, knowing assuredly that he is divine, to the mass kneeling or the puritan's prayer rising, or sitting patiently in a pew, ranting and frothing in his insane crisis, or waiting dead-like till his spirit aroused him, looking forth on pavement and land, or outside of pavement and land, belonging to the winders of the circuit of circuits.

Even though Whitman might feel that his nature was unrestricted by any particular form and although he might claim to speak not for one creed or sect or party only, but for all, it was not that he had achieved a state in which forms were no longer significant to him. As a matter of fact, the formal aspects of a limited and particularized activity were obviously fascinating. He was not disinterested. Sometimes with the passive emotionality of a movie audience, he imagined himself in a long succession of situations.

"I go hunting polar furs and the seal," he said, "leaping chasms with a pike-pointed staff, clinging to topples of brittle and blue.

I ascend to the foretruck,
I take my place late at night in the crow's nest,
We sail the arctic sea, it is plenty light enough,
Through the clear atmosphere I stretch around on the wonderful beauty,
The enormous masses of ice pass me and I pass them, the scenery is plain in all directions,
The white-topt mountains show in the distance, I fling out my fancies toward them,
We are approaching some great battle-field in which we are soon to be engaged,
We pass the colossal outposts of the encampments, we pass with still feet and caution,
Or we are entering by the suburbs some vast and ruin'd city,
The blocks and fallen architecture are more than all the living cities of the globe.

I am a free companion, I bivouac by invading watchfires,
I turn the bridegroom out of bed and stay with the bride myself,
I tighten her all night to my thighs and lips.

My voice is the wife's voice, the screech by the rail of the stairs,
They fetch my man's body up dripping and drown'd."

It is instantly evident in Whitman's writing that his interest was less in the essential nature of the similitude which he discovered than in the objects which it included. It was as though he made a strict connection between particularized form and an absence of the consciousness of lack, whether in fancy he projected himself into a limited occupation, or merely watched others who were engaged in it.

"The butcher boy puts off his killing-clothes, or sharpens his knife at the stall in the market,
I loiter enjoying his repartee and his shuffle and breakdown," he said.

"Blacksmiths with grimed and hairy chests environ the anvil,
Each has his main-sledge, they are all out, there is a great heat in the fire."

"From the cinder-strew'd threshold I follow their movements,
The lithe sheer of their waists plays even with their massive arms,
Overhand the hammers swing, overhand so slow, overhand so sure,
They do not hasten, each man hits in his place."

Watching a wrestling match, Whitman noted in quick succession its details,—the two apprentice boys who were in it, lusty, quite-grown, good-natured, native-born; the vacant lot at sundown after work; the coats and caps thrown down; the embrace of love and resistance; the upper-hold and under-hold; the hair rumpled over and blinding the eyes. He saw the firemen marching in their special costumes, the play of masculine muscle through clean-setting trowsers and waist-straps, the slow return from the fire, the pause when the bell strikes suddenly again, and the listening on the alert, the natural, perfect, varied attitudes, the bent heads, the curved necks and the counting.

"Such-like I love," he said, "I loosen myself, pass freely, am at the mother's
    breast with the little child,
Swim with the swimmers, wrestle with the wrestlers, march in line with
    the fireman, and pause, listen, count."

"I knew a man, a common farmer, the father of five sons," Whitman also
    wrote,
"And in them the fathers of sons, and in them the fathers of sons.

This man was of wonderful vigor, calmness, beauty of person,
The shape of his head, the pale yellow and white of his hair and beard, the
    immeasurable meaning of his black eyes, the richness and breadth of his
    manners,
These I used to go and visit him to see, he was wise also,
He was six feet tall, he was over eighty years old, his sons were massive,
    clean, bearded, tan-faced, handsome,
They and his daughters loved him, all who saw him loved him,
They did not love him by allowance, they loved him with personal love,

141

He drank water only, the blood showed like scarlet through the clear-
brown skin of his face,
He was a frequent gunner and fisher, he sail'd his boat himself, he had a
fine one presented to him by a ship-joiner, he had fowling-pieces presented to him by men that loved him,
When he went with his five sons and many grand-sons to hunt or fish, you
would pick him out as the most beautiful and vigorous of the gang,
You would wish long and long to be with him, you would wish to sit by him
in the boat that you and he might touch each other.

I have perceived that to be with those I like is enough,
To stop in company with the rest at evening is enough,
To be surrounded by beautiful, curious, breathing, laughing flesh is
enough,
To pass among them or touch any one, or rest my arm ever so lightly round
his or her neck for a moment, what is this then?
I do not ask any more delight, I swim in it as in a sea."

In his relation to personality, or to any definite role as opposed to the
whole play of life on the earth, Whitman was like a perennial audience
acting with every character and between shows living in the spell of one
play until the next one was performed; like the sea which out of its great
shapelessness, and under the influence of a constant urge, raised itself up
into the various transitory shapes of waves and found a final cumination in
contact with the shore. Paradoxically, it was the urgency and desirability
of form which led Whitman to cultivate his sea-like formlessness, for not
only was he able by this means to project himself at liberty into forms
which were attractive to him, but the very attractiveness of those forms
and his yearning after them was increased almost to the point of ecstasy by
his polarity with them. He endeavored to maintain this polarity, not wishing to limit himself or restrict his nature. In one poem, he speaks of a bride,
a wife, as more resistless than he could tell, and calls his love for her fast
anchored and eternal; yet the loss of his fast anchorage was also pleasurable
to him, and he speaks in the same poem of the love of a man as the last
athletic reality, his consolation, under the force of which he became disem-
bodied and ethereal. "I ascend, I float in the regions of your love O man,"
he said. The ecstasy of polarity to form, so close to the ecstasy of the sea's
desire which he was not soon willing to forgo, precluded in Whitman any

form of his own. When Whitman speaks of form's excitement and compulsion, it is to mark himself off as one not possessing it, but as one who exists in a sphere of pure and almost absolute intensity of feeling.

"To be in any form, what is that?" he says,
"(Round and round we go, all of us and ever come back thither,)
If nothing lay more develop'd the quahaug in its callous shell were enough.

Mine is no callous shell,
I have instant conductors all over me whether I pass or stop,
They seize every object and lead it harmlessly through me.

I merely stir, press, feel with my fingers, and am happy,
To touch my person to some one else's is about as much as I can stand."

Whitman who had diligently avoided taking particular form himself, found that his nature was nevertheless so attracted and compelled to form that when it was encountered in another, he was reduced to allegiance by it, as a weaker light coming too near a stronger is virtually extinguished. But this was satisfying to him. He did as we do when we make a region of darkness around us the better to see a light. After searching for a long time for some form of his own, he found that external form was more satisfying and splendid, and finally abandoned himself to the ecstatic pleasures of disintegration.

"Long I thought that knowledge alone would suffice me—O if I could but obtain knowledge!" he said.
"Then my lands engrossed me—Lands of the prairies, Ohio's land, the southern savannas, engrossed me—For them I would live—I would be their orator;
Then I met the examples of old and new heroes—I heard of warriors, sailors, and all dauntless persons—And it seemed to me that I too had it in me to be as dauntless as any—and would be so;
And then, to enclose all, it came to me to strike up the songs of the New World—And then I believed my life must be spent in singing;
But now take notice, land of the prairies, land of the south savannas, Ohio's land,

Take notice, you Kanuck woods—and you Lake Huron and all that with
you roll toward Niagara—and you Niagara also,
And you, California mountains—That you each and all find somebody
else to be your singer of songs,
For I can be your singer of songs no longer,—One who loves me is jealous
of me and withdraws me from all but love,
With the rest I dispense—I sever from what I thought would suffice me,
for it does not—it is now empty and tasteless to me,
I heed knowledge and the grandeur of The States, and the examples of
heroes, no more,
I am indifferent to my own songs—I will go with him I love,
It is enough for us that we are together—We never separate again."

He was grateful for the consolations of this relationship which he called
adhesive love. He found that in dependence upon it, he could be relieved
of the doubts which tormented him, and no longer need question the
world.

"Of the terrible doubt of appearances," he said,
"Of the uncertainty after all that we may be deluded,
That may-be reliance and hope are but speculations after all,
That may-be identity beyond the grave is a beautiful fable only,
May-be the things I perceive, the animals, plants, men, hills, shining and
flowing waters,
The skies of day and night, colors, densities, forms, may-be these are (as
doubtless they are) only apparitions, and the real something has yet to
be known,

. . .

To me these and the like of these are curiously answered by my lovers, my
dear friends,
When he whom I love travels with me or sits a long while holding me by the
hand,
When the subtle air, the impalpable, the sense that words and reason hold
not, surround us and pervade us,
Then I am charged with untold and untellable wisdom, I am silent, I
require nothing further,

I cannot answer the question of appearances or that of identity beyond the
  grave,
But I walk or sit indifferent, I am satisfied,
He ahold of my hand has completely satisfied me."

This was not yet an unswerving attitude. Whitman was still to make
excursions from it. And yet if at any time we attempt to discover the essential Whitman, he is to be found not in any peculiar and irreducible form
but in an unrealized potentiality of form, an energy too little organized
into matter and therefore extravagant of it, an emotion out of hand and
unfastened, with no one there to take the risks or accept the products of its
freedom. Whitman really found himself not in knowledge, not in love of
the land, nor in heroism, nor in the songs of the New World, but in the
maintenance of a state of constant emotional excitement. Formless and
yearning, his personal version of the cosmic and elemental passion of the
sea represented the whole passion much as decay, the most sensational
aspect of metabolism is representative of the whole of life. Whitman, eager
for feeling, anxious for his own disintegration in the face of the great power
of external form, made an apotheosis of death and found in it his final
reality. The longing for death, to be sure, had been part of Whitman's
desire from the very first. On that same night when by the influence of the
sea and a singing bird he had first been made aware of his yearning and
unsatisfied love, the sea had whispered to him through the night and very
plainly before daybreak, 'death' as a clew to his unknown want. Edging
near, as privately for him, rustling at his feet and creeping thence steadily
up to his ears and laving him softly all over, it had given him the key, the
word of the sweetest song and of all songs, that strong and delicious word.

In *When Lilacs Last in the Dooryard Bloomed*, the second poem which
deals with this same experience, there is no longer any need for the sea to
give a clew. The song of the bird is not equivocal now.

"Come lovely and soothing death," it sang,
"Undulate round the world, serenely arriving, arriving,
In the day, in the night, to all, to each,
Sooner or later delicate death.
Prais'd be the fathomless universe,
For life and joy, and for objects and knowledge curious,

And for love, sweet love—but praise! praise! praise!
For the sure-enwinding arms of cool-enfolding death.

Dark mother always gliding near with soft feet,
Have none chanted for thee a chant of fullest welcome?
Then I chant it for thee, I glorify thee above all,
I bring thee a song that when thou must indeed come, come unfalteringly.

Approach strong deliveress,
When it is so, when thou hast taken them I joyously sing the dead,
Lost in the loving floating ocean of thee,
Laved in the flood of thy bliss O death."

On the sea-shore, that suggesting, dividing line, as Whitman described it, the line of contact and junction, when the solid was married to the liquid, Whitman commonly pictured himself as the liquid element.

Identity

There were times when Whitman felt the necessity for taking form himself, and on several occasions he stated the thesis that whatever identity we gathered for ourselves in this world determined our whole existence throughout eternity.

"There is, in sanest hours," he said, "a consciousness, a thought that rises, independent, lifted out from all else, calm, like the stars, shining eternal. This is the thought of identity,—yours for you, whoever you are, as mine for me. Miracle of miracles, beyond statement, most spiritual and vaguest of earth's dreams, yet hardest basic fact, and only entrance to all facts. In such devout hours, in the midst of the significant wonders of heaven and earth, (significant only because of the Me in the center,) creeds, conventions, fall away and become of no account before this simple idea. Under the luminousness of real vision, it alone takes possession, takes value. Like the shadowy dwarf in the fable, once liberated and look'd upon, it expands over the whole earth, and spreads to the roof of heaven."

It was in aspiration toward the marvelous thing, identity, that Whitman, who had no intrinsic form but felt form desirable,—who had once been Walter Whitman, a newspaper writer and gentleman of the town, who had worn a frock coat and silk hat and carried a stick,—now altered his costume to that of a workman, shortened his name, and began to create that character of simplicity and directness and deep affection which led him to call himself, a few years later, the Good Gray Poet. But at first the elements of age and paternal kindliness were less in evidence.

"Walt Whitman, a kosmos, of Manhattan the son," he announces himself
    in *Leaves of Grass*,
"Turbulent, fleshy, sensual, eating, drinking and breeding,
No sentimentalist, no stander above men and women or apart from them,
No more modest than immodest."

Or, as he said enthusiastically of the author of *Leaves of Grass*, in a review written by himself in another name, "An American bard at last! One of the roughs, large, proud, affectionate, eating, drinking, and breeding, his costume manly and free, his face sunburnt and bearded, his posture strong and erect, his voice bringing hope and prophecy to the generous races of young and old. We shall cease shamming and be what we really are.

"For all our intellectual people," he said, indicating his knowledge of Emerson's teachings, "followed by their books, poems, novels, essays, editorials, lectures, tuitions and criticisms, dress by London and Paris models, receive what is received there, obey the authorities, settle disputes by the old tests, keep out of rain and the sun, retreat to the shelter of houses and schools, trim their hair, shave, touch not the earth barefoot, and enter not the sea except in complete bathing dress. Where are the gristle and beards, and broad breasts, and space, and ruggedness, and nonchalance, that the souls of the people love?" he asks.

And then by way of answer, he says, "Self-restraint, with haughty eyes, assuming to himself all the attributes of his country, steps Walt Whitman into literature, talking like a man unaware that there was ever hitherto such a production as a book, or such a being as a writer. . . . He drops disguises and ceremony, and walks forth with the confidence and gayety of a child. . . . If health were not his distinguishing attribute, this poet would be the very harlot of persons. Right and left he flings his arms, drawing men and women with undeniable love to his close embrace, loving the clasp of their hands, the touch of their necks and breasts, and the sound of their voices. All else seems to burn up under his fierce affection for persons."

Whitman was deeply fond of this character he had created for himself. In his last years, writing of himself again under a pseudonym, he said he had never known a man who—for all he took an absorbing interest in politics, literature, and what is called 'the world'—seemed to be so poised on himself alone. And in like manner, he had once asked,

"What am I after all but a child, pleased with the sound of my own name?
    repeating it over and over;
I stand apart to hear—it never tires me."

But this was no simple selfishness. The character which Whitman had created for himself was that of a bard; and although his identity might be intense and pleasurable, it was also diffuse. His egocentricity which was magnanimous after its fashion, was not for his own sake alone, but as he said,

"For the sake of him I typify, for the common average man's sake, your sake, if you are he."

Whitman had become a poet, and his actions and attitudes are properly seen only in the light of his mission. It was a large mission.

"Of these States," he said, "the poet is the equable man,
Not in him but off from him things are grotesque, eccentric, fail of their full returns,
Nothing out of its place is good, nothing in its place is bad,
He bestows on every object or quality its fit proportion, neither more nor less,
He is the arbiter of the diverse, he is the key,
He is the equalizer of his age and land,
He supplies what wants supplying, he checks what wants checking,
In peace out of him speaks the spirit of peace, large, rich, thrifty, building populous towns, encouraging agriculture, arts, commerce, lighting the study of man, the soul, health, immortality, government,
In war he is the best backer of the war, he fetches artillery as good as the engineer's, he can make every word draw blood,
The years straying toward infidelity he withholds by his steady faith,
He is no arguer, he is judgment, (Nature accepts him absolutely,)
He judges not as the judge judges but as the sun falling round a helpless thing,
As he sees the farthest, he has the most faith, His thoughts are the hymns of the praise of things,
In the dispute on God and eternity he is silent,
He sees eternity less like a play with a prologue and denouement,
He sees eternity in men and women, he does not see men and women as dreams or dots."

"Are you faithful to things?" Whitman asks of anyone who would assume a place to teach or be a poet here in the States.

"Do you teach what the land and sea, the bodies of men, womanhood,
amativeness, heroic angers teach?
Have you sped through fleeting customs, popularities?
Can you hold your hand against all seductions, follies, whirls, fierce con-
tentions? are you very strong? are you really of the whole People?
Are you not of some coterie? some school or mere religion?"

Whitman loved the People. He described himself as the credulous man
of qualities, ages, races, advancing from the people in their own spirit
crying "Omnes! Omnes! Let others ignore what they may! Here is what
sings unrestricted faith."

"The People!" he said; "Like our huge earth itself, which, to ordinary
scansion, is full of vulgar contradiction and offense, man viewed in the
lump, displeases, and is a constant puzzle and affront to the merely educated classes. The rare, cosmical, artist-mind, lit with the Infinite, alone
confronts his manifold and oceanic qualities. . . .

"Literature, strictly consider'd has never recognized the People, and,
whatever may be said, does not today. Speaking generally, the tendencies
of literature, as hitherto pursued, have been to make mostly critical and
querelous men. It seems as if, so far, there were some natural repugnance
between a literary and professional life, and the rude rank spirit of the
democracies. There is, in later literature, a treatment of benevolence, a
charity business, rife enough it is true; but I know nothing more rare even
in this country, than a fit scientific estimate and reverent appreciation of
the People—Of their measureless wealth of latent power and capacity,
their vast, artistic contrasts of lights and shadow—with, in America, their
entire reliability in emergencies, and a certain breadth of historic grandeur, of peace or war, far surpassing all the vaunted samples of book-
heroes, or any *haut ton* coteries, in all the records of the world.

"The average man of a land at last only is important. He in these States,
remains immortal owner and boss, deriving good uses, somehow, out of
any sort of servant in office, even the basest; (certain universal requisites,
and their settled regularity and protection being first secured,) a nation
like ours, in a sort of geological formation state, trying continually new
experiments, choosing new delegations, is not served by the best men
only, but sometimes more by those that provoke it—by the combats they
arouse. Thus national rage, fury, discussions, etc., better than content. . . .

"Then still the thought returns, (like the thread passage in overtures,) giving the key and echo to these pages. When I pass to and fro, different latitudes, different seasons, beholding the crowds of the great cities, New York, Boston, Philadelphia, Cincinnati, Chicago, St. Louis, San Francisco, New Orleans, Baltimore—when I mix with these interminable swarms of alert, turbulent, good-natured, independent citizens, mechanics, clerks, young persons—at the idea of this mass of men, so fresh and free, so loving and so proud, a singular awe falls upon me. I feel, with dejection and amazement, that among our geniuses and talented writers and speakers, few or none have yet really spoken to this people, created a single image-making work for them, or absorbed the central spirit and the idiosyncrasies which are theirs—and which, thus, in highest ranges, so far remain entirely uncelebrated, unexpress'd."

But it was not only with dejection and amazement that Whitman as one of the people felt this lack of an image-making work. He was frightened by it. He saw the States with all their variety of origins and their diverse climes, cities and standards, and the diverse characters and aims, moreover, of the people, and nothing was plainer to him than the need, for a long period to come, of the fusion of the states into a moral and artistic identity. He was continually haunted, he said, by the fear of conflicting and irreconcilable interiors and the lack of a common skeleton, knitting all close. In a crisis, he felt, it would take more than the written law, or self-interest, or common pecuniary or material objects to act as the true nationality, the genuine union of the States. This diversity and conflict he saw, must have to counteract it the fervid and tremendous Idea, melting everything else with resistless heat, and dissolving all lesser and definite distinctions in vast, indefinite, spiritual, emotional power. There must be consistency at any rate. "For how can we remain, divided, contradicting ourselves, this way?" he asked. "I say we can only attain harmony and stability by consulting ensemble and the ethic purports, and faithfully building upon them." Politics might serve admirably here. He felt that in America they had already been established for good in their own native, sound, long-vista'd principles, never to be overturned. Therefore they offered a sure basis for all the rest, and some of the dangerous diversity might be dissolved if future religious forms, sociology, literature, teachers, schools, costumes, etc., were to make a compact whole, uniform, on tallying principles, with politics.

Something must be done, Whitman felt, to prevent the malformations he saw around him wherever he went; someone must express and make images for the people. For everywhere, in shop, street, church, theatre, barroom, official chair, he saw pervading flippancy and vulgarity, low cunning, infidelity—everywhere the youth puny, impudent, foppish, prematurely ripe—everywhere an abnormal libidinousness, unhealthy forms, male, female, painted, padded, dyed, chignon'd, muddy complexions, bad blood, the capacity for good motherhood deceasing or deceas'd, shallow notions of beauty, with a range of manners, or rather lack of manners, (considering the advantages enjoy'd) probably the meanest to be found in the world. "The spectacle is appalling," he said. "We live in an atmosphere of hypocrisy throughout. The men believe not in the women nor the women in the men. A scornful superciliousness rules in literature. The aim of all the litterateurs is to find something to make fun of. A lot of churches, sects, etc., the most dismal phantasms I know, usurp the name of religion. Conversation is a mass of badinage. From deceit in the spirit, the mother of all false deeds, the offspring is already incalculable. An acute and candid person, in the revenue department in Washington, who is led by the course of his employment to regularly visit the cities, north, south, and west, to investigate frauds, has talk'd much with me about his discoveries. The depravity of the business classes of our country is not less than has been supposed, but infinitely greater. The official services of America, national, state, and municipal, in all their branches and departments, except the judiciary, are saturated in corruption, bribery, falsehood, maladministration; and the judiciary is tainted. The great cities reek with respectable as much as non-respectable robbery and scoundrelism. In fashionable life, flippancy, tepid amours, weak infidelism, small aims, or no aims at all, only to kill time."

These considerations led Whitman to state that the fruition of democracy, on aught like a grand scale, resided altogether in the future. From the sordidness of the present, Whitman saw two alleys of escape. There was, of course, the fusion of all in the vast indefinite Idea. But besides this, there was his other dependence,—identity, personalism, and he saw the hope of America in the copious production of perfect characters among the people. "Singleness and normal simplicity and separation," he said (and in his extremity seemed even to deny fusion), "amid this more and more complex, more and more artificialized state of society—how pensively we yearn for them! how we would welcome their return!"

Therefore, in addition to established sciences, he suggested a science, as it were, of 'healthy average personalism, on original-universal gounds,' the object of which should be to raise up and supply through the States a copious race of superb American men and women, cheerful, religious, ahead of any yet known. But it was no elite or special class that he thought to erect. He would demand of the programme of culture inaugurated by his new science a scope generous enough to include the widest human area. It must have for its spinal meaning the formation of a typical personality of character, eligible to the uses of the high average of men and not restricted by conditions ineligible to the masses. It must aim to form over this continent an 'idiocrasy of universalism' and 'vitalize all men's free play of special Personalism.'

Whitman himself, sensing the great need of identity and the benefits it could give, attempted a basic model or portrait of personality for the general use for the manliness of the States; "—and doubtless," he said, "that is most useful which is most simple and comprehensive for all, and toned low enough." He believed that for such a portrait the canvas should be prepared well beforehand. "Parentage must consider itself in advance," he said. "(Will the time hasten when fatherhood and motherhood shall become a science—and the noblest science?) To our model, a clear-blooded, strong-fibred physique, is indispensable; the questions of food, drink, air, exercise, assimilation, digestion, can never be intermitted. Out of these we descry a well-begotten selfhood—in youth, fresh, ardent, emotional, aspiring, full of adventure; at maturity, brave, perceptive, under control, neither too talkative nor too reticent, neither flippant, nor sombre; of the bodily figure, the movements easy, the complexion showing the best blood, somewhat flush'd, breast expanded, an erect attitude, a voice whose sound outvies music, eyes of calm and steady gaze, yet capable also of flashing—and a general presence that holds its own in the company of the highest. (For it is native personality, and that alone, that endows a man to stand before presidents or generals, or in any distinguished collection, with *aplomb*—and *not* culture, or any knowledge or intellect whatever.")

Having thus provided for the physical qualifications of his model, Whitman found that with regard to the mental-educational part, the enlargement of the intellect, stores of cephalic knowledge, etc., the customs of the age, especially in America, so fully provided that it hardly needed his attention. It only seemed necessary to provide for the model's spiritual and political life. Religion was commonly neglected, and although Whitman had little regard for priests or churches, he said he felt it essential that one's isolated Self should enter the pure ether of veneration, reach the divine levels, and commune with the unutterable. And likewise he felt that to practically enter into politics was an important part of American personalism, and he therefore advised every young man north and south who was earnestly studying his pages, to always inform himself, always do the best he could, and always vote. "So much," he said, "(hastily tossed together, and leaving far more unsaid,) for an ideal, or intimations of an ideal, toward American manhood."

This then, was what Whitman would do,—he would provide a model for the men and women of the States. The consideration which prompted him in this is best apparent in the light of his perception of what he termed the plentiful meanness and vulgarity of the ostensible masses. This was his means to overcome it. "It must still be reiterated," he said, ". . . that all else in the contributions of a nation or age, through its politics, materials, heroic personalities, military eclat, etc., remains crude, and defers, in any close and thorough-going estimate, until vitalized by national, original archetypes in literature." He took it as a matter of course that he must entirely recast such models as traditional literature supplied, because the types of highest personality must be changed from what the oriental, feudal, ecclesiastical worlds bequeathed us. "Of course, the old undying elements remain," he said. But he felt that America must, for her purposes, cease to recognize a theory of character grown of feudal aristocracies, or formed by merely literary standards, or from any ultramarine, full-dress formulas of culture, polish, caste, etc., and must sternly promulgate her own new standard, yet old enough, and accepting the old, the perennial elements, and combining them into groups, unities, appropriate to the modern, the democratic, the west, and to the practical occasions and needs of our own cities, and of the agricultural regions. It was for this reason that he demanded races of orbic bards with unconditional uncompromising sway. "Come forth," he said, "sweet democratic despots of the west!"

It was as if he wooed his own identity. That only the rare and cosmical artist's mind, lit with the infinite, confronts his manifold and oceanic qualities, his measureless wealth of latent power and capacity, had been Whitman's judgement of the People. And therefore, this lovely world with its swarms of alert, turbulent, good-natured, independent citizens, mechanics, clerks, young persons, its masses of men so fresh and so free, so loving and so proud,—this lovely world, so like a projection of that earlier ecstatic world in which there was no imperfection and could be none,—was indeed, no more than such a projection. Whitman was never able to make it exist beyond his poet's vision, or to believe that it existed in any but the purest, most absolute state, where no evil, no doubt, no ennui was ever admitted. These last were things of the present, nebular world, which to the sober judgment was full of vulgar contradiction and offense. Whitman thought that if he could only become a bard, with unlimited power, the lovely world might be restored, for nothing could trouble the God-like accomplished sureness of the bard. Whitman saw the solution of his own and the national problem as one and the same,—the achievment of form. Considering in *Democratic Vistas* the difference between that actual America in which he lived and the America which would content him and which he thought fit and suitable, "It is, in some sort, no less a difference," he said, "than lies between that long continued nebular state and vagueness of the astronomical worlds, compared with the subsequent state, the definitely form'd worlds themselves, duly compacted, clustering in systems, hung up there, chandeliers of the universe, beholding and mutually lit by each other's lights, serving for ground of all substantial foothold, all vulgar uses—yet serving still more as an undying chain and echelon of spiritual proofs and shows. A boundless field to fill! A new creation, with needed orbic works launch'd forth, to revolve in free and lawful circuits,— to move self-poised, through the ether, and shine like heaven's own suns."

Who but a God with limitless powers, Whitman felt,—who but one beyond boredom, complaints, or scornful criticisms, would be equal to such a task! Since the identity of the poet was to be his salvation from the terrors of the nebular world, it seemed to him that part of the test of the great literatus should be the complete absence in him of the idea of the covert, the lurid, the maleficent, the devil, the grim estimates inherited from the puritans, hell, natural depravity, and the like. Since the poet was to create the duly compacted, definitely formed world without imperfection and without impurity, the poet, himself, would be perfect and pure. He would not be preyed upon by the tormenting doubts and insufficiencies which preyed upon Whitman before he became a poet. The great literatus would be known by his cheerful simplicity, his adherence to natural standards, his limitless faith in God, his reverence, and by the absence in him of doubt, ennui, burlesque, persiflage, or any strained or temporary fashion. He would master obedience, not be mastered by it. High up out of reach he would stand, turning the pivot of a concentrated light with his finger. He would baffle the swiftest runners as he stood, and easily overtake and envelop them. By his steady faith he would withhold the times straying toward infidelity and confections and persiflage. The poet was the Answerer.

"Him all wait for, him all yield up to, his word is decisive and final
Him they accept, in him lave, in him perceive themselves as amid light
Him they immerse and he immerses them."

. . .

"The gentleman of perfect blood acknowledges his perfect blood,
The insulter, the prostitute, the angry person, the beggar, see themselves
    in the ways of him, he strangely transmutes them,
They are not vile any more, they hardly know themselves they are so grown

. . .

"The maker of poems settles justice, reality, immortality,
His insight and power encircle things and the human race,
He is the glory and extract so far of the human race.

. . .

"The sailor and traveler underlie the maker of poems, the Answerer,
The builder, geometer, chemist, anatomist, phrenologist, artist, all these
    underlie the maker of poems, the Answerer."

Walt Whitman, like the sea formless himself, never conceived of form as other than external. Although he sang the song of himself steadily, he was different from other individualists of his time because he was unaware of a personality within himself to be explored and explored for. It was a thing of the external world, he thought, to be acquired in order that one might exploit it. It was from this premise that he thought he might be useful to American democracy and hasten its achievement, if he were to furnish it with models of perfect personality, and when he came to do this dealt with the apparent, not the virtual aspects. By the same process of reasoning, he thought to become, as he conceived it, a bard, the highest, most God-like form. Form was beautiful to Whitman, and its persuasiveness led him, since he found no single form within himself, to a kind of emotional eclecticism, not interested in the achievement of form as the resolution of such contradictory and chaotic materials as were at hand, but rather in the as-

sumption of ready-made form, in avoidance of the materials. The particular realities of a role were not important to Whitman; it was important
chiefly that it was a role, a definite part, and that through it he might share,
by impersonation, in the objective beauty which it had. There was no
single world within himself to content Whitman with a special appropri-
ateness and sufficient space; lacking this, his hunger for life and identity
was uncontrolled. "It is not enough to have this globe or a certain time," he
cries in *A Song of Joys*, "I will have thousands of globes and all times." And
then with a peculiar happiness,—sometimes like a child planning his future, sometimes like one longing for escape from emotional drabness into
life as the movies live it, he begins to recount the divergent joys which
strike his eclectic fancy:

"O the engineer's joys! to go with a locomotive!
To hear the hiss of steam, the merry shriek, the steam whistle, the laughing
  locomotive!
To push with resistless way and speed off in the distance.

. . .

"O the fireman's joys!
I hear the alarm at dead of night,
I hear bells, shouts! I pass the crowd, I run!
The sight of the flames maddens me with pleasure.

. . .

"O to have been brought up on bays, lagoons, creeks, or along the coast
To continue and be employed there all my life,
The briny and damp smell, the shore, the salt weeds exposed at low water,
The work of fishermen, the work of the eel-fisher and clam-fisher;
I come with my clam-rake and spade, I come with my eel-spear,
Is the tide out? I join the group of clam-diggers on the flats,
I laugh and work with them, I joke at my work like a mettlesome young
  man;
In winter I take my eel-basket and eel-spear and travel out on foot on the
  ice—I have a small axe to cut holes in the ice,
Behold me well-clothed going gaily or returning in the afternoon, my
  brood of tough boys accompanying me,

157

My brood of grown and part-grown boys, who love to be with no one else
    so well as they love to be with me,
By day to work with me and by night to sleep with me.

       . . .

"(O something pernicious and dread!
Something far away from a puny and pious life!
Something unproved! something in a trance!
Something escaped from anchorage and driving free)

       . . .

"O to resume the joys of the soldier!
To feel the presence of a brave commanding officer—to feel his sympathy!
To behold his calmness—to be warmed in the rays of his smile!
To go to battle—to hear the bugles play and the drums beat!

To hear the crash of artillery—to see the glittering of the bayonets and the
    musket-barrels in the sun!
To see men fall and die and not complain!
To taste the savage taste of blood—to be so devilish!
To gloat so over the wounds and deaths of the enemy.

       . . .

O the old manhood of me, my noblest joy of all!
My children and grand-children, my white hair and beard,
My largeness, calmness, majesty, out of the long stretch of my life.

       . . .

O the joy of my soul leaning pois'd on itself, receiving identity through
    materials and loving them, observing characters and absorbing them,

       . . .

O the joy of a manly self-hood!
To be servile to none, to defer to none, not to any tyrant known or un-
    known,
To walk with erect carriage, a step springy and elastic,
To look with calm gaze or with a flashing eye,
To speak with a full and sonorous voice out of a broad chest.
To confront with your personality all the other personalities of the earth.

. . .

O to sail to sea in a ship!
To leave this steady unendurable land,
To leave this tiresome sameness of the streets, the sidewalks and the
    houses,
To leave you O you solid motionless land, and entering a ship,
To sail and sail and sail!

To have life henceforth a poem of new joys!
To dance, clap hands, exult, shout, skip, leap, roll on, float on!
To be a sailor of the world bound for all ports,
A ship itself, (see indeed these sails I spread to the sun and air,)
A swift and swelling ship full of rich words, full of joys."

Whitman would have the ordered, the duly compacted world, the world without doubt, without evil, the achievement of perfect form even if he needed to become formless himself to reach it. Wishing that life might always be a poem of new joys, he relied so completely on the external world that he had no refuge from imperfection in it, and therefore it must somehow be made to appear perfect. The character of the omnipotent poet was an expedient for this purpose. But there were others; even beyond the eclectic roles of which poet was one, there was a mechanical naturalism, a further expedient to obviate a personal reference or responsibility. Whitman sometimes promulgated a world in which whatever existed was right and perfect.

"Meditating among liars and retreating sternly into myself, I see that there
    are really no liars or lies after all," he said,
"And that nothing fails its perfect return, and that what are called lies are
    perfect returns,
And that each thing exactly represents itself and what had preceded it,
And that the truth includes all, and is compact just as much as space is
    compact,
And that there is no flaw or vacuum in the amount of the truth—but that
    all is truth without exception;
And henceforth I will go celebrate any thing I see or am,
And sing and laugh and deny nothing."

His premise, that all was truth without exception, caused him some-times to have difficulty in defining his position exactly. "To the heights of such estimate of Nature indeed ascending, we proceed to make observa-tions for our Vistas, breathing rarest air," he says in *Democratic Vistas*. "What is I believe called Idealism seems to me to suggest, (guarding against extravagance, and ever modified even by its opposite,) the course of inquiry and desert of favor for our New World metaphysics, the foun-dation of and in literature, giving hue to all. . . . Fearless of scoffing, and of the ostent, let us take our stand, our ground, and never desert it, to confront the growing excess and arrogance of realism. To the cry, now victorious—the cry of sense, science, flesh, incomes, farms, merchandise, logic, intellect, demonstrations, solid perpetuities, buildings of brick and iron, or even the facts of the shows of trees, earth, rocks, etc., fear not my brethren, my sisters, to sound out with equally determin'd voice, that conviction brooding within the recesses of every envision'd soul— illusions! apparitions! figments all! True we must not condemn the show, neither absolutely deny it, for the indispensability of its mean-ings. . . ." In his eclecticism, Whitman wished he had been brought up on bays, lagoons, creeks, or along the coast, where in some circumscribed surroundings his whole existence and identity might have been deter-mined by his environment. He wished he might be a soldier to live in the presence of some brave commanding officer, feeling his presence and sym-pathy. In order to regain a world which had had no imperfections, and thereby to so far simplify the problem of his identity, he was eager to cir-cumscribe his nature, whether by the uniform of a soldier, the restrictions of environment or the denial of his consciousness. For this last purpose, he reaches in a poem called *The Sleepers* a queer half world of lost detail and faded images.

"I wander all night in my vision," he says,
"Stepping with light feet, swiftly and noiselessly stepping and stopping,
Bending with open eyes over the shut eyes of sleepers . . . .

. . .

I go from bedside to bedside, I sleep close with the other sleepers each in turn,
I dream in my dream all the dreams of the other dreamers,
And I become the other dreamers.

. . .

Double yourself and receive me darkness
Receive me and my lover too, he will not let me go without him.
I roll myself upon you as upon a bed, I resign myself to the dusk.

. . .

The antipodes, and everyone between this and them in the dark,
I swear they are averaged now—one is no better than the other,
The night and sleep have liken'd them and restored them.

I swear they are all beautiful . . . everything in the dim light is beautiful,

. . .

The universe is duly in order, everything is in its place,

. . .

The diverse shall be no less diverse, but they shall flow and unite—they
    unite now.

The sleepers are very beautiful as they lie unclothed.
They flow hand in hand over the whole earth from east to west as they lie
    unclothed,
The Asiatic and African are hand in hand, the European and American are
    hand in hand,
Learn'd and unlearn'd are hand in hand, and male and female are hand in
    hand. . . ."

Such was the dream he had of society. Sometimes he wished he might
be an old man, serenely liberated from the passions of his youth and maturity, his identity objectified by the passage of time. He grew old while
still in his thirties; and it was as an aged father that he went to Washington
at the time of the Civil War to tend the sick and the wounded in the army
hospitals there. "Dear sons and comrades," he called them. "O," he said,
"what a sweet unwonted love (these good American boys of good stock,
decent, clean, well-raised boys, so near to me)—what an attachment,
grows up between us, started from hospital cots, where pale young faces
lie and wounded or sick bodies. My brave young American soldiers—now

---

for so many months I have gone around among them, where they lie. I have long discarded all stiff conventions (they and I are too near to each other, there is no time to lose, and death and anguish dissipate ceremony here between my lads and me)—I pet them, some of them it does so much good, they are so faint and lonesome—at parting at night sometimes I kiss them right and left—the doctors tell me I supply the patients with a medicine which all their drugs and bottles and powders are helpless to yield."

It was a medicine he thought specific for wider uses as well. Over the carnage of the war, there rose a voice of prophecy to assure him that affection should solve the problems of freedom yet, that those who loved each other should become invincible, that they should yet make Columbia victorious.

"It shall be customary in the houses and streets to see manly affection," he
    said,
"The most dauntless and rude shall touch face to face lightly,
The dependence of Liberty shall be lovers
The continuance of Equality shall be comrades.

These shall tie you and band you stronger than hoops of iron,
I, ecstatic, O partners! O lands, with the love of lovers tie you."

What indeed, he wondered, was finally beautiful except death and love! He thought it was not for life he was chanting his chant of lovers; he thought it must be for death. He said that in the future of the States, poets immenser far must arise and make great poems of death. Such a poem, he felt, was his own *Passage to India*. He gave it a prominent place in the Centennial Edition of *Leaves of Grass*, ". . . not," he said, "as in antiquity, at highest festival of Egypt, the noisome skeleton of death was sent on exhibition to the revellers for zest and shadow to the occasion's joy and light—but as the marble statue of the normal Greeks at Elis, suggesting death in the form of a beautiful and perfect young man, with closed eyes, leaning on an inverted torch—emblem of rest and aspiration after action—of crown and point which all lives should steadily have reference to, namely, the justified and noble termination of our identity, this grade of it, and outlet preparation for another grade."

HERMAN MELVILLE; OR, THE AMBIGUITIES

The Social Problem

As the man with whom he had been drinking quickly withdrew, another stranger advanced, and touching the Cosmopolitan said, "I think I heard you say you would see that man again. Be warned; don't you do so."

The Cosmopolitan protested. "What is your prejudice against my friend?" he asked. "What is he?"

But the stranger shrugged his shoulders and his sad look grew more intense. "What are you?" he said with a mixture of impatience and fervor as though annoyed by the Cosmopolitan's innocence, and yet eager for the opportunity it gave him. "What am I? Nobody knows who anybody is. The data which life furnishes towards forming a true estimate of any being are as insufficient to that end as in geometry, one side given would be to determine the triangle."

But this skeptical attitude the speaker expressed was partly denied by the statement which followed: "I warned you against him however, because he is suspected for what on these boats is known—so they tell me—as a Mississippi operator, an equivocal character. That he is such, I little doubt, having had him pointed out to me by one desirous of initiating me into any little novelty of this western region, where I never before traveled. And sir, if I am not mistaken, you also are a stranger here (but, indeed, where in this strange universe is not one a stranger?) and that is a reason why I felt moved to warn you against a companion who could not be otherwise than perilous to one of a free and trustful disposition."

In Herman Melville's novel *The Confidence Man*, these remarks are made by two of the travelers on the steamboat *Fidèle*, as it passes from St. Louis to New Orleans, one First of April, sometime in the 1850's. The *Fidèle* was a strange boat. Its passengers have only an insubstantial, shifting reality. And yet they were faithful delineations of the people Melville knew. It was the models from which these portraits were drawn that seemed incredible to him. *The Confidence Man* is a book of richness and depth, ingrained with terror. It is a picture of the world in which Melville lived at that time, a world in which he had arrived after gradual and difficult progress. He was born in 1819, two years after Thoreau was born, and in the same year as Whitman. He lived through most of his century and died in 1891. Before he went to sea for the first time, on a merchant-ship to Liverpool, he had worked at various places,—his Uncle Peter's bank, his Uncle Tom's farm, his brother's store. Then, returning from Liverpool, he taught school for a while. When he was twenty-one, he joined the crew of a whaling-ship, and went to sea for the second time. This time he was gone more than three years and came back as a sailor on board a naval frigate. He began to write books about his adventures in the south seas, and they sold fairly well. When his books gradually became more serious and less saleable, he took to farming to supplement his income. Meantime, he married and had children. Sometimes he traveled about the country, to give lectures. For twenty years, during which he wrote almost nothing, he worked as a customs inspector in New York. When he died, the few people who read the brief notice were surprised to learn he had not died long before. They had forgotten him.

"It was with a heavy heart and full eyes, that my poor mother parted with me; perhaps she thought me an erring and willful boy, and perhaps I was; but if I was, it had been a hard-hearted world, and hard times that made me so. I had learned to think much and bitterly before my time; all my young mounting dreams of glory had left me; and at that early age, I was as unambitious as a man of sixty." It was not until he was thirty that Melville wrote in this way about the attitude of mind with which he had undertaken his first voyage, twelve years before. The book was called *Redburn*, and like two south seas books already written, it was essentially Melville's own story. His bitterness at that age was largely a boy's romantic bitterness. It was true that he had known poverty and disappointment and an insecure world. His father had died, and his once prosperous family was no longer so. But the bitterness he later learned, the poverty and cruelty he began now to see in the outer world, made his own past life seem warm and comfortable by contrast. The attitudes with which he went to sea—the desperation and recklessness of poverty, and the misanthropy of a disappointed boy,—attitudes which made the world seem to stretch away before him in a long, muddy road, bitter cold and bleak as December, so that he felt as if the warm soul had been flogged out of him by adversity,— these attitudes found their reflection in the crew, who had been confirmed in them by much wider and longer experience. But the crew's own bitterness and desperation caused them to feel no sympathy for Pillgarlic, as the mate first called him. They felt rather the contempt that the bitterly experienced feel for even the bitter novice, and looked upon him as one whom they could victimize and abuse as the world had victimized and abused them. When, on the first night at sea, they were all frightened by one of their number who rose from the drunken sleep in which he had been brought aboard and, in a fit of delirium, dashed overboard and was drowned, they assumed that Melville shared their fright even more than he did. He had indeed been frightened but he was proud of not showing it, and he saw that they had been frightened too. But they claimed not to be, and said that this was the kind of hard, wicked life he had embarked upon, and that they were so used to it that they took no notice, but as for him, that he had better run as far inland as he could as soon as he got home from this voyage again, and thereafter never go near the sea. When he protested that he could stand the sea as well as they could, they all united to abuse him as a white-handed gentleman, and threatened to push him overboard some day out of the rigging. "I loathed, detested, and hated them," he said, "with all that was left of my bursting heart and soul, and I felt myself the most forlorn and miserable wretch that ever breathed. May I never be a man, thought I, if to be a boy is to be such a wretch. And I wailed and wept, and my heart cracked within me, but all the time I defied them through my teeth, and dared them to do their worst."

It was this defiance that saved him, the defiance and another feeling of response to the sea and to all the wild commotion of the outer world so that he felt a wild exulting, a bubbling and bursting at his heart, as if a hidden spring had burst out there, and his blood ran tingling along his frame like mountain brooks in spring freshets.

In the busy dock section of Liverpool, he was to see more of the dark and bitter side of things, of the wild commotion of the outer world. The whole waterfront region was crowded with beggars such as he had never seen in America, so that it seemed to him hard to believe that such an array of misery could be furnished by any town in the world. Old women drying up like mummies with slow starvation and age; young girls, incurably sick; sturdy men with the gallows in their eyes, who were whining and lying; young boys, hollow-eyed and decrepit; and puny mothers, holding up puny babies in the glare of the sun: these were the ordinary and principle features of the scene. But the more unusual beggars displayed terrible sores or deformities, or pointed silently to pictures or chalked writing on the pavement which described their condition.

In Launcelott's Hey, a tiny street or alley among the warehouses, Melville one day found a woman and two children dying from starvation under a grating in the sidewalk. There was a baby already dead in the woman's arms. He tried for three days to get help to them, but he met with indifference everywhere, and on the third day he found a heap of quicklime where they had been.

On the voyage home, the group of emigrants who were carried as part of the west-bound cargo were so poorly provided for that many of them died. And then there was the crew again, although by now the crew and Melville had begun to accept one another, and things had not gone so badly had it not been for a man named Jackson. This Jackson was physically the weakest and ugliest man of the crew. He might have been thirty years old from his appearance, or he might have been fifty, but by his own account he had been at sea since he was only eight, when he first went as a cabin-boy in an Indiaman and ran away at Calcutta. Since that time, he had passed through every kind of dissipation and abandonment in the worst parts of the world, and now nothing was left of him but the foul lees and dregs of a man. In spite of his physical weakness, he was the tyrant and bully of the crew. They all stood in mortal fear of him, so that instead of showing him the hatred that they felt, they cringed and fawned about him, treated him with the utmost consideration, did all manner of menial services for him, and accepted him as arbiter in all their disputes. Jackson's particular hatred was for Melville, or for anyone else among the men who had any wholeness of health or strength. There was a remarkably robust and good-humored young man from Belfast, who Melville thought should have been a leader in the crew, but he was on the contrary a person of no mark or influence, and was abused and snubbed by Jackson, and the crew hooted at him and trampled on him. Jackson seemed to be full of hatred and gall against everything and everybody in the world, as if all the world were one person and had done him some dreadful harm that was rankling and festering in his heart. During the long night, he would enter into arguments to prove that there was nothing to be believed, nothing to be loved, and nothing worth living for, but everything to be hated in the wide world; and thus he went about corrupting and searing every heart that beat near him. But there seemed to Melville to be even more woe than wickedness about the man, and his wickedness seemed to spring from his woe. For all his hideousness, there was something in his eye at times that was ineffably pitiable and touching.

Melville was well aware of his own position as a mere boy among the

168

sailors. He kept quiet and had very little to say, and well knew that his best plan was to get along peaceably with everybody, and endure a good deal before showing fight; but he was unable to avoid Jackson's evil eye or escape his enmity. "And his being my foe," he said, "set many of the rest against me; or at least they were afraid to speak out for me before Jackson; so that at last I found myself a sort of Ishmael in the ship, without a single friend or companion; and I began to feel a hatred growing up in me against the whole crew—so much so, that I prayed against it, that it might not master my heart completely and so make a fiend of me, something like Jackson."

By the time that Melville wrote in *Redburn* this account of the crew on his first voyage, he had already written in earlier books of the crews he sailed among on subsequent voyages. They were much alike, outcasts and victims for the most part of a harsh civilization. But the most raw and savage of a lawless lot of humanity was the crew of the *Julia*, of which he writes in his second book, *Omoo*. The events in *Omoo* take place in the South Seas, waters where sailor characteristics showed up in wilder aspects than anywhere else. Most of the ships there were whalers, and whalers not only attracted the most reckless men of all nations, but in various ways fostered the greatest license in them. Such crews could be governed by only the harshest sort of discipline. The captain of the *Julia* was a young cockney who had emigrated to Australia and got command of the ship through favoritism, though he was in no way competent. He was essentially a landsman, and though a man of education, no more meant for the sea than a hairdresser. Everyone made fun of him. They called him 'the Cabin Boy,' 'Paper Jack,' and a half-dozen other undignified names. The men made no secret of their derision, and he knew it all very well, and bore himself with becoming meekness. He left everything to the chief-mate, a courageous, good seaman, who was always more or less drunk, but whose bluff, drunken energy was almost what was needed to keep the riotous crew in some sort of noisy subjection. But he was not always able to do so, and on one occasion was beaten and forced to yield a point to a man who refused to work or to come on deck. Two of the crew, also, were drunk constantly from liquor they secretly stole from the hold. The captain took sick and seemed to be dying, and when the ship put in to Tahiti in order to take the captain off, the men, who were eager themselves to go ashore but were not allowed to, refused to take the ship to sea again or to do any duty. They were not without reasonable grievances. Many of their number were sick, and the well men were not numerous enough to work the ship properly. The ship's provisions had been bought at an auction of condemned navy stores in Sydney, and they were very poor. The pork looked as if preserved in iron rust; the beef was a mahogany-colored, fibrous substance, tough and tasteless to chew; the biscuit was honey-combed through and through with worms, and there was little or nothing else to eat.

The upshot of the matter was that the crew refused to yield to the empty threats of punishment made by the British consul at Tahiti, and still refusing duty, were taken ashore to a kind of jail, from which after being confined for several weeks, they were allowed to escape.

This mutiny aboard the *Julia*, if mutiny it was, was not Melville's first revolt from the cruel abuses aboard the ships of his time. Several months before, with a single companion, he had deserted a ship at Nukuheva, an island in the Marquesas group, the place at which he later joined the *Julia*. He refers to the ship from which he ran away as the *Dolly*, and it was presumably the *Acushnet*, on which he had embarked for his second voyage in January 1841. It was not uncommon for sailors to leave ship at islands in the South Seas, and Melville justifies his failure to keep the agreement he had made in signing the ship's articles by saying that the ship itself had failed to keep its part of the agreement, and so nullified it. "In numberless instances," he says, "had not only the implied but the specified conditions of the articles been violated on the part of the ship in which I served. The usage on board of her was tyrannical; the sick had been inhumanly neglected; and her cruises were unreasonably protracted. The captain was the author of these abuses; it was in vain to think that he would either remedy them, or alter his conduct, which was arbitrary and violent in the extreme. His prompt reply to all complaints and remonstrances was—the butt end of a hand-spike, so convincingly administered as effectually to silence the aggrieved party. To whom could we apply for redress? We had left both law and equity on the other side of the Cape; and unfortunately, with a very few exceptions, our crew was composed of a parcel of dastardly and mean-spirited wretches, divided among themselves, and only united in enduring without resistance the unmitigated tyranny of the captain. It would have been mere madness for any two or three of the number, unassisted by the rest, to attempt making a stand against his ill-usage. They would only have called down upon themselves the particular vengeance of this 'Lord of the Plank,' and subjected their shipmates to additional hardships."

As a consequence of all this, Melville and his companion, Toby, determined to seclude themselves in an interior valley of Nukuheva where it was believed there were friendly natives, until the *Dolly* should be forced to sail again without them. Almost dead, they reached a valley after several days of difficult travel through jungle and over mountains, during which Melville contracted a painful and disabling infection in one of his legs. It was not the valley they had intended to enter, and as the days went on, they learned from almost certain signs that they were living among cannibals. They were held in a sort of captivity in the valley, but they were not unkindly treated, and indeed they lived a gentle, idyllic life with the natives. The people of the valley of Typee had such simplicity and grace and kindliness as Melville had never seen before. No one was sick here; no one starved or begged to keep from starving; no one was dirty or frightened or cruel. Their warfare was a rare and brief skirmish with the people of the adjoining valley in which it might happen that no one was injured, although it was apparently true that if any of the enemy should be killed, his body was brought back and eaten by the warriors. This was their cannibalism. But cannibalism, whatever particular form it might take, was repellent to white European society, and its existence in the South Seas served as one justification for the influx of the white enlighteners. Under their influence, cannibalism ceased to be practiced, but wherever Melville traveled in the South Seas, he nevertheless found the natives degraded by contact with the whites, and the older and more frequent the contact, the greater the degradation. To a simple and gentle people who actually practiced with the greatest naturalness most of the precepts of Jesus, the missionaries brought a bewildering and puritanical consciousness of sin. And simultaneously, as though it were a necessary concomitant for such an innocent people, the other white men, the traders and sailors, brought the means and mechanisms of sin. The result was corruption and disease and slaughter. It was only after the missionaries had come that there was any reason for their coming,—as though a fire company were to carry with it some other group of men to start the fires which were to be put out. All in all, it was like a repetition of the expulsion of man from Eden. The heathen images and temples, for which the islanders had little reverence anyway, were demolished, and the islanders were converted to nominal Christians, and disease and vice and premature death made their appearance. The Europeans moved in, and the savages found themselves interlopers in what had been their own lands. The Christians appropriated all the natural food and ate it themselves, or traded it to the many ships that now began to call at the harbors; the natives were told to work and earn their support if they did not wish to starve. The Europeans were opposed to indolence, and they Christianized and evangelized the natives into draught horses.

Among many similar sights that Melville saw, he would remember a robust and very lady-like wife of a missionary, who every day used to take her little outings in a go-cart drawn by two naked islanders, an old man and a young boy. Riding along in this elegant rig, the lady would look about her as magnificently as a queen going to coronation. But outside of town there was a sandy rise of ground where, to avoid dismounting and walking up on foot, she would bawl at the natives and beat them over the head with the handle of a heavy fan she carried, though back home in New England she had walked often enough, as Melville said, driving the cows home from pasture. But this was different. And whenever there was a service in the American Chapel in the town where this lady lived in Christian humility, a score of similar go-carts could be seen outside, each with its pair of squalid natives waiting to draw their superiors home.

Melville, quite naturally, could not avoid contrasting these scenes of degradation with the dignity and grace of native life in those areas where civilization had not yet penetrated. The Typees, for example, were so pure and upright in all the relations of life, he said that after passing a few weeks in this valley of the Marquesas, he formed a higher estimate of human nature than he had ever before entertained. "But alas! since then I have been one of the crew of a man-of-war," he said, "and the pent-up wickedness of five hundred men has nearly overturned my previous theories."

After living with the cannibals in Typee, and after sailing in the *Julia* and joining in the mutiny aboard her, Melville spent several more months wandering about the islands of the Pacific and finally shipped aboard the American Frigate, *United States*, which in *White Jacket*, the book that recounts this experience, he calls the *Neversink*.

On merchant-ships and whalers, which had been Melville's previous experience, the line between those who sailed forward and those who sailed aft was not very sharp, but it did exist. Melville was aware of social distinctions not only afloat but ashore, where he was quite conscious not only of the aristocratic traditions of his family, but also of its present poverty and of the treatment he had sometimes been given in the world because of that poverty. But now, in the Navy, he was for the first time made acutely aware of how enormous and artificial distinctions of rank could be.

At one time, he saw the terrible fear felt by one seaman that he might be forced to come face to face with his brother who was an officer and thought to be aboard another ship lying near them in harbor. Another time, he saw a former officer, whom drink had brought down to a common seaman, included in a draught of men sent aboard the *Neversink*, where he was snubbed and humiliated by one of the Lieutenants, his cabin-mate in other days.

There were many men in the crew of the *Neversink* who had come there through adversity of one sort or another. When the man who served the ship as a cooper was lost overboard and had to be replaced, thirteen men who had followed that trade offered to fill his place. Melville saw from this and from other observations that a frigate's crew included men of all callings. For the Navy was the asylum of the perverse, the home of the unfortunate. "Here," he said, "the sons of adversity meet the children of calamity and here the children of calamity meet the offspring of sin. Bankrupt brokers, boot-blacks, black-legs and blacksmiths here assemble together; and castaway tinkers, watch-makers, quill-drivers, cobblers, doctors, farmers and lawyers compare past experiences and talk of old times."

A man-of-war was a city afloat, with long avenues set out with guns instead of trees. Melville quotes the old sailor saying that the gallows and the sea refuse nothing, and he was reminded of the truth of the final print in a Hogarth series, in which the Idle Apprentice, after consorting with harlots and gambling on tombstones, is at last shown as being pushed off to sea in a boat, with a ship and the gallows in the distance.

Aboard the frigate, the cast-offs of society had their failing heightened by the close cribbing and confining of so many mortals in one oaken box on the sea. "Like pears close packed," Melville said, "the crowded crew mutually decay through close contact, and every plague-spot is contagious. Still more, from this same close confinement—so far as it affects the common sailors—arise other evils so direful that they will hardly bear even so much as an allusion. What too many seamen are when ashore is very well known; but what some of them become when entirely cut off from shore indulgences can hardly be imagined by landsmen. The sins for which the cities of the plain were overthrown still linger in some of these wooden-walled Gomorrahs of the deep. More than once complaints were made at the mast of the *Neversink* from which the deck-officer would turn away with loathing, refuse to hear them, and command the complainant out of his sight."

Such was the general character of the crew among which Melville found himself; but many men aboard by no means conformed to this general character. Neither Jack Chase, the captain of the main-top, the section of the ship to which Melville was assigned, nor Bland, the master-at-arms, the chief police officer of the ship, conformed to it. Melville observed them closely. They were both polite, gentlemanly men, apparently educated, and were fascinating conversationalists and story-tellers. Physically there was some difference between them. Jack Chase had all the appearance of youth and good health and strength,—'tall and well-knit, with a clear open eye, a fine broad brow and an abounding nut-brown beard.' Bland, while there was a fine polish about his whole person, had a mouth that seemed to Melville somewhat small, Moorish-arched, and delicate, and a black, snaky eye. But the great difference was in their characters, a difference which their physical appearance reflected only partially. Jack was all frankness and freedom, good sense and good feeling. At one time, he had deserted from the American Navy and joined a revolution in Peru, for though he bowed to naval discipline afloat, he was a stickler for the rights of man and the liberties of the world. When he was discovered as an officer on a Peruvian warship, he came back to his own ship with an unprotesting good will, and no charge of desertion was ever brought against him. The action had made him an even greater hero than he had been before. He was loved by all the sailors, and admired by the officers, and even the captain spoke to him with a certain air of respect.

Bland, however, was hated by the seamen to a degree that exceeded the hatred they would normally have felt toward any man who held his loveless office. He was an implacable police officer, vigilant, cruel and remorseless. Unsuspected by either officers or crew, he was for a long time the clever head of a smuggling ring which brought illegal liquor aboard the ship and sold it at outrageous prices to the sailors,—sailors who in most cases would be flogged the next day at the gangway for drunkenness, with Bland standing by to assist them off with their shirts. Yet it was when he was at last discovered, deprived of his office, and after a short confinement in the brig, sent out among the crew, that he showed his greatest power. He had tyrannized over five hundred men who hated and loathed him, and while in office even, his life had been secretly attempted by men he had brought to the gangway; and yet he blandly smiled, politely offered his cigar-holder to a perfect stranger, and laughed and chatted right and left as if with an angelic conscience, and sure of kind friends wherever he went both in this life and in the life to come.

At first, the men gave him a wide berth and returned scowls for his smiles. "But who can resist the very devil himself, when he comes in the guise of a gentleman, free, fine, and frank?" asks Melville. And it was as a devil that he saw Bland. It was again Jackson of Melville's first voyage, but a disguised and subtle Jackson, a Jackson in whose conversation there was no trace of evil, who studiously shunned an indelicacy, never swore, and abounded in puns and witticisms and tastefully narrated anecdotes. The figures of Bland and Jack Chase became permanent concepts in Melville's mind.

It was not long after Melville first came aboard the *Neversink* that he heard the cry, 'All hands witness punishment, ahoy!' a cry that no matter how often repeated always sounded to him as dreadful as doom, and he saw what he saw again many times, a flogging. Four sailors had been found fighting in some part of the ship. Now they were to be punished for it. They were forced to admit to the captain that it was true they had been fighting, and this bare fact was the only thing pertinent. No circumstances were inquired into or allowed to be told. The first of the four, who happened to be the one responsible for the fracas, was tied to the grating; the captain's finger was lifted, and the first boatswain's-mate came forward, combing out the nine tails of his cat with his hand, and then sweeping them around his neck, brought them with the whole force of his body down on the man's back. Again, and again, and again, until a dozen lashes had been given, and at every blow the long purple bars on the prisoner's flesh rose higher and higher. The man was taken down, and joined the crew with a smile, saying that it was nothing when you were used to it. The second and third prisoners were quiet, sober, middle-aged men, more or less innocent parties in the fight. The first of them, a Portuguese, surged from side to side under the lash with every blow, and all the while poured out a torrent of involuntary blasphemy, though no one had ever heard him curse before. He went among the men when he was set free, swearing to have the life of the captain. The third man had some pulmonary complaint, and he only cringed and coughed under his punishment. He was off duty for several days after the flogging, which was the first he had ever received, and he felt the insult more than the injury, and was silent and sullen for the rest of the cruise.

The last of the four was a handsome lad about nineteen years old, and a great favorite in his part of the ship. He had often boasted of never having been flogged, and as he was tied to the gratings you could see the shuddering and creepings of his dazzlingly white back. At the first blow, the boy, shouting, "My God! Oh! My God," writhed and leaped so as to displace the gratings, and so scatter the nine tails of the scourge all over his person. At the next blow, he howled, leaped, and raged in unendurable torture. The dozen lashes were given through to the end and he was cut down, and wept, going among the crew, "I don't care what happens to me now. I have been flogged once and they may do it again, if they will. Let them look out for me now!"

Melville determined that he, for one, would never be scourged, and he was ready to do almost anything to avoid it. He attended carefully to all his duties, and when he had no duties, kept a good deal to himself and out of sight to avoid trouble. But one day toward the end of the cruise, his name was called through the ship, and he was summoned to the mast in great fear and loathing. He had failed to loose some sail which he had never known was assigned to him to be loosed. He stated his innocence boldly, but the captain refused to listen to him.

"There are times when wild thoughts enter a man's heart," he said, "when he seems almost irresponsible for his act and deed. The captain stood on the weatherside of the deck. Sideways, on an unobstructed line with him, was the opening of the lee gangway, where the side-ladders are suspended in port. Nothing but a slight bit of sinnet-stuff served to rail in this opening, which was cut right down to the level of the captain's feet, showing the far sea beyond. I stood a little to windward of him, and, though he was a large powerful man, it was certain that a sudden rush against him, along the slanting deck, would infallibly pitch him head-foremost into the ocean, though he who so rushed must needs go over with him. My blood seemed clotting in my veins; I felt icy cold at the tips of my fingers, and a dimness was before my eyes. But through that dimness the boatswain's mate, scourge in hand, loomed like a giant, and Captain Claret, and the blue sea seen through the opening at the gangway, showed with an awful vividness. I cannot analyze my heart, though it then stood still within me. But the thing that swayed me to my purpose was not altogether the thought that Captain Claret was about to degrade me, and that I had taken an oath with my soul that he should not. No, I felt my man's manhood so bottomless within me, that no word, no blow, no scourge of Captain Claret could cut me deep enough for that. I but swung to an instinct in me—the instinct diffused through all animated nature, the same that prompts even a worm to turn under the heel. Locking souls with him, I meant to drag Captain Claret from this earthly tribunal of his to that of Jehovah, and let Him decide between us. No other way could I escape the scourge."

At the last moment Melville was saved from being a murderer and a suicide by an almost unprecedented action on the part of Jack Chase and a corporal of Marines, both of whom defied tradition by speaking out for Melville, saying that they knew him to be a man who would not neglect a duty if he knew of it. The captain hesitated a moment in surprise, but he was not willing to ignore the pleas of two such respected men in the ship, and Melville was released. But Melville had been stirred as deeply as it is possible for a man to be stirred.

When he returned to America in October 1844, after his long voyage, he began to consider the things he had seen, and with a mind conditioned by his experiences, to reflect upon them and write his experiences and reflections down in his books. He was concerned by the contrast between European life and the life of the people of the islands, and with the tragic results of the meeting of these two cultures. He saw that the actions of the white men were based on a series of mistaken ideas,—ideas that the islanders were savages living in darkness, and that therefore they could properly be destroyed as wild animals or criminals are destroyed, and that thereafter, those whom it had not been necessary to kill could be benefitted by contact with the learning and the customs of an enlightened European civilization. Melville discovered, as any perceptive man might have done, that though the islanders were obviously not intellectuals, nor familiar with Christian doctrine, neither were they naturally savage, nor living in entire darkness. In some cases, they had been exasperated into savages by horrible cruelties committed against them by the Europeans, and Melville said that there was many a petty trader that had navigated the Pacific, whose course from island to island might be traced by a series of cold-blooded robberies, kidnappings and murders. Actions of this kind were justified by the comparative superiority the Europeans felt by virtue of their greater civilization. "Indeed, it is almost incredible," Melville said, "the light in which many sailors regard these naked heathens. They hardly consider them human. But it is a curious fact that the more ignorant and degraded men are, the more contemptuously they look upon those whom they deem their inferiors."

The more closely Melville observed native life, the deeper became his admiration for Polynesian culture, and the more detached his perspective on what was generally termed civilization. Not only did the islanders seem to him infinitely more happy than civilized man; the differences went deeper than surface happiness. He wondered for a long time how social order could exist among the Typees, as it surely did, when there were no laws, no courts, and no police. "It must have been by an inherent principle of honesty and charity towards each other," he said. "They seemed to be governed by that sort of tacit common-sense law which, say what they will of the inborn lawlessness of the human race, has its precepts graven on every breast. The grand principles of virtue and honor, however they may be distorted by arbitrary codes, are the same all the world over: and where these principles are concerned, the right or wrong of any action appears the same to the uncultivated as to the enlightened mind. It is to this in-dwelling, this universally diffused perception of what is *just* and *noble* that the integrity of the Marquesans in their intercourse with each other is to be attributed. In the darkest nights they slept securely, with all their worldly wealth around them, in houses the doors of which were never fastened. The disquieting ideas of theft or assassination never disturbed them. Each islander reposed beneath his own palmetto thatching, or sat under his own bread-fruit tree, with none to molest or alarm him. There was not a padlock in the valley, nor anything that answered the purpose of one: still there was no community of goods."

Melville saw that civilization did not engross all the virtues of humanity, and had not even her full share of them. They flourished in greater abun-dance and attained greater strength among many barbarous people. He cited the hospitality of the Arab, the courage of the North American In-dian, and the faithful friendships of some of the Polynesian nations, as far surpassing anything of a similar kind among the polished communities of Europe and America. But civilization had its full share of vices and misery. Melville asks if the infrequent cannibalism which the Marquesans prac-ticed as a way of revenging themselves on their enemies, was really more barbarous than the drawing and quartering of criminals as it had been done in enlightened England until a very few years before,—a practice by which a convicted traitor, perhaps a man found guilty of honesty, patriotism, and such heinous crimes, had his head lopped off with a huge axe, his bowels dragged out and thrown into a fire, while his body, carved into four quarters, was with his head exposed upon pikes, and permitted to rot and fester among the public haunts of men.

"The fiend-like skill we display in the invention of all manner of death-dealing engines, the vindictiveness with which we carry on our wars, and the misery and desolation that follow in their train, are enough of themselves to distinguish the white civilized man as the most ferocious animal on the face of the earth."

"And what's the use of bein' *snivelized*?" asks one of the characters in *Redburn*, "snivelized chaps only learns the way to take on 'bout life, and snivel. You don't see any Methodist chaps feelin' dreadful about their souls; you don't see any darned beggars and pesky constables in *Madagasky*, I tell ye. . . . Are *you* now, Buttons, any better off for bein' snivelized? No; you ar'n't a bit—but you're a good deal worse for it, Buttons. I tell ye, ye wouldn't have been to sea here, leadin' this dog's life, if you hadn't been snivelized—that's the cause why, now. Snivelization has been the ruin on ye; and it's spiled me complete; I might have been a great man in Madagasky; it's too darned bad! Blast Ameriky, I say."

Surely, Melville must have felt considerable sympathy with this attitude, and yet he was a complex and honest enough person not to be entirely unsympathetic with another sailor who was this sailor's conversational adversary in *Redburn*,—a man who had seen a good deal of the civilized world and loved it, and found it a good and comfortable place to live in.

Melville found a certain amount of goodness and comfort even in the naval life aboard the frigate, though not a great deal, and there was much of it that he hated. He revolted against the very nature of the ship itself,—an armed man-of-war, bristling with guns, and signifying the whole savage system of civilized warfare, an activity which, it seemed to Melville, was one that struck both common sense and Christianity in the face, so that everything that was connected with it was foolish and brutal. Though Melville served in the Navy in a time of peace, it was a time of tension with England over the northwest boundary question, and rumors of a threatened war reached the *Neversink* in South American harbors. Melville found that the crew hated the idea of going into action, almost to a man. They had nothing to expect from a war but harder work and harder usage, wounds, a wooden leg or arm, and death. The officers, however, became increasingly cheerful and lively, for war, which held nothing for the sailor, might mean promotion and glory for the officers. How were the officers to be promoted, Melville asks, but over the buried heads of killed comrades and messmates; or how were they to gain glory but by the distinguished slaughter of their fellow-men? And he wonders when the time would come in which no class of men would hail the gathering of war clouds, and invoke them to burst. He felt that standing armies and navies kept the spirit of war alive during peace, and that as long as they existed, such a time would not come.

Melville also saw the contrast between the crew's reaction to rumors of war and the officers' reaction to the same rumors, as a single instance, among many that might be cited, showing the antagonism of their interests. He believed that this antagonism, in which they continually dwelt together in the ship, was not only inimical to any true fraternity amongst them, but also that it was a false antagonism that had been created and was maintained for just that purpose. He saw that the whole system of naval discipline was based on the setting of one man against another, of marine against sailor, and rank against rank: a system of cruel cogs and wheels, systematically grinding up in one common hopper everything that might help the moral well-being of the crew. If the sailor mutinied, it needed no urging for the marine to run a bayonet through his heart; or if the marine revolted, the sailor was eager to charge with his pike. If the captain had a grudge against a lieutenant or a lieutenant against a midshipman, how easy it was to torture him by official treatment which would not lay his superior officer open to legal rebuke. And if a midshipman had a grudge against a sailor, how easy for him by cunning practices born of a boyish spite to arrange to have the sailor flogged at the gangway. Melville saw a sinister vein of bitterness running through all the ramifications of rank and station aboard a man-of-war, an observation which might have been of less significance were it not for the fact that he saw a man-of-war as a picture in little of the world at large.

The bitter discipline of the Navy was framed and supported by the Articles of War, which the crew were required to hear read at monthly muster, and whose operation they witnessed daily. "How comes it that, by virtue of a law solemnly ratified by a Congress of freemen, the representatives of freemen, thousands of Americans are subjected to the most despotic usage, and, from the dockyards of a republic, absolute monarchies are launched, with the 'glorious stars and stripes' for an ensign?" Melville asks. "By what unparalleled anomaly, by what monstrous grafting of tyranny upon freedom did these Articles of War ever come to be so much as heard of in the American Navy?" He discusses their origin and application at length, and with detachment as well as indignation, and he compares them with other less savage laws that had been devised in other times and places for the less savage government of seamen. Bad as the Articles of War might be in themselves, he saw that they were made more unjust by their execution in which those which were designed to punish sailors were strictly enforced, while those which applied to officers and sailors alike were ignored, at least insofar as they might be used against officers.

The most ordinary punishment aboard ship, and one from which officers were exempt, was flogging, which was administered at the discretion of the captain for almost any offense. This punishment, as has been seen, filled Melville with a special horror. He maintained vehemently that flogging was not lawful, since in its use on American ships it was opposed to the spirit of the Constitution, and was inconsistent with the legal principles developed by Blackstone and even Justinian; and beyond this, he asserted that flogging was opposed to the essential dignity of man which no legislator had a right to violate. "No matter then," he says, "what may be the consequences of its abolition; no matter if we have to dismantle our fleets, and our unprotected commerce should fall a prey to the spoiler. . . . It is not a dollar and cents question of expediency; it is a matter of *right* and *wrong*. And if any man can lay his hand on his heart, and solemnly say that this scourging is right, let that man but once feel the lash on his own back, and in his agony you will hear the apostate call the seventh heavens to witness that it is *wrong*."

Though Melville did not feel that expediency was the right grounds on which to adjudge flogging, he knew that there was really nothing inexpedient about its abolition. Admiral Collingwood in England, and Commodore Stockton in America, had both demonstrated that flogging was not necessary to govern even the most desperate crews. And it had been the converse experience of many other captains that flog as hard and as often as they would, crime and disorder did not disappear. But, in any event, he felt that depravity in the oppressed was no apology for the oppressor, nor was the ignorance of men an excuse for tyrannizing over them.

Melville's plea for the abolition of flogging is so impassioned and so straightforward, that it may be surprising to find his realization elsewhere in *White Jacket*, that flogging was not an isolated problem,—that to abolish the scourge would not be to abolish tyranny. He felt that that tyranny was an outgrowth of the basic antagonism and unequal division of strength within the ship, and a reflection again of the nature of a man-of-war, the object of which, as its name indicated, was to fight those battles which its crew was averse to fighting.

He saw that all these factors somehow worked together to produce what was considered the ideal type of sailor, the model citizen of the man-of-war world, a man so used to a hard life, so drilled and disciplined to servitude that he seemed to resign himself cheerfully to his fate. He had plenty to eat, spirits to drink, clothing to keep him warm, a hammock to sleep in, tobacco to chew, a doctor to medicine him, a parson to pray for him; to a man who had been a castaway and penniless, this could hardly help but seem a luxurious bill of fare.

A man whom Melville calls Landless was such a sailor. His back was scarred all over with years of floggings, and yet he enjoyed life with the zest of everlasting boyishness. He walked the prison-like decks of the frigate as though they were as broad as the prairie. Nothing ever disconcerted him; nothing could change his laugh into anything resembling a sigh. "Rum and tobacco," said Landless, "what more does a sailor want?"

"This Landless was a favorite with the officers, among whom he went by the name of 'Happy Jack,' " said Melville. "And it is just such Happy Jacks as Landless that most sea-officers profess to admire; a fellow without shame, without a soul, so dead to the least dignity of manhood that he could hardly be called a man. Whereas, a seaman who exhibits traits of moral sensitiveness, whose demeanor shows some dignity within; this is the man they, in many cases, instinctively dislike. The reason is, they feel such a man to be a continual reproach to them, as being mentally superior to their power. He has no business in a man-of-war; they do not want such men."

Before Melville had finished writing the four books that deal with his actual voyages,—when he had written only the first two, *Typee* and *Omoo*,—he embarked on a purely imaginary voyage in which he searched through the philosophies and social structures of the world for some frame of belief in which man could live in truth and dignity and freedom. This was his book *Mardi* where the world is represented as a South Seas archipelago, through which Melville and certain companions travel from island to island, searching for Yillah, the lost maiden of man's happiness.

Herman Melville was a fervent man who was unusually conscious of Christian teachings, and who read the English Bible not only as a writer might read it for its richly beautiful language, but also as one who was moved by its religious ardor. His religious feeling was too intense and personal to find much ease in the Christian Church. It seemed to him that the church cast a joyless shadow on the world, that its priests were frequently hypocritical, mercenary and ignorantly dogmatic, and its chronicles were a catalogue of horrors committed in the name of goodness. He felt that its greatest hostility was directed not against the ungodly, but against those men who felt God so deeply that they searched,—even with humility,—for religious truth in the world outside of the dogmas and complex formalities of the church.

Desirous as Melville was of believing in the divine mission of Jesus, he nevertheless reflected that Jesus came to dissipate errors, but thousands of errors originated in the various constructions of his principles had been added to the various errors that survived from the past; that Jesus came to do away with all gods but one, but since His day the idols of the church had more than quadrupled; that Jesus came to make men more virtuous and happy, but along with all the previous good, the same wars and crimes and miseries were still extant; that Jesus came to guarantee our eternal felicity, but according to what was held by the church, that felicity rested on so hard a proviso that, to a thinking mind, very few of our sinful race might secure it. Melville therefore was tempted to reject the whole doctrine of Christ, not because of all that was hard to be understood in the Gospels, but because of obvious and undeniable things in the world all around him which seemed to him at war with Christian doctrine as promulgated by the church. Even if he were not to make the rejection himself, he knew that the world had done so, that the maxims they so busily taught to the heathen in the hope of bringing about a millenium, were disregarded by the teachers. The whole social framework seemed opposed to the meekness of Christianity. On the one side was the heavenly wisdom of Jesus, and on the other side the practical wisdom of the earth, with its due appreciation of the necessities of nations, which at times demanded bloody wars and massacres, and its proper estimation of rank, of title, and of money.

Suppose there were a place where the heavenly and the worldly wisdoms were in accord. Melville made such a supposition. He called the imagined land Serenia, the place where reason and revelation were found to support one another. It is explained by one of the inhabitants of Serenia that right-reason and Christian precepts are the same,—that otherwise they would reject the precepts. For it is a reasonable, a rationalist, society which they have formed, a society which rejects the perfection of man but believes in a germ of goodness in man's heart which can be fostered to the benefit of society. Similarly, they have rejected the immediate perfection of the state because of the imperfection of its citizens. It seems to them a denial of the laws of reason to seek to breed equality by breeding anarchy, and there are therefore economic and social inequalities. But they are not so wide that any few men are happily supported by the miseries of many, nor does anyone starve while others feast. The vicious members of society are made to live apart from it until reclaimed by love and by reason.

There are no churches in Serenia, despite its religious basis, no prayers, no fasting, and no priests. The whole land is considered as God's church, the aspirations of men as their prayers, Jesus as a sufficient priest, and joyous Christian living a more acceptable form of worship than lugubrious fasting. All formal and verbal pieties are replaced by living practice: for "Of what merit, his precepts, unless they may be practiced?"

Melville supposed the land of Serenia and praised it. He thought that by its beauty it would seem desirable to a poet, by its rationality to a philosopher, by its enlightenment to an historian, and by its dignity and political wisdom to a king. For his own part, he rejected it.

Rejecting religious doctrine as an absolute faith, Melville also rejected political doctrines. He saw his own country, America, as the best political hope of the world, but he was disturbed by deep doubts about it. In a way, America was like the church, professing what it neither believed or practiced. The system of negro slavery was a continuous denial of the American doctrine of the freedom and equality of all men. It is apparent that in other respects, he thinks of America in the same terms as he thought of Serenia, as a mistaken millenium, a relative good misjudged as an absolute. Melville's *Mardi* was written during the period of the republican revolutions of mid-century Europe. He noticed the way in which America hailed the news of revolutionary successes as though they were the final and liberating victories in man's long social struggle,—victories, moreover, for which America had furnished the political inspiration. He felt, himself, that these revolutions were repellently violent and destructive, and yet that they were needed and some good would come from their violence,—a good that would in large part justify their destruction. They were not the final victory. He felt that the grand error of his age was the general belief that the very special Diabolus was abroad, whereas the very special Diabolus had been abroad since the world began. And he felt that the grand error of

184

his nation was the conceit that the world was now in the last scene of the last act of her drama, and that all preceding events had been ordained to bring about what they now believed to be at hand,—a universal and permanent Republic. "May it please you," he said, "those who hold to these things are fools, and not wise."

Thinking of the transitory nature of freedom in other ages and other countries, Melville wondered how long America could remain free. He knew that free horses needed wide prairies and that so far we had had room enough to be free, but that our physical space would not last forever. Or he saw America as a boy, free because young, full of fiery impulses and hard to restrain, his strong hand working to champion his heart, defying the oppressor and scaling at a bound the high walls of old opinion, at once generous and acquisitive. But the years elapse and the bold boy is transformed. His heart is shut up as a vice. Seeking no more acquisitions, he is only intent on preserving his hoard. The maxims once trampled underfoot are now printed on his forehead, and he who hated oppressors, is become an oppressor himself. Americans were a great and glorious people, and this the best and happiest land under the sun, but not wholly because in our wisdom we had decided to have it so. It was partly due to our geography and our newness.

Melville could not separate the idea of universal freedom and equality from something else he had seen which worked counter to it,—the inbred servility of mortal to mortal, and the organic causes which seemed inevitably to divide mankind into brigades and battalions with captains at their head. It was in much that way that the men in the *Neversink* had been divided, and now the division seemed natural and unavoidable. Moreover, if it were true that it is easier to govern others than to govern oneself, and it seemed to be true, then a nation of free men would require that all men be better and wiser than the wisest of governors had ever been. But Melville had never heard of a stable democracy in which all men governed themselves. "Though an army be all volunteers," he said, "martial law must prevail."

He saw that individual freedom in a democracy was in double danger from a people's tyranny on one side, and from a lawless anarchy on the other. Freedom was not the exclusive property of democracy; there had been free men under caesars and kings. And indeed it was better on all hands that peace should rule with a sceptre, than that the tribunes of the people should brandish their broadswords; better to be the subject of a just and upright king than to be a free man in France with the executioner's axe on every corner; better to be secure under one king than to be exposed to the violence of twenty million monarchs where every man was king. What was called political freedom, therefore, was good as a means only. It was not the prime end or the chief blessing. The freedom which Melville desired was more social than political, and its real felicity was not to be shared. "That is of a man's own individual getting and holding," he said. "It is not who rules the state, but who rules me."

He turned again to the past and its alternations, to the bloody wars and tyrannies that sooner or later had always and inevitably followed the periods of peace and liberality. If time could be reversed and the future change places with the past, the past would cry out against us and our future as we cry out now against the savagery of the past. There was evil in the world and though it might be assuaged, it could not be done away with. Where, then, was the final answer to man's social problem?

There was no answer.

The whole world was like that world in *Typee*, in which the idyllic life was an isolation and captivity; like that world of the South Seas, in which the apostles of goodness and enlightenment necessarily brought evil and destruction with them; like the world of the desertion from the *Dolly* and the mutiny aboard the *Julia*, where freedom and protest against social abuses were aspects of disorder and anarchy. It was like the world in a man-of-war aboard the *Neversink*, a world committed to hostility and violence, where the magnanimous Jack Chase was side by side with the deceptively evil Bland, and where tyranny and degradation were so ingrained that to abolish flogging would hardly touch them. These were not temporary problems which any one generation could solve for themselves and all the generations to come. They were permanent and constantly recurrent problems. The 'very special Diabolus' of social evil had been abroad since the world began.

Evil was too persistent and man too equivocal for a final answer. Melville saw this truth and believed it. But no such belief can be easily acceptable to a man. It is one thing to see and another to believe; it is one thing to believe and another to accept belief.

To one who strove toward social goodness for man, it must often have seemed that man himself is the chief obstacle to goodness.

"Man's vicious: snaffle him with kings," says one of the speakers in *Clarel*.

"Or if kings cease to curb, devise
  Severer bit."

But man was not entirely vicious and some men were hardly so at all. A social answer based on man's viciousness would be wrong. On the other hand, it would be foolish and equally wrong to base a society on complete confidence in the goodness of man. In his relations to good and evil, man was ambiguous. The terror of this ambiguity is the substance of Melville's novel, *The Confidence Man*, which he wrote in 1856, in the harsh light and heavy shadows of the deeps of despair. Melville had arrived at the knowledge that the answer to man's social problem would need to be based on a judgment of man's nature, and would involve a distinction between what was good and what was evil. But simultaneously, he arrived at the further knowledge that the conflict between good and evil was like a wrestling match, where the opponents are not only at variance, but are deeply entangled. This same knowledge, which Melville found so hard to accept, came to most of his contemporaries as a cynical perception which they accepted and used to such immediate advantage as they could. He began to see the whole world as though it were a river steamboat, swarming with petty swindlers who show the ambiguity of man at the same time that they make a mockery of it. The confidence men on the boat work their little swindles by an apparently disinterested preaching of trust in mankind, or by pleading the magnitude of wrongs charitably endured, the long-suffering of which has not deprived them of their kindness. They speak consequently of the good and evil usages to which people subject one another, and of the attitudes such usage should prompt. For their part, the gulls, who are also led to speak of these matters, are victimized because they are made to feel ashamed of so wretched and coarse a sentiment as mistrust, or because their expectation of great gain blinds them to swindles, or because apparent misfortune reminds them more that misfortune is commonplace and real and hard to bear, than it reminds them that misfortune is easily simulated. But few of the victims yield without a struggle. And therefore, just as the *Fidèle* shifts from bank to bank, and town to town, as she passes slowly down the river, so the course of the narrative shuttles from side to side, as in case after case the claims of trust and mistrust are alternately presented. But this struggle which goes on between the passengers of the ship, some of whom play philanthropist in order to steal better, and some of whom preach misanthropy in order to protect what they have, is only a kind of trivial and unreal masquerade in which high moral terms are the costumes beneath which the actual protagonists are seen to be only simplicity and craft, and the prize only a pocketbook. However unreal the struggle is in itself, it does reflect nevertheless a real uncertainty which in Melville's mind underlay it. Finding himself in the situation of a masquerade, in which all the issues had become almost intolerably confused, in which as a matter of fact, their very existence as issues of any importance was denied when they were used to conceal the actual swindling concerns of the masqueraders, Melville tenaciously clutched his own uncertainty like a golden bough. The reality of his uncertainty gave to even the figures of the masquerade, unreal and yet all-inclusive as they were, a certain relevance and even authority, just as an acute need for some mislaid object will lead a person to search once more in the places where he has already looked several times without being able to find it.

In *The Confidence Man* Melville writes about a world in which it is impossible to arrive at any unequivocal belief. He was a man to whom it would have been superfluous to give the warning which is given in the conversation quoted from *The Confidence Man* at the beginning of this essay, that someone was an equivocal character. The knowledge of equivocation was the common ground which he had with the swindlers. It was also the basis of a considerable difference. For tne confidence men, equivocation was a deliberate device which they could use to accomplish certain material ends. They could put on or throw off their disguise whenever it was desirable to do so, without being affected by the thought that their natures were therefore indeterminate, since the disguise was after all their own origination, and subject to their will, and indeed was simply a cloak that had nothing to do with their actual natures. Moreover, the success of their dissembling depended on their not representing but concealing their doubleness, so that equivocation forced them into the argumentativeness and narrow singleness of the conversations which they, the apparent philanthropists, had with the misanthropes. But they were not, themselves, convinced by the assertions which they made, and therefore were not, in their own eyes, ambiguous. Melville, who was aware of their dissembled belief and their actual beliefs, valued the two equally, since both were partly convincing and neither fully so. To him, therefore, they were not only ambiguous, but their ambiguity was inescapable and beyond their control.

The torture of an intolerable ambiguity caused Melville to cry out against the very structures he had found to be the finest and most hopeful in the world,—against Christianity and against American freedom. In the long philosophical poem, *Clarel*, most of which was written at various periods during the late eighteen-fifties and early sixties, a man stands in Jerusalem near the arch called Ecce Homo, where Jesus is said to have been displayed to the people by Pilate before the crucifixion.

No raptures which with saints prevail,
Nor trouble of compunction born
He felt, as there he seemed to scan
Aloft in spectral guise, the pale
Still face, the purple robe, and thorn;
And inly cried—*Behold the Man!*
Yon man it is this burden lays:
Even He who in the pastoral hours,
Abroad in fields, and cheered by flowers,
Announced a heaven's unclouded days;
And, ah, with such persuasive lips—
Those lips now sealed while doom delays—
Won men to look for solace there;
But, crying out in death's eclipse,
When rainbow none His eyes might see,
Enlarged the margin for despair—
My God, My God, forsakest Me?

Upbraider! we upbraid again;
Thee we upbraid; our pangs constrain
Pathos itself to cruelty.
Ere yet Thy day no pledge was given
Of homes and mansions in the heaven—
Paternal homes reserved for us;
Heart hoped it not but lived content—
Content with life's own discontent,
Nor deemed that fate ere swerved for us;
The natural law men let prevail;
Then reason disallowed the state
Of instinct's variance from fate.
But Thou—ah, see, in rack how pale

Who did the world with throes convulse;
Behold Him—yea—behold the Man
Who warranted if not began
The dream that drags out its repulse.

   Nor less some cannot break from Thee;
Thy love so locked is with Thy lore,
They may not rend them and go free:
The head rejects; so much the more
The heart embraces—what? the love?
If true what priests avouch of Thee,
The shark Thou mad'st, yet claim'st the dove.

   Nature and Thee in vain we search:
Well urged the Jews within the porch—
'How long wilt make us still to doubt?'
How long?—'Tis eighteen cycles now—
Enigma and evasion grow;
And shall we never find Thee out?
What isolation lones Thy state
That all we else know cannot mate
With what Thou teachest? Nearing Thee
All footing fails us; history
Shows there a gulf where bridge is none!
In lapse of unrecorded time
Just after the apostles' prime,
What chance or craft might break it down?
Served this a purpose? By what art
Of conjuration might the heart
Of heavenly love, so sweet, so good,
Corrupt into the creeds malign,
Begetting strife's pernicious brood,
Which claimed for patron Thee divine?

  Anew, Anew,
For this Thou bleedest, Anguished Face;
Yea, Thou through ages to accrue,
Shalt the Medusa shield replace:

In beauty and in terror too
Shalt paralyse the nobler race—
Smite or suspend, perplex, deter—
Tortured, shalt prove a torturer.
Whatever ribald Future be,
Thee shall these heed, amaze their hearts with Thee—
Thy white, Thy red, Thy fairness, and Thy tragedy.

And in the same poem, a humorless man, an idealistic southerner who has exiled himself from his country, embittered by the bitterness of the Civil War, speaks out a feeling that was partly, if not always and entirely Melville's. Addressing a man who has lost both an arm and a leg in the war for Mexican freedom, he says,

Ay, Democracy
Lops, lops; but where's her planted bed?
The future, what is that to her
Who vaunts she's no inheritor?
'Tis in her mouth, not in her heart.
The Past she spurns, though 'tis the Past
From which she gets her saving part—
That Good which lets her Evil last.
Behold her whom the panders crown,
Harlot on horseback, riding down
The very Ephesians who acclaim
This great Diana of ill fame!
Arch-strumpet of an impious age,
Upstart from ranker villanage,
'Tis well she must restriction taste
Nor lay the world's broad manor waste:
Asia shall stop her at the least
That old inertness of the East.

Yet during the period of the Civil War, he reached a kind of equilibrium of doubt, which though not an entire peace with himself and the world, was nevertheless more than a merely negative resignation to the problem. Since there was no final answer to be found for man's social problem, and no complete definition of man, then the ambiguity of man should be positively maintained in opposition to any solution offered and claimed as final.

YEA AND NAY—
EACH HATH HIS SAY;
BUT GOD HE KEEPS THE MIDDLE WAY.
NONE WAS BY
WHEN HE SPREAD THE SKY
WISDOM IS VAIN AND PROPHECY.

"Let us revere," he said at this period, "that sacred uncertainty which forever impends over men and nations."

Melville's poems of the Civil War show him as subject to variant emotions, and the symbol which he offers himself is that of a harp placed in the window and played on by the wind. War and slavery were both repugnant to him, and as the darkness and brutality of war closed in, so far as this was a war against slavery, he exulted in it. Moreover, he could not be insensitive to the courage, the sacrifice and the magnanimity which the war brought with it along with its many evils. In the reconstruction period, he spoke out in a plea for understanding for the South. He felt that patriotism need not be narrow, or base, or inhumane, and that the northern zeal for complete and immediate reform of the conquered states was not necessarily patriotism. To rejoice in the triumph of the North was right only insofar as that triumph implied an advance for the whole country and for humanity. The triumph had been won by superior resources and crushing numbers, rather than by greater skill, or bravery, or righteousness. It was not in itself an advance or pacification; nor could pacification be brought about by law-making, however anxious or energetic or repressive, if unaided by generosity of sentiment. He saw that emancipation had not been brought about by legislation but by agonized violence. And now he said, "Let us be Christians toward our fellow-whites, as well as philanthropists toward the blacks, our fellow-men. In all things we are enjoined to do as we would be done by. Nor should we forget that benevolent desires, after passing a certain point, can not undertake their own fulfillment without incurring the risk of evils beyond those sought to be remedied. Something may well be left to the graduated care of future legislation, and to heaven. . . . With certain evils men must be more or less patient."

He had learned a little patience and was willing to leave something to heaven. "Let us pray," he said, "that the terrible historic tragedy of our time may not have been enacted without instructing our whole beloved country through terror and pity."

Problems of Confidence and Evil

A knowledge of ambiguity was an early awareness with Herman Melville, and it became a principal instrument of his mind, just as ambiguity itself was a pervasive and abiding characteristic of his world. Ambiguity appears in concrete and simple terms in *Typee*, which was the first of his books. The island of Nukuheva, to which Melville and his shipmate Toby fled from the whaleship *Dolly*, was divided into series of valleys which were separated from each other by steep ranges radiating outward from the central mountains. Melville and Toby meant to lose their pursuers in the mountains and then come down into the valley of the Happars, who were said to be a gentle and well-disposed people. They intended to avoid at all costs the valley of Typee, where the natives were ferocious cannibals. But they lost their way in the mountains, and came down into that valley without knowing where they were, and hardly caring, so close to death were they from fatigue and hunger and injuries. When they were challenged by the suspicious natives, some presentiment or stroke of luck led Melville to express approval of the Typees and contempt for the Happars. The ferocious savages were immediately delighted, affectionate and kindly. The Typees thought of the Happars with horror for their coarseness and brutality. Actually, the two tribes were alike, capable of both gentleness and savagery, and their similarity extended to the fear and hatred with which each one regarded the other.

It was hard for Melville himself to resolve the incongruous elements in Typee life. In every household in the valley, he was received with consideration and respect and an affectionate happiness for his company. Yet when he talked of leaving the valley and finding a ship for home, they were cold or even threatening, and made it clear that he was not to be allowed to leave. He wondered despairingly if they could be saving him for an eventual feast. Nothing in their daily lives, in their simple and innocent employments, in their cleanliness, beauty and kindness, was consistent with the generally held ideas of heathen cannibals.

Melville found that almost nothing in the world resembled his expectations. As a boy, he had romantic notions of distance. On his first voyage, the real strangeness of Liverpool was not in its unfamiliarity, but in its

194

surprising resemblance to New York or even to Albany. He carried with him on this trip a guide book which had belonged to his father, and he studied it carefully aboard the ship. But the city had changed so greatly in the almost half a century since the guide book was printed, that it was nearly useless to him. It was not entirely false. There were ghosts and recollections of what he had expected to see. Where the guide book had shown a fort, there now stood a place called the Old Fort Tavern.

A very large amount of Melville's later experience was of this same character. He looked about the world as at a strange city and often had a feeling almost of mistaken destination such as he might have had if having set out for one place and taken the proper road, at the last minute he had unaccountably arrived at some other place whose existence had been unsuspected, and which in its jumbling of barely recognizable and totally alien elements, seemed less a second place than an elusive suggestion and cruel disguise, or new and threatening manifestation of the first. It was impossible to assume that the original conception, though mistaken in particulars, was entirely false.

For a long time and in spite of contrary evidence, he clung to a belief which was shared by many men of his time, a belief that America was indeed a New World. "The other world beyond this, which was longed for by the devout before Columbus' time, was found in the New," he says in *Redburn*, "and the deep-sea-lead, that first struck these soundings, brought up the soil of Earth's Paradise. Not a Paradise then, or now; but to be made so at God's good pleasure, and in the fullness and mellowness of time. The seed is sown, and the harvest must come; and our children's children on the world's jubilee morning shall go with their sickles to the reaping." It was not a lack of the desire or will to believe that led to his subsequent political detachment.

One day while Melville was living with the Typees, a stranger appeared in the valley and was greeted with pleasure and enthusiasm by all the natives. This was a most unusual event, for the stranger was not one of the Typees, and so far as Melville had been able to learn, there was a complete absence of friendly intercourse among the mutually hostile tribes of Nukuheva. But Melville discovered later that there could be exceptions to the general hostility. A member of one tribe might ratify a friendship, perhaps, with one of a neighboring tribe; and so great was the Polynesian respect for friendship that his person would be tabooed in the adjoining valley, and he would be able to come amongst the enemy people unharmed so long as he came without hostility or design. The stranger who appeared that day amongst the Typees was such a person. He was tabooed in all the valleys of the island and so wandered about freely, carrying the news, and was received with special respect and interest because he had one time sailed on a ship with the white men and had lived for a while in Australia. Melville saw in this man's position certain likenesses to his own, and he called his second book *Omoo*, a dialect term which signified a rover, a wanderer, one who moved about from island to island protected by the operation of the taboo, which was at once a passport and an isolation and detachment. He had begun to feel isolated and detached in the world. His nature was warm and enthusiastic; but his warmth was often met with a cold stare, and his initial enthusiasms were moderated by the changing lights of experience. The Omoo title might almost have been extended to the long allegorical novel *Mardi*, his third book, in which he travels through the island archipelago of the world of behaviors, ideas, and politics. In large portions of this book Melville himself quite disappears except as an impersonal narrator, and his own attitudes merge variously with those of the island king and his companions, the philosopher, the poet, and the historian. It appears, though, that an element of vindictiveness is slowly being introduced into what had been an impassive relationship with the world, and the figure of Omoo changes, fearfully at first and then with resignation, to the Biblical figure of Ishmael who was the son of the barren Sarah's handmaid, and who was cast out with his mother into the desert to become a wild man and a wanderer. In *Redburn* he spoke of an unwilling isolation from the crew, of the loneliness of being without a single friend or companion, and of the hatred which began to grow in his heart as a reaction to the loneliness. He looked on this feeling with such horror that he said he prayed against it.

There is a somewhat similar isolation in *White Jacket*. He said he had not been aboard the frigate long before he discovered that it would not do to be intimate with everybody. He kept to his own section of the ship and to a few trusted companions because he saw that an indiscriminate mingling led to sundry annoyances and scrapes which were likely to end up in a flogging, the great fear which hung over that ship like the fear of death in a plague. He makes his attitude doubly evident by speaking of a friend of his, a man called Nord, as a wandering recluse among the man-of-war mob, and one who had apparently reached the same conclusion.

Coupled with his isolation, however, was another feeling of identification with the crew, an identification that he might have shunned at an earlier period. "Whenever employed in killing time in harbor," he said, "I have lifted myself up on my elbow and looked around me, and seen so many of my shipmates all employed at the same common business; all under lock and key; all hopeless prisoners like myself; all under martial law; all dieting on salt beef and biscuit; all in one uniform; all yawning, gaping and stretching in concert, it was then that I used to feel a certain love and affection for them, grounded, doubtless, on a fellow-feeling.

"And though in a previous part of this narrative, I have mentioned that I used to hold myself somewhat aloof from the mass of seamen on board the *Neversink*; and though this was true, and my real acquaintances were comparatively few, and my intimates still fewer, yet, to tell the truth, it is quite impossible to live so long with five hundred of your fellow beings, even if not of the best families in the land, and with morals that would not be spoiled by further cultivation; it is quite impossible, I say, to live with five hundred of your fellow beings, be they what they may, without feeling a common sympathy with them at the time, and ever after cherishing some sort of interest in their welfare."

Melville's early concept of evil was simple and straightforward, and is well exemplified in the *Redburn* portrait of Jackson, the sailor who was his bitter and corrosive enemy on the first voyage. Jackson was ugliness rather than beauty, hatred rather than love; he was malevolent, destructive, and an enemy of whatever was gentle or kindly or lovely, of anything that had health and wholeness. At the same time, he noted a certain gallantry and daring in Jackson. It was one of his characteristics that though he would shy away from dull work in a calm, yet in tempest-time he always claimed the van and would yield it to no one; and Melville reflected that this, perhaps, was one cause of his unbounded dominion over the men. Jackson was killed before the voyage was up, when he fell from the extreme weather-end of the topsail-yard while reefing the sails in a gale. And when Melville says, "I have pitied no man as I have pitied him," or elsewhere, "And I sometimes fancied, it was the consciousness of his miserable, broken-down condition, and the prospect of soon dying like a dog, in consequence of his sins, that made this poor wretch always eye me with such malevolence as he did," then it is evident that the ambiguities of Melville's attitudes are at work, and the concept of evil which he had expressed in a faulty and obscure way in his third book, *Mardi*, are still operative in his mind.

This is the framework of *Mardi*: the narrator in a small boat in the South Seas, together with a primordial sailor and a primordial savage, rescues the beautiful maiden, Yillah, the soul, the serenity of man, from an island priest and his sons who have been taking her to be sacrificed. In the course of the rescue the old priest is killed. The narrator and Yillah live blissfully until Yillah suddenly disappears. Then with new companions, the narrator starts a search of all the islands of Mardi in order to find Yillah again. Throughout the journey, the searchers are pursued by avengers, the sons of the priest, and repeatedly encounter the messengers of Hautia, the darkly beautiful queen, sensuous and evil, who seeks to allure them to her island. When everywhere else has been searched, the narrator finally goes to Hautia's island, and though Yillah is not found there, there are indications that she may have been held there captive, during the search, or in any event that Hautia has the key to the mystery. The book ends obscurely and inconclusively with the narrator embarked on a new search which is endless and despairing.

At one point in the narrative, the companion philosopher has an apocalyptic vision in which it is revealed to him that the unique characteristic of God, the basis of the universe, is the understanding of evil, and the path to salvation and holiness is knowledge.

It is not surprising, therefore, that the portrait of the evil man, Bland, in *White Jacket*, is more ambiguous and subtle, more sympathetic, than that of Jackson in *Redburn*. Bland's nature is not outwardly repulsive; it is not known to most of the men of the ship. Moreover, he is helpless in his evil as though he were a necessary and blameless part of the universe, and his wicked deeds the legitimate operation of his whole infernal organization. "But, however it was," said Melville, "I, for one, regarded this master-at-arms with mixed feelings of detestation, pity, admiration, and something opposed to enmity. I could not but abominate him when I thought of his conduct; but I pitied the continual gnawing which under all his deftly-donned disguises, I saw lying at the bottom of his soul. I admired his heroism in sustaining himself so well under such reverses. And when I thought how arbitrary the *Articles of War* are in defining a man-of-war villain; how much undetected guilt might be sheltered by the aristocratic awning of our man-of-war quarter-deck; how many florid pursers, ornaments of the ward-room, had been legally protected in defrauding the *people*, I could not but say to myself, well, after all, though this man is a most wicked one indeed, yet he is even more luckless than depraved."

When Melville identifies himself, the narrator, as Ishmael, at the very beginning of *Moby Dick*, it is done so casually and briefly that it may pass unnoticed that this is an identity against whose consequences he had spoken of praying in *Redburn*, and it may not be remembered that the Biblical Ishmael was one of whom the angel said, 'his hand will be against every man, and every man's hand against him; and he shall dwell in the presence of all his brethren.' Similarly, the character of Ahab, the protagonist of the story, is drawn so sympathetically, and the reader so easily identifies himself for the moment with this heroic figure, that it may be forgotten Ahab is an evil man, one of a series of portraits of evil men. That these things are so, is an indication of Melville's increased understanding of evil, his growing awareness of its complex ambiguity, and his equally growing sympathy with it.

Toward the end of the book, when the wild chase is nearly over, and the fiercely vindictive Ahab is softened momentarily by the mildness of the weather and the sad fatality of the nearing end, he thinks back with sorrow on his forty years of whaling, forty years of peril and privation, and storm-time, and desolate solitude, on the pitiless sea, forty years of forsaking the peaceful land to make war on the horrors of the deep, and he calls himself a fool.

"What is it," he asks, "what nameless, inscrutable, unearthly thing is it; what cozening, hidden lord and master, and cruel, remorseless emperor commands me; that against all natural lovings and longings, I so keep pushing and crowding, and jamming myself on all the time; and recklessly making myself ready to do what in my own proper, natural heart, I durst not so much as dare?" Ahab refuses the humanitarian action begged of him by the captain of the *Rachel*,—assistance in the search for the *Rachel*'s lost whaleboat whose castaways included the captain's son. For Ahab, when the request was made, was closing in on Moby Dick, the whale, the *great* inhumanity. At another time, he has no interest in casting the chains of his lightning-rods over the side in a storm, and tells the mate he'll contribute though to raising rods on the Himmalehs and Andes that all the world may be secured. The nameless, inscrutable, unearthly thing, the cruel, remorseless emperor, that has made Ahab vindictive, and cruel, and inhumane, is the inhumanity of the natural world, and the realization that, in acknowledging his fullest stature, in becoming truly human rather than merely humane, man is forced to share in the organic evil of the universe. This is the trap against which Ahab is fighting, a trap like one of those ingenious mechanisms in which one is more deeply ensnared the harder one fights against it. Ahab is the strong man, the real master of the crew, not merely because he is the ship's captain, but because he is the maimed man who lives with more force and clearer focus, by virtue of a quarrel with the world. He is not content to live a cautious, inoffensive life, like a well-trained servant.

There was a great whale in the sea, larger and fiercer than other whales, white-skinned, solitary and elusive, known to the men of the fishery as Moby Dick. Many ships had tried to take him, but he was a killer that chewed their boats to matchwood and crushed the occupants in his great, crooked jaw, or dumped them drowning into the sea. In one such encounter, Ahab had lost a leg. Enraged and maddened by the frustration and physical pain, he came to identify the whale with not only his bodily woes but all his intellectual and spiritual exasperations. "The White Whale swam before him as the monomaniac incarnation of all those malicious agencies which some deep men feel eating in them, till they are left living on with half a heart and half a lung. That intangible malignity which has been from the beginning; to whose dominion even the modern Christians ascribe one-half of the worlds; which the ancient Ophites of the east reverenced in their statue devil;—Ahab did not fall down and worship it like them; but deliriously transferring its idea to the abhorred White Whale, he pitted himself, all mutilated, against it. All that most maddens and torments; all that stirs up the lees of things; all truth with malice in it; all that cracks the sinews and cakes the brain; all the subtle demonisms of life and thought; all evil, to crazy Ahab, were visibly personified and made practically assailable in Moby Dick. He piled upon the whale's white hump the sum of all the general rage and hate felt by his whole race from Adam down; and then, as if his chest had been a mortar, he burst his hot heart's shell upon it."

Melville himself, as Ishmael, rounds out Ahab's concept of the whale, and broadens it. The whale is the source of evil to Ahab, but as he knows without expressing it, there would be no point in seeking to gain mastery over him unless the whale were also the source of satisfaction. Ahab's struggle is against the center of life, and Ishmael makes this clear. He speaks of the sailor superstition that Moby Dick was both ubiquitous and immortal; but the source of the greatest awe inspired by the whale was in his whiteness as a symbol of horror, and of the frustration inherent in the infinite. The association of horror with whiteness is an unreasoning thing, but the feeling is real. Melville believed in the reality of horror, 'the instinct of the knowledge of the demonism of the world,' and he knew that somewhere behind the material objects which arbitrarily or foolishly inspire it, the real things must exist; that though 'in many of its aspects this world seems formed in love, the invisible spheres were formed in fright.'

"But not yet," he said, "have we solved the incantation of this whiteness, and learned why it appeals with such power to the soul; and more strange and far more portentous—why, as we have seen, it is at once the most meaningful symbol of spiritual things, nay, the very veil of the Christian's Deity; and yet should be as it is, the intensifying agent in things most appalling to mankind.

"Is it that by its indefiniteness it shadows forth the heartless voids and immensities of the universe, and thus stabs us from behind with the thought of annihilation, when beholding the white depths of the milky way? Or is it that as in essence, whiteness is not so much a color as the visible absence of color, and at the same time the concrete of all colors; is it for these reasons that there is such a dumb blankness, full of meaning, in a wide landscape of snows—a colorless, all-color of atheism from which we shrink? And when we consider that other theory of the natural philosophers, that all other earthly hues—every stately or lovely emblazoning—the sweet tinges of sunset skies and woods; yea and the gilded velvet of butterflies, and the butterfly cheeks of young girls; all these are but subtile deceits, not actually inherent in substances, but only laid on from without; so that all deified Nature absolutely paints like the harlot, whose allurements cover nothing but the charnel-house within; and when we proceed farther and consider that the mystical cosmetic which produces every one of her hues, the great principle of light forever remains white or colorless in itself, and if operating without medium upon matter, would touch all objects, even tulips and roses with its own blank tinge—pondering all this, the palsied universe lies before us a leper; and like willful travelers in Lapland, who refuse to wear colored and coloring glasses upon their eyes, so the wretched infidel gazes himself blind at the monumental white shroud that wraps all the prospect around him. And of all these things the Albino whale was the symbol. Wonder ye then at the fiery hunt?"

The realities which the white whale represented for Melville were so large and important that they could not all be contained in Moby Dick, but extended outward to include all whales. "Who can show a pedigree like Leviathan?" he asks, thinking of the great age of the species. "Ahab's harpoon had shed older blood than the Pharaoh's. Methuselah seems a schoolboy. I look round to shake hands with Shem. I am horror-struck at this ante-mosaic, unsourced existence of the unspeakable terrors of the whale, which, having been before all time, must needs exist after all humane ages are over." And again, "Wherefore, for all these things, we account the whale immortal in his species, however perishable in his individuality. He swam the seas before the continents broke water; he once swam over the site of the Tuilleries and Windsor Castle, and the Kremlin. In Noah's flood, he despised Noah's Ark; and if ever the world is to be again flooded, like the Netherlands, to kill off its rats, then the eternal whale will still survive, and rearing upon the topmost crest of the equatorial flood, spout his frothed defiance to the skies."

Beyond Moby Dick, or whales as a species, the symbol of tantalizing and elusive reality is extended to the sea itself, as when Melville speculates on the fascination that the sea or any water holds for us, and says, "Surely all this is not without meaning. And still deeper the meaning of that story of Narcissus, who because he could not grasp the tormenting, mild image he saw in the fountain, plunged into it and was drowned. But that same image, we ourselves see in all rivers and oceans. It is the image of the ungraspable phantom of life; and this is the key to it all."

Beyond whales or the sea, the symbol of impersonal, indifferent, resistant reality was extended to one of the whaler's crew, the carpenter. The carpenter was a 'stript abstract,' an 'unfractioned integral.' He worked with wood, or bone, or any material indifferently, and was expert at all manner of mechanical trades. There was an impersonal stolidity about him that so shaded off into the surrounding infinite of things 'that it seemed one with the general stolidity discernible in the whole visible world; which while pauselessly active in uncounted modes, still eternally holds its peace and ignores you though you dig foundations for cathedrals.' And this half-horrible stolidity seemed to involve an all-ramifying heartlessness.

It was with a similar impersonal stolidity and heartlessness that Moby Dick attacked the boats of whaling vessels whether they pursued him or not. The attack was effortless, swift, and final; and the first sight of the whale swimming through the waters, so beautifully, with such calm and serenity, gave no indication at all of the full terror of his submerged trunk and hideous jaw. It is as against indifferent heartlessness that Ahab's defiance of the whale gains much of its significance, as in his declaration that 'in the midst of the personified impersonal, a personality stands here,' or in his assertion that 'nor White Whale, nor man, nor fiend can so much as graze old Ahab in his own proper and inaccessible being,' or in his final act of defiance when he addresses Moby Dick as, 'thou all-destroying but unconquering whale; to the last I grapple with thee; from hell's heart I stab at thee; for hate's sake I spit my last breath at thee.'

This is a notably serene and objective book in spite of all Ahab's intense and bitter passions. Ahab is foredoomed by his very nature, and though there is no lack of suspense, his final destruction is impending and inevitable from the first. Ishmael is a participant and yet retains a little area of detachment, and he is the sole survivor of the general disaster, picked up from the water and saved by the cruising *Rachel*, humanely searching the sea for her own castaways. It is the triumphant serenity of the natural world which sounds the final note in the book. But in a sense, the temptation not to survive, to be only Ahab, must have been very strong for Melville as can be seen in subsequent books. The cost of maintaining a serene objectivity was high indeed. The existence in a single world and at the same time of Ahab's titanic and inhuman tortures, and the homely, kindly humanities of Starbuck, who was Ahab's chief mate, and the need to acknowledge their equal truth, was nearly insurmountable. One is reminded of Melville's figure of the Wandering Jew, in the masque scene in *Clarel*, in which the Jew who is forced to share in every guilt in the world, says,

"Go mad I cannot: I maintain
The perilous outpost of the sane."

It was an almost heroic action not to go mad in Melville's lonely world of dubieties and incongruous elements, to maintain some vestige of a faith in a world of doubts and ambiguous evils. Melville had tried to explain his world in the previous book, *Mardi*. It was a failure. *Moby Dick*, which was a much greater book, deeper and more accurate and exacting, a plainer exposition of reality, was written with an evident faith in public acceptance and understanding. But it, too, was a public failure, and ignored by Melville's contemporaries. The desert outcast Ishmael had made every overture consistent with truth to his comfortably housed and accepted brothers, and all the overtures went unnoticed. The disappointment and the economic hardship which resulted could not help but influence his later attitudes.

There is a new element in *Moby Dick*, an element which gives Melville's

work the dimension of greatness, the element of wonder. As much as anything else no doubt, it sustained him through disappointment. "The great
floodgates of the wonder world swung open," he said. This attitude is
recurrent. In the next book, *Pierre*, he speaks of the face of Isabel as one of
those faces which "compounded so of hell and heaven, overthrow in us
all foregone persuasions, and make us wondering children in this world
again." He knew that such a response to the world was a reflection of the
mystery which man is within himself, and he said that we had no cause
ever to fancy that a dog or a horse or a fowl would stand transfixed by the
majesty of the sky, as men do. And indeed, it was only man's sense of his
own wonder, only the arches of the soul underfitting the sky's arches,
which could prevent the upper arch from falling on us with an inscrutable-
ness we could not sustain. Again he asks, "Is it possible, after all, that spite
of bricks and shaven faces, this world we live in is brimmed with wonders,
and I and all mankind, beneath our garbs of common-placeness, conceal
enigmas that the stars themselves, and perhaps the highest seraphim can
not resolve?"

Israel Potter, the book which followed *Pierre*, was a straightforward
historical novel, written primarily for the money it might bring in, and yet
it is as though Melville speaks of himself, when he says of Israel, ". . . now,
for the first time, he had time to linger, and loiter, and lounge—slowly
absorb what he saw—meditate himself into boundless amazement. For
forty years he never recovered from that surprise—never, till dead, had
done with his wondering."

Ahab's struggle against the whale, in terms of which Melville saw most
of the significance of man's life, was a struggle, which like a war, forced a
disregard for the ordinary humanities and kindnesses, and led Ahab to be
heedless of his own life and safety, and of the lives and safety of his crew.
Yet Melville was not contemptuous of life or the value of a man. The
friendship between Ishmael and Queequeg, the savage harpooneer, led
Ishmael to say that his splintered heart and maddened hand were no longer
turned against the wolfish world, that the soothing savage had redeemed
it. For Melville himself, of course, the redemption was not complete; the
strong sympathies with Ahab show that. He felt that men might seem
detestable as joint stock companies and nations, that man in the mass
might seem a mob of unnecessary duplicates, that often men might be
knaves or fools or murderers, but man in the ideal was so noble and so
sparkling, such a grand and glowing creature, that over any ignominious

blemish in him all his fellows should run to throw their costliest robes. Man was a wonder, a grandeur, and a woe. There was an innate dignity in him which was not dependent on any high station in the world, an immaculate manliness which could remain intact when all the outer character seemed gone. On this inward dignity, which was independent of all economic and social differences, Melville based the justification of democratic government. He said that democratic dignity radiated from God, in whose omnipresence lay our divine equality. Melville found that man's identity was so far within him that it remained untouched and untouchable in the great crises of life, and he illustrates this in his own life and in those of his characters,—as in his reaction when he was about to be flogged on the *Neversink*, or as in Ahab's final defiance of the whale, or as in Pierre's apparent but not actual loss of identity when he breaks with all the ties of his family and hereditary station. Since man's dignity was so immaculate and indestructible, he felt that no government or social action was right which tried to destroy it, or which failed to recognize it. Feeling this way, he was reverent also of human life, and it was difficult for him to reconcile himself to the loss of life in such struggles as Ahab's with good and evil.

When the heroic balance and synthesis of *Moby Dick* was ignored by the world, and when it showed within itself so complete an ambivalence of forces which Melville believed but found hard to accept, it was inevitable that the deadlock struggle should be renewed, and *Pierre, The Confidence Man*, and *Clarel* be written in increased despair and frustration. *Pierre* is a compounding of many elements: the old realization of ambiguities, the sorrow caused by the inhumanities of the waste and loss of human life, and Melville's own disappointments. The book's full title is *Pierre, or the Ambiguities*. The heart of the ambiguity in Melville's life is seen in a paragraph in which Pierre reflects on his present and past conditions after he has been disowned by his mother and deprived in other ways of all the happiness and beauty which life had promised him. How different is Melville's attitude here from that earlier one in *Redburn*, when he considered that evil sailor, Jackson, whose hate and fury, to Melville's astonishment and disgust, had been turned on the robust and good-humored, the strong, the fine, and the handsome. Pierre resolves all of his mother's love to pride, and doubts she would ever have loved him had he been, for example, a cripple. "Me she loveth with pride's love," Pierre exclaims, in the archaic diction which fills the book to its detriment but fails to destroy its import. "In me she thinks she seeth her own curled and haughty beauty; before my glass she stands,—pride's priestess—and to her mirrored image, not to me, she offers up her offerings of kisses. Oh, small thanks I owe thee, Favorable Goddess, that didst clothe this form with all the beauty of a man, that so thou mightest hide from me all the truth of a man. Now I see that in his beauty a man is snared, and made stone-blind, as the worm within his silk. Welcome then be Ugliness and Poverty and Infamy, and all ye other crafty ministers of Truth, that beneath the hoods and rags of beggars hide yet the belts and crowns of kings. . . . Oh, now methinks I a little see why of old the men of Truth went barefoot, girded with a rope, and ever moving under mournfulness as underneath a canopy."

This insight of Pierre's was inherent in Melville's previous books, particularly in *Moby Dick*, but it was never before expressed so directly. Jackson, and all other evil figures in Melville are thrown into a new light by the realization that evil is real, and that beauty blinds man to the truth. *Pierre*, as befits its title and its author, is replete with ambiguities both obvious and subtle. There are the double images of reflections in looking glasses, and the reflection of living faces by faces in portraits. There is the less concrete double image of Pierre's dead father, worshipped and idealized until his illegitimate daughter, Isabel, reveals herself. Pierre and his mother address each other as brother and sister, and his half-sister Isabel is forced to pose as his wife, as indeed she is in all but fact. Lucy, the sweet, fair image of innocent beauty, who was to have been his wife, is renounced and later comes to live with Pierre and Isabel as a cousin. There is irony in the whole story. Pierre is forced to abandon the pretty illusions, sentimentalities and secure insulations of his life to live by the truth and the realities of human existence, and finds himself more and more entangled in lies and deceptions. By his own sacrifice, he sets out to make up for his father's wrongs and their resultant cruelties, and becomes the source of more wrongs and cruelties which finally lead to complete disaster for himself and the people he loves. Plotinus Plinlimmon, one of the peripheral characters in the book, gives a most persuasive reason why this should have been so. In his theory of Chronometricals and Horologicals, he considers that the truth of heavenly wisdom and the conventions of earthly wisdom are like the two times carried by a ship on a voyage, the Greenwich time on the chronometer, and the local time on an ordinary clock. And as a man would be foolish to keep Greenwich time in China, so is the heavenly wisdom of God an earthly folly to man. "Literally speaking this is so," he said. "Nor does the God at the heavenly Greenwich expect common men to keep Greenwich wisdom in this remote Chinese world of ours." Plinlimmon taught that the effort to live in this world according to the strict letter of the chronometricals is likely to involve inferior beings, such as we are, in strange, unique follies and sins. But to live by the horological, as he advocated, did not involve the justification of wickedness, since a downright wicked man sinned as much against his own horologe as against the heavenly chronometer. "A virtuous expediency, then," he concluded, "seems the highest desirable or attainable earthly excellence for the mass of men, and is the only earthly excellence that their creator intended for them. When they go to heaven, it will be quite another thing."

The moral position represented by Plotinus Plinlimmon is so widely held and so rarely stated that one might well admire the courage of its frank acknowledgement as well as the sweet and sound reasonableness of the position itself. The story of Pierre, with the woe and destruction which he wrought in keeping to what he took to be chronometrical wisdom in the sacrifice of himself for the benefit of others, might almost be offered in substantiation of Plinlimmon's theories. Melville was thoroughly versed in contradictory, incongruous knowledge. He knew that the most Mammonish parts of the world were owned by the Christian nations, who gloried in the owning and seemed to have reason therefore, although Christianity called on all men to renounce the world. He had read what he called the greatest real miracle of all religions, the Sermon on the Mount, and had exulted in it and believed it as final truth, and knew in his heart it was divine, not human in its origin. With this exultation and belief in his mind, he looked back on the world and knew the world was a lie. All this should have inclined him to an acceptance of Plinlimmon's explanations, offering as they did, a reasonable path to spiritual peace after spiritual torture. Melville, speaking of Pierre or any other enthusiast, said that unless he prove recreant, or unless he prove gullible, or unless he can find the talismanic secret to reconcile this world with his own soul, then there is no peace for him, no slightest truce for him, in this life. Pierre, as representing Melville's own experience, had found that a near approach to truth or reality or the heart of existence, was like a near approach to the pole, where all directions are south, and the compass, which was effective at a distance, is no longer of value.

"In those Hyperborean regions, to which enthusiastic Truth, and Earnestness, and Independence, will invariably lead a mind fitted by nature for profound and fearless thought, all objects are seen in a dubious, uncertain and refracting light. Viewed through that rarefied atmosphere the most immemorially admitted maxims of men begin to slide and fluctuate, and finally become wholly inverted; the very heavens themselves being not innocent of producing this confounding effect, since it is mostly in the heavens themselves that these wonderful mirages are exhibited.

"But the example of many minds forever lost, like undiscoverable Arctic explorers, amid those treacherous regions, warns us entirely away from them; and we learn that it is not for man to follow the trail of truth too far, since by so doing he entirely loses the directing compass of his mind; for arrived at the pole, to whose barrenness only it points, there, the needle indifferently respects all points of the horizon alike."

Melville considered the silence which seemed both to precede and attend every profound thing and its emotions. Like the whiteness of Moby Dick, it was at once the most harmless and the most awful thing in all nature. The common source of both good and evil, and the source to which man was constantly impelled, Silence alone was the only voice of God. That talismanic secret to reconcile the world with man's soul had never yet been found, and in the nature of things it seemed that it never could be. Philosophers had time and again pretended to have found it, but if they had not later discovered their own delusion, some other man had discovered it for them, and their philosophies had been let glide away into oblivion. That profound Silence, that only voice of our God, from that divine thing without a name, philosophers had pretended to get an answer. How could a man get a voice out of silence? That was the problem; in recognition of his necessities, Melville who was neither recreant nor gullible, lived with it without peace. The false peace offered by Plotinus Plinlimmon was not a solution to the problem but an escape from it by denying its existence. That kind of insulation was not what Melville wanted.

Horror, barrenness, and negativism were inescapable aspects of reality in that polar world in which Melville found himself. He describes them in three pieces of short fiction, written at about the same time as *Pierre*, which are as great and remarkable as any ever written in America. *Benito Cereno* is a story of a ship carrying African slaves as part of her cargo. It seems to Amasa Delano, an able, good-hearted Yankee shipmaster, who visits aboard in a remote island harbor and tries to alleviate the ship's unseaworthy distress, that the Spanish captain is a tyrant and an incompetent weakling. The whole state of affairs on the foreign ship gradually becomes more strange to Captain Delano. There is a threatening fear which grows stronger and stronger; and though he repeatedly dismisses it from his mind, circumstances always force its return. He finally learns that the negroes are the real masters of the ship, that they had revolted a few weeks previous, had hideously slaughtered most of the whites aboard, and are now forcing the Spanish captain, a victim of almost insane terror, to carry them to Africa.

The Encantadas, or Enchanted Isles is a series of sketches concerned with the life and absence of life on a group of barren equatorial islands off the coast of Ecuador, which today are generally called the Galapagos. The ocean currents were strong around them; navigation was difficult; the islands themselves seemed to shift positions: and the sailors thought them enchanted. Nearly a month had been spent by a ship going from one isle to another though there was only thirty miles between, for nowhere else in the world was the wind so light and baffling or so given to calms. The islands themselves were volcanic,—barren places of ashes and cinders at the dead center of the world where change never came and where, already reduced to the lees of fire, ruin itself could work little more on them. The islands had been only rarely and sparsely inhabited, and tortoises were the principal animals that abounded there. Their long languid necks protruded from the lifeless thickets; the vitreous island rocks were worn down and grooved into deep ruts by ages and ages of the slow draggings of tortoises in quest of pools of scanty water. The creatures were black as widower's weeds and heavy as chests of plate, with vast shells medallioned and orbed like shields, and dented and blistered like shields that have breasted a battle,—shaggy too, here and there, with dark green moss, and slimy with spray from the sea. The great feelings inspired by them were of dateless, indefinite endurance and hopeless, toiling persistence. Melville had known them in their journeyings across the islands to ram themselves heroically against rocks and long abide there, nudging, wriggling, wedging, in order to displace them and so hold on their inflexible path, cursed by a drudging impulse to straightforwardness in a belittered world.

The Encantadas was so accurate a description of one side of human existence, overshadowing a brighter side, as the dark shells of the tortoises hid the shining yellow carapace covering their bellies, that it was possible to change the locale completely and not have a story very different after all. The story called *Bartleby the Scrivener* substitutes for the desolate racks of the islands an equally barren and desolate office in Wall Street in Melville's New York. The windows at one end of the office looked out on the white wall of an airshaft, and at the other end on the age-blackened brick of the nearest building, ten feet away. Bartleby, a copyist in this office, gradually gave up his work and everything else in his life to stare constantly at the blank wall outside his window. He ate and slept miserably at his desk, and never went out of the office until the police were forced to carry him away. He offered them no resistance.

These then, this horror and this blank-walled desolation, were aspects of human existence as Melville saw it, aspects of his own existence. He stared at the blank wall of public indifference, of moral ambiguity, of loss of faith. Everything in the world stirred and wavered unresistingly to his hand and remained unchanged, as objects underwater seem to shift and stir at every disturbance of the surface, while actually maintaining all the time the same blank stolidity of shape and position. His own identity even, for which like most men he was searching as one fixed point perhaps in a faltering, ambiguous world, lay too deep down to be reached or calculated. ". . . So strange and complicate is the human soul," he had found in *Pierre*, "so much is confusedly evolved from out itself, and such vast and varied accessions come to it from abroad, and so impossible is it always to distinguish between these two, that the wisest man were rash, positively to assign the precise and incipient origination of his final thoughts and acts. Far as we blind moles can see, man's life seems but an acting upon mysterious hints; it is somehow hinted to us to do thus or thus. For surely no mere mortal who has at all gone down into himself will ever pretend that his slightest thought or act solely originates in his own defined identity." To both our security and peril, we were inseparably linked to one another as, in *Moby Dick*, Queequeg, over the ship-side, cutting-in the blanket of blubber from a whale, was attached by a monkey-rope to Ishmael on deck, thus merging their individualities in a joint stock company of two in which the mistake or misfortune of one might plunge the other, all innocent, into unmerited disaster and death.

"I thought that man was no poor drifting weed of the universe," someone is made to say in *The Confidence Man*, ". . . that, if so minded, he could have a will, a way, a thought, and a heart of his own." Yet how could this be so in a world where man was so helplessly prone to evil that you could conclude nothing absolute from the human form, where the human form, short of being conclusive evidence of humanity, seemed rather to be a kind of unpledged and indifferent tabernacle. One of the clever beggars in *The Confidence Man* is dressed in mourning, and tells an affecting story as a preliminary to asking for money to take him back to his daughter. He learns the identity of the passenger to whom he tells the story from an accidentally dropped business card, and equipped with the information written on it, pretends to recognize the passenger as an old acquaintance and a messenger from heaven to one who in such deplorable circumstances was thrown among utter strangers. He said that he had been married to a vicious woman,—one who delighted in subtler forms of evil which though not recognized as criminal, or indeed not recognized at all, were nevertheless in their destructive nature, in their constant premeditation, and in the sense of fulfillment they gave to their perpetrator, more vicious than crime. She delighted in coarseness and cruelty and malice, which would drive her victims into a sad nervousness. But she never practiced these pleasures in a way or to an extent which would exclude her from society, but only to a degree that made her dreaded, and sometimes dreaded for things which were apparently trivial and innocent. In company, for example, she had a strange way of touching as if by accident, the arms or hands of the young men who happened to be there, seeming to reap a secret delight from it. But her husband, engaged in conversation with someone, would suddenly perceive her, moving about the room bestowing her mysterious touches, and his distress became acute when he saw that the strangeness of the thing seemed to strike upon the touched person, who nevertheless hesitated to speak of it then and there, or even in the future to complain of an offense which was after all so vague and indefinite. These unpleasant peculiarities of his wife could have been borne well enough were it not for the fact that she also began an artful torment of her little daughter, waiting until the child had reached the end of her endurance, and then playing the maternal hypocrite with her, fussing and petting until the child was comforted and the torment could be resumed. Knowing that his wife would neither confess nor amend, and might possibly become even worse than she was, the unfortunate man knew that the only thing he could do was to take the child and leave. The upshot of this action was that his wife brought suit against him who, in the eyes of the court, had simply deserted his wife for no reason that could be discovered rationally, and had moreover attempted to deprive her of her own child. Then, hearing that his wife was trying to have him committed to an insane asylum on the grounds that all the things he had alleged against her during the trial were hallucinations,—as indeed they could appear to be, he fled. And now, he was an innocent outcast, as he said, wandering forlorn in the great valley was an innocent outcast, as he said, wandering forlorn in the great valley of the Mississippi, with a weed on his hat for the loss of his wife; for he had lately seen by the papers that she was dead and thought it but proper to comply with the prescribed form of mourning in such cases. For some days past, he had been trying to get money enough to return to his child and was but now started with inadequate funds.

This was an affecting story. It sounded authentic, presenting men, as it did, as almost helpless creatures preyed upon by an evil which was ambiguous, elusive, and inescapable,—a view which Melville had reason to agree with and accept. And yet it is actually a fabrication told for the purpose of duplicity and with the same spoofing cynicism and unreality which another of the book's characters used when he, achieving on his side too a sound of authenticity, convinced the ship's barber that men, from their goodness and soundness of heart, were worthy of trust. The barber immediately acted on his new conviction, took down his 'No Trust' sign, and was swindled by the man who convinced him.

Evil as well as goodness could be counterfeited and used in a deliberate masquerade, as the man with the weed had used it. How, without denying all confidence in man, a denial which was undesirable, was it possible not to be victimized? The matter of *The Confidence Man* is not a simple opposition of good and evil, but a three-sided question in which prudence, which is really a desire for truth, is opposed both by confidence and by loss of faith, either of which can be supported by empirical evidence in a world in which good and evil are already ambiguous and confused without any attempt by man to masquerade them deliberately. "You flock of fools under this captain of fools, in this ship of fools," one passenger is made to cry out. He was a man who had charity but had sufficient intelligence also to see the possibility of sham. And after his outcry, people who had neither charity nor intelligence, set upon him and reproached him, in the name of charity, for his cynicism.

A story is told of Colonel John Moredock who was an Indian-hater. It is said that his mother was three times widowed by a tomahawk, and he himself was the only child to survive a massacre in which the mother and all the other children were scalped. When the news of the massacre reached him, he became an Indian-hater, and began at once to seek out and kill the murderers of his family. When after a number of years the last member of this band was dead, the killing of Indians had become his passion to which he devoted most of his life, and it was believed he never let pass an opportunity. Indian-hating was not an unusual phenomenon. All backwoods-

men were taught from childhood to regard the Indians as a race of assas-
sins, horse-thieves and treaty-breakers. These teachings, fortified by actual
instances of Indian crime, were so firm in the backwoodsman's mind, that
neither the kindly acts nor the protests of individual Indians were able to
uproot them. Some people thought that one cause of the Indians' returning the antipathy of the backwoodsmen as sincerely as they did, was their
moral indignation at being so libeled by them. On the other hand, the
backwoodsmen claimed that those redmen who were the greatest sticklers
for the theory of Indian virtue and loving-kindness were sometimes the
arrantest horse-thieves among them.

"It were to err to suppose," the judge who often recited the narrative of
Colonel Moredock and Indian-hating, would say, "that this gentleman
was naturally ferocious, or peculiarly possessed of those qualities, which,
unhelped by provocation of events, tend to withdraw man from social life.
On the contrary, Moredock was an example of something apparently self-
contradicting, certainly curious, but, at the same time, undeniable: namely
that nearly all Indian-haters have at bottom loving hearts; at any rate hearts,
if anything, more generous than the average."

Melville gives the judge this last reflection not by way of excuse or exten-
uation of Moredock's actions. The old Colonel was an invention whose
existence in truth was only metaphorical. But even had he been actual,
Melville's interest would still have been less in his praise or blame, than in
the contradiction of his nature,—that contradiction, or ambiguity, or in-
direction, which vetoes an action or reverses appearances or brings directions full circle, and is so much a part of existence that the deliberate dissembling of the confidence men can suggest it but hardly comprise it. It
had made so deep an impression on Melville's mind that he would have
been, as a matter of fact, unable to judge the Colonel. He was uncertain,
hesitant, sometimes almost nullified in his mind, and his whole intellectual power was turned toward an examination of the circumstances of these
feelings which he felt were not accidental nor exclusively his, but represented a true, if unaccountable, state of existence. To whom was an evil
basis to be assigned, and who indeed was entirely innocent?

Before the river steamer first left dock, a man in a cream-colored suit
and a white hat came aboard with neither baggage nor friends. He was
apparently a deaf mute. He walked along the lower deck until he was attracted by a large group of people crowded around a placard posted by the
captain's office which offered a reward for the capture of a mysterious
imposter supposed to have recently arrived from the East. Pushing his way

through this crowd until he stood beside the placard, he produced a slate on which he wrote, "Charity thinketh no evil." Being jostled by the crowd so that his hat was crushed down on his head, he replaced the first sentence with this other,—"Charity suffereth long, and is kind." Then leaving his station by the placard, he passed back and forth along the deck, changing his slate at intervals by substituting a new conclusion for the previous one so that he successively announced that charity, "endureth all things," "believeth all things," and finally, "never faileth." His behavior caused considerable comment among the passengers. But when, at length, he went to the rear of the lower deck and fell asleep there, he was soon forgotten and apparently left the boat before many stops had been made.

The apparent deaf mute of Christian charity may have been in actual league with the confidence men and then again, perhaps he was not. The issue was left in doubt. In either event, his attitudes were more help than hindrance to their swindling operations. Perhaps it was only that even with the best intentions in the world, one inevitably played into the hands of evil. Melville did not know. He had reached the very bottom of doubt where doubts themselves seemed questionable, and an assured heretic a man of greatest faith. Melville's doubt was at the same time spiritual and social, and rightly so; it is part of the irony that the expression of this idea in *The Confidence Man* should be left to the Cosmopolitan, a pompous hypocrite of a character, the same one who took such pains to swindle the barber out of the price of a shave. ". . . They are coordinates," he says. "For misanthropy, springing from the same root with disbelief of religion, is twin with that. It springs from the same root, I say; for set aside materialism, and what is an atheist, but one who does not, or will not, see in the universe a ruling principle of love; and what is a misanthrope, but one who does not, or will not, see in a man a ruling principle of kindness? Don't you see? In either case the vice consists in a want of confidence."

In 1856, in the fall, Melville started on a journey abroad which included a visit to the Holy Land. He had long wanted to go there for reasons that had partly to do with faith. *Clarel*, the narrative and philosophical poem, which was one result of his journey, is largely a discussion of faith and of lack of faith. Melville almost seems to have hoped that the influence of Jerusalem might work some restoration of belief or some complete conversion on his mind and spirit. Most of the people in the poem are uncertain what Palestine may have to offer, but its great age and the very barrenness of its desolation seem to promise fertility. Here at any rate, they seem to be saying, is the neglected and homely source, the forgotten foundation of our world. Clarel himself is a young and bewildered student who has found the world full of contrary natures. "What clue, what clue?" he asks. Rolfe is determined to get behind the parrot-lore of convention, but beyond that he is unable to describe what the lurking thing may be that he hopes to find on 'Jewry's inexhausted shore of barrenness.' Both Rolfe and Clarel are Americans. A hunchbacked Italian, Celio, is dissatisfied by all political and religious creeds and is not tempted by any of the various careers that his ability and family might have opened to him. But he is not yet through with life; he hopes that somewhere there is something more than negation, and Palestine's great age may reveal it to him. There is a Swede, Mortmain, who has been a romantic reformer in Europe with a large following. But now he feels that the optimist basis of his thinking was false, and that reform is futile. Discouraged and fiercely embittered by the reactions and reversals in European politics, the dry dust of Palestine seems like wisdom to him in which he sits down to rust. A third American, Ungar, though he held a low opinion of slave-holding, had been so torn by the Civil War, and so incapable of accepting its verdict, that he had exiled himself from his native Maryland.

"Man sprang from deserts:

Rolfe remarks,

                       at the touch
Of grief or trial overmuch
On deserts he falls back at need;
Yes, 'tis the bare abandoned home
Recalleth then."

These sorrowful and bewildered men, these variant Ishmaels in the desert of the Holy Land, are cruelly set off by a bustling Anglican priest called Derwent, who is undiscouraged by a world whose realities he has never allowed to touch him, and unbothered by spiritual questions or loss of faith because he has never had any faith, nor ever missed it. The terrible feeling through all this long poem is not cynical bitterness—though there are bitter and cynical people in it—but a tortured feeling of loneliness, as though man were an exile and a stranger in his own world. Even a single friend, or the smallest, firm, unequivocal basis for a faith, might have relieved the strangeness and the exile. But these were the very things that seemed impossible, and Clarel is filled with a desire to believe and a warmth that both fail to find any expression. One day, Clarel tries to speak of himself to Vine, who seems the most sympathetic of the various people who are his traveling companions. But though there was no spoken rebuke, Vine nevertheless immediately withdraws into himself, and Clarel is effectively discouraged from further confidence. Vine's unspoken attitude seemed to say that each man had his own sorrows which made other men's sorrows unwanted and superfluous; that he was neither the first nor the last man to be tried by doubts, and that he would have somehow to live them through by himself, since no one living could help him; and moreover that the 'negatives of flesh' should be adequate indication of the impossibility of spiritual sympathy between one man and another.

There are many echoes in *Clarel* of Melville's previous experience and writings, as though he were casting about again in his past with Clarel's expression, "What clue, what clue?" Derwent is reminiscent of the socially proper and spiritually empty Reverend Mr. Falsgrave who was of so little assistance to Pierre. The landscape of the Holy Land recalls the landscape of the Encantadas, and Agath, who had been a sailor, makes the comparison directly, and describes the islands to the travelers as they ride along. Rolfe had also been a sailor, and the sight of a palm tree at Mar Saba reminds him of a beautiful palm-covered island that he lived on once and ran away from. It is the thought of Typee returning. He thinks of the truant ship-boy who climbed down from the mountains over the perilous cliffs and into the beautiful orchards where he was hailed as though he were a god, and was urged to luxuriate forever with the simple, friendly people in the lovely and bountiful valley. But he had left the valley, feeling that there he had gone astray from the world. And now his renunciation seemed to him like Adam's flight from Paradise, but a willful flight, lacking the compulsion and the sin which had given Adam no choice but to flee. He had been free to stay, and the thought of the valley haunted him like an avenger.

It is also Rolfe, the former sailor, who speaks of 'nature with her neutral mind,' in telling the story of a strong-willed and indomitable sea captain, somewhat like Ahab, who was pursued by an indomitable fate, was shipwrecked by a whale and at last, unlike Ahab, became as meek and unresisting as Bartleby.

Besides this recurrence and mingling of old themes, there is a forecast of a remaining and final one. A brief section, called 'Of Rama,' which is arbitrarily introduced into the narrative, speaks of natures which are at one time innocent and lawless, and which alone are familiar with 'strange things that dwell repressed in mortals,'—natures which survive everything that may be brought against them.

"Though black frost nip, though white frost chill
Nor white frost nor the black may kill
The patient root, the vernal sense
Surviving hard experience
As grass the winter. Even that curse
Which is the wormwood mixed with gall—
Better dependent on the worse—
Divine upon the animal—
That cannot make such natures fall."

In 1866, Melville was offered a post as Inspector of Customs in New York. He stayed there nineteen years, writing almost nothing. After he left this post, and when he was nearly seventy, he wrote *Billy Budd*. It was the resolution and summary of the whole meaning and experience of his life.

In the days when Melville had gone to sea, one might often have encountered around the docks and the waterfront streets, a whole group of sailors or marines, like an informal guard of honor, surrounding and escorting one of their number in whom they quite obviously took great pride. Some of the reason for their pride would be apparent in the very appearance of the man, in his great health and beauty and physical well-being. Any seafarer would have known that he was also an unusually proficient seaman, a leader and champion and spokesman among the crew, a man of great moral value and courage. Such a man was known as the Handsome Sailor. Such a Handsome Sailor had been Jack Chase on board the *Neversink*, to whom this book is dedicated ('wherever that great heart may now be here on earth or harbored in Paradise'). Such a man too, was Billy Budd, in whom physical and moral strength and beauty were all united.

He had been impressed into the English Navy from a merchant-ship called, symbolically enough, the *Rights of Man*; and the merchant captain was very sorry to lose him since Billy had been, as he said, his peacemaker, keeping the whole burly crew in harmony, working together. Nevertheless, he came aboard the naval vessel, the *Indomitable*, happily enough and in good spirit, and though he did not occupy so high a position there as aboard the smaller merchant craft, he was still a striking figure, an unusually expert seaman, and was well-liked and respected by both officers and crew. At the climax of the story, after he had been aboard for several months during which the respect and the liking grew, he was hanged for mutiny and murder, of both of which crimes he was undoubtedly guilty although he had not the slightest intention of either.

The murdered man was Claggart, the master-at-arms (or call him Bland or Jackson). Nothing was known of his antecedents. It was apparent that he had not been bred to the sea and since he was a man in his middle thirties, he must have had some previous history ashore. The sailors, who disliked any master-at-arms, sensed a special evil in Claggart; and thinking of evil, as they did, in the most direct and obvious terms, they rumored that he had been some swindler or forger who was forced into the Navy to escape the jails. Such a thing was not uncommon in the British Navy at that time,—the time of the Napoleonic Wars.

The Master-at-Arms had always a pleasant word for Billy Budd, and Billy was unaware that Claggart had conceived an antipathy toward him. He only knew that he began to find himself in a series of little troubles over the infraction of very minor matters of discipline, such as the stowage of his gear. He told his troubles to one of the oldest sailors on the ship who warned him that Claggart was down on him, but Billy saw no outward sign or reason for it and couldn't believe the warning. There was indeed no reason, and every reason. There was, first of all, the evil nature of Claggart, his natural depravity, so that evil was born into him as into the scorpion for which the Creator alone is responsible. Though he might hide his nature, he could not change it, and he had no choice but to live it out to the end. Civilization is auspicious to such a natural depravity as Claggart's which folds itself in a mantle of respectability. It has no vices or small sins, is never mercenary or avaricious, and partakes nothing of the sordid or sensual. It is suggested that what first moved Claggart against Billy Budd was the latter's significant personal beauty. For though Claggart was far from an ugly man himself, and was well enough aware of his good points as to be always neat and well-groomed, yet Billy's form and face were heroic. There were envy and antipathy mingled when the Master-at-Arms eyed Billy's good looks, cheery health, and frank enjoyment of young life, and saw that these things in some way reflected or revealed a moral quality underneath, which in its innocence had never willed malice nor experienced its bite. The Master-at-Arms was almost the only person in the ship who was intellectually capable of adequately appreciating the moral phenomenon presented in Billy Budd. That insight intensified his passion. He disdained the innocence that he saw. To be nothing more than innocent! Yet he saw the charm of it, the courageous free and easy temper of it, and he would have shared it, but he despaired of being able to do so. Into the gall of envy and despair, according to his nature, he infused the vitriol of contempt. He was not entirely the willing agent. When, unobserved, his glance would happen to light on Billy walking about the deck, it would follow him with a settled melancholy and meditative expression, his eyes strangely infused with incipient feverish tears. Then he would look, as Melville said, like a man of sorrows, and his melancholy expression would have in it a touch of yearning. But this was an evanescence, and quickly repented of, as it were, by an immitigable look, pinching and shriveling the visage into the semblance of a wrinkled walnut. It was this latter look which was translated into action, first by an attempt actually to involve Billy in a mutinous conspiracy with the other impressed men in the ship, and finally, when this failed completely, by reporting to the incredulous Captain, a series of false and circumstantial details which seemed to so involve him. The Captain, who greatly doubted Billy's guilt, determined to bring the accuser and the accused face to face in his cabin. Here, when the accusation was repeated, the wholly innocent Billy Budd was unable to speak in reply, first because he was so astounded by the unjust accusation, and additionally because he had a natural stammer even under ordinary circumstances. Outraged, and helpless to speak, yet driven to some form of protest, he struck Claggart with his fist with such force that he killed him.

The other person of importance in this story was Captain Vere, in whose presence the murder was committed, and to whom it now fell to decide the moral issues involved and the action to be taken. He knew that Billy Budd was entire goodness and was blameless; he knew that Claggart deserved the death he had gotten; without the slightest question in his mind as to where innocence and guilt really lay, he knew as well that in the eyes of the law under which the case must be judged, innocence and guilt would be effectively reversed. Captain Vere had proved himself in naval engagements a man of great if unspectacular and personally colorless courage, and as if deliberately so. He was, moreover, a learned man, who read deeply and widely on long voyages, and though practical enough whenever the occasion demanded, he would sometimes betray a dreaminess of mood and stand absently gazing off at the black sea. He was a strict disciplinarian, but no lover of authority for mere authority's sake, and he was very far from seizing to himself the perils of moral responsibility when that responsibility could be rightly avoided. And yet he was preeminently a responsible man. That moral ambiguity of good and evil of which he was so well aware in the case between Claggart and Billy Budd, did not make him incapable of action, nor lead him, Pilate-like, to absolve himself of all responsibility in the case. The responsibility fell squarely upon him and he accepted it. It was the year of the great mutiny in the English Navy. Any further hint or appearance of insurrection needed to be dealt with promptly and courageously. Moreover, the *Indomitable* might at any moment encounter ships of the enemy fleet. Any delay or any leniency would be dangerous, and particularly so since the crew, like all sailors, were the greatest sticklers for the traditional usages of the sea. "With mankind," Captain Vere would say,—(and who has a better right to say it than Vere or Melville with their deep realization of the inadequacy of forms)—"with mankind, forms, measured forms, are everything; and that is the import couched in the story of Orpheus, with his lyre, spell-binding the wild denizens of the woods." There was no choice but to call a summary court whose ultimate verdict, even before the calling, was never a matter of doubt. Captain Vere was necessarily the chief witness before the court; he gave his testimony directly and clearly and without rancor; Billy Budd willingly confirmed him in all he had said. Everyone in the room was aware that Billy was innocent in nature and guilty under the law. The path by which they were led out of this dilemma was Captain Vere's willing responsibility to take a measure of guilt upon himself. The buttons they wore on their uniforms were the King's, and attested the fact that their allegiance was to the King, not to nature; and though they needed to condemn, it was with an assurance that the Last Assizes would acquit. It was an act of very great faith expressed with passion and responsibility, partaking nothing of the cold, self-satisfied liberation of Plotinus Plinlimmon. Surely Melville expressed in the sacrifice of Billy Budd his own departure from Typee and rejection of Serenia, and Pierre's fall from felicity.

The faith, as it were, was reciprocated in a benediction. As Billy Budd stood beneath the main-yard with the rope around his neck, his only words, which he called out clearly and loudly, were, "God bless Captain

Vere!" And the whole crew, helplessly and without any volition, took up the cry. It was Melville's great cry of affirmation and acceptance. For that little moment, in an irreparably evil and ambiguous world, ambiguity and evil with all their consequences were acquiesced in, and Jackson and Bland, Ahab, Claggart, and Ishmael, and the evil Whale itself, were drawn up and absorbed in a clear act of conviction and faith. Herman Melville was at peace. God bless Captain Vere!

Design by David Bullen
Typeset in Mergenthaler Imprint
by Wilsted & Taylor
Printed by Maple-Vail
on acid-free paper

triumphant legions came, the consuls, and the emperors, to receive the honors of a triumph at Rome, while behind them came the pack animals loaded with their booty, and the prisoners with hands and feet in chains, their backs bare to show the marks of the floggings.

The Appian Way was the queen among all highways and became more sumptuous as it neared the city of Rome. It stretched for miles between two rows of cypress trees, and prepared the eye for the great sight of the city itself, the center of the world. Along its length, among the cypress, were those white marble monuments, gleaming in the sun, with their inscription lists telling of victories and glorious achievements; the names and titles of notable persons; now and then statues of idols and busts of ancestors, as if these last were to witness the passing pageant of life from some window in Eternity. It was a road that made one think of Rome and of death.

As all great people do, the Romans cared for the bodies of the dead and preserved their memory by putting their last resting places along her beautiful highways, under the transparent arch of the sky among the flowers and greenery in order to have her dead remembered. Round mausoleums of red bricks or sheathed in marble rose up like fortresses with ramparts and towers, real houses of death—or, shall we say, resistance to death? Before Christ came, the world was obsessed by a fear of death. It was conscious of sin for which death is the price; but that little man in chains was the bearer of tidings of liberation. He would proclaim a definite victory over death.

All around and beyond there stretched an expanse of bleak plain, broken here and there by marshes; on the left, in the distance, the sea; on the right, the plain ended in groves of willows, clumps of ferns at the foot of the Lepini [2] mountains whose villages and temples could be seen in the distance. Stagnant water, full of croaking frogs, invaded broken places in the consular road so that travellers had to wade through the water almost to their knees.

Where the Appian Way began to descend for a level stretch, if Paul had stopped for a few minutes to look and admire (the escort

[2] Lepini—a continuation of the Appenines.

would never refuse a request to gaze upon such delightful and superb beauty), he would have seen the road ahead ascending a hill and ending at its top in a slender spire piercing the blue sky, narrowed in by a mortuary chapel on one side and on the other by a solitary pine. Paul's ardent mind imagined that it continued even to the Heavenly Sion, to which end all his travels had been leading him for years and years—the place of his eternal meeting with his Master and Saviour.

When he turned his eyes to the right or the left as he walked, Paul shook his head sadly that people could be so vain or so foolish as to wall up ashes and lifeless bodies within stones or columns of stones. When the resurrection of the dead takes place, these stone ramparts will break open as easily as the pomegranates whose green stems could be seen among the hedges. After the same manner as the pomegranates open, so the graves will open at the resurrection, and future men will blossom forth as new creatures ready for reward or punishment. The spectacle of that imperial road and funereal way revealed a reverence for the human body. Such reverence illumined by the light of the Gospel and made complete by faith, would have transformed the body into a temple of the Holy Spirit! The body would be like a chalice to receive the Blood of the Son of God. It would be an edifice from which would flash out the perfections of the Eternal Builder, God Himself.

And behold, some of the faithful came to meet him the following day at the "Three Taverns." They had started the day before and had walked all night in order to welcome him there. St. Luke relates that when Paul saw them he thanked the Lord and was filled with new joy and courage. He realized how far the Word of God had travelled, and that in Rome also a fruitful work was being done. He entered the city through the Capena Gate, walking between the soldiers and the faithful; in the eyes of the Roman Institution, he was an accused; in the eyes of the Roman Church, he was a conqueror.

At Rome, where the Christian Community was composed mostly of converted pagans, Paul was already known for his Apostolate among the Gentiles and for his letter to that Church. He also had personal friends and relatives who lived in Rome. The Jews frequently travelled from one business center to another. Perhaps some of these who knew him came to greet him at the gateway of the city. Paul must have been deeply moved to tears at seeing and meeting all these brethren, known or unknown to him, but in whom the devotion to the Gospel was solid and upright against all the influences of heresy. With transports of joy he thanked God, that being now in their midst, he had reached one of the principal goals of his travels.

If Paul's arrival had chanced to be on a sunny day with the limpid blue sky of a Roman spring smiling down upon him, he must have been dazzled as he lifted his eyes, full of keen interest in the spectacle of life before him. There were the unending stretches of little houses closely packed together, the narrow streets crowded with people and with the din of labor; the imposing marble monuments (looking so strong and secure), and the high palaces that crowned the hills.

As the cortege neared the center of the city, Paul found himself in the midst of a curious crowd of magistrates in cap and gown; of soldiers in shining armor. Then they reached the *miliarium aureum,* the gilded column erected by Augustus from which point radiated Roman roads to all parts of Italy. Paul must have been filled with admiration and surprise at the evidence of so much power and with the outward show of wealth. Any ordinary man coming from the rural districts would have felt small and insignificant in the midst of the great amphitheaters, the great basilicas and arches of the Forum, the comings and goings of gilded chariots, luxurious litters with their numerous escorts; and an ordinary prisoner would have felt his last bit of courage oozing away. On the contrary, Paul admired all those marvels of human achievement and saw in them the genius of God. If he felt his own nothingness more keenly, he was also keenly conscious of the power of the Lord Whom he served and for Whom he wore those chains.

He never doubted but that the city would be won for Christ— but won only through bloodshed and persecutions. The barrier of idolatry would fall, and the whole Empire become a realm of Christian justice. The prisoner Paul had high ambitions. He knew Christ could—and that He would—make that great metropolis the center of His Kingdom upon earth.

Certainly by temperament and because of the nature of the Gospel message, Paul would prefer Rome to Athens. The monuments of Rome testified that her subjugation of nations had been by force and by power, but Athens only bewildered men to no purpose by her monuments to human intellectuality. Paul found in the Romans far more spontaneity and more sincerity.

So the strange procession, tired from its long march, traversed the dingy streets crowded with artisans, laborers, slaves and idlers, which gave the thickly populated city an oriental aspect. In the midst of noisy voices Paul went up the street between the Quirinal and the Esquiline hills, towards the Praetorian Camp. And there finally, he halted in a prison.

GLADSTONE

By the same Author

Gladstone and the Bulgarian Agitation, 1876
The Crisis of Imperialism, 1865–1915